A Crisis of Births

Population Politics and Family-Making in Italy

Elizabeth L. Krause
The University of Massachusetts, Amherst

 Case Studies on Contemporary Social Issues:
John A. Young, Series Editor

THOMSON
———— ✳ ————™
WADSWORTH

Australia • Canada • Mexico • Singapore • Spain
United Kingdom • United States

THOMSON

✶

™

WADSWORTH

Anthropology Editor: *Lin Marshall*
Assistant Editor: *Nicole Root*
Editorial Assistant: *Kelly McMahon*
Marketing Manager: *Matthew Wright*
Marketing Assistant: *Tara Pierson*
Project Manager, Editorial Production:
  Rita Jaramillo
Print/Media Buyer: *Rebecca Cross*

Permissions Editor: *Sarah Harkrader*
Production Service: *Mary E. Deeg,*
  Buuji, Inc.
Copy Editor: *Cheryl Hauser*
Cover Designer: *Rob Hugel*
Cover Image: *Elizabeth L. Krause*
Cover and Text Printer: *Webcom*
Compositor: *Buuji, Inc.*

The logo for the Contemporary Social Issues series is based on the image of a social group interacting around a central axis, referring both back to a tribal circle and forward to a technological society's network.

Printed in Canada
1 2 3 4 5 6 7 08 07 06 05 04

For more information about our products, contact us at:
Thomson Learning Academic Resource Center
1-800-423-0563

For permission to use material from this text, contact us by:
Phone: 1-800-730-2214   **Fax:** 1-800-730-2215
Web: http://www.thomsonrights.com

Library of Congress Control Number: 2003113821

ISBN 0-534-63693-4

Wadsworth/Thomson Learning
10 Davis Drive
Belmont, CA 94002-3098
USA

Asia
Thomson Learning
5 Shenton Way #01-01
UIC Building
Singapore 068808

Australia/New Zealand
Thomson Learning
102 Dodds Street
Southbank, Victoria 3006
Australia

Canada
Nelson
1120 Birchmount Road
Toronto, Ontario M1K 5G4
Canada

Europe/Middle East/Africa
Thomson Learning
High Holborn House
50/51 Bedford Row
London WC1R 4LR
United Kingdom

Latin America
Thomson Learning
Seneca, 53
Colonia Polanco
11560 Mexico D.F.
Mexico

Spain/Portugal
Paraninfo
Calle Magallanes, 25
28015 Madrid, Spain

For Mom, who endured my birth,
and in memory of Josie (1997–2002)

Contents

List of Illustrations

FIGURES

TABLES

Foreword

ABOUT THE SERIES

This series explores the practical applications of anthropology in understanding and addressing problems faced by human societies around the world. Each case study examines an issue of socially recognized importance in the historical, geographical, and cultural context of a particular region of the world while adding comparative analysis to highlight not only the local effects of globalization, but also the global dimensions of the issue. The authors write with a readable narrative style and include reference to their own participation, roles, and responsibilities in the communities they study. Their engagement with people goes beyond being merely observers and researchers, as they explain and sometimes illustrate from personal experience how their work has implications for advocacy, community action, and policy formation. They demonstrate how anthropological investigations can build our knowledge of human societies and at the same time provide the basis for fostering community empowerment, resolving conflicts, and pursuing social justice.

ABOUT THE AUTHOR

Betsy Krause practiced journalism in Missouri and Oregon before obtaining her master's degree (Oregon State University) in applied anthropology and her doctorate degree (The University of Arizona) in cultural anthropology. She has conducted fieldwork in Micronesia, Italy, Oregon, and Arizona. Her numerous articles have appeared in a range of publications, including *Human Organization, Journal of Historical Anthropology, Transforming Anthropology, Cultural Anthropology, Journal of Modern Italian Studies* as well as *Newsday.* She has contributed chapters to several edited books, including *The Greenwood Encyclopedia of Women's Issues Worldwide: Europe* and *Barren States: The Population Implosion in Europe* (forthcoming). She is currently assistant professor in the Department of Anthropology at the University of Massachusetts, Amherst.

ABOUT THIS CASE STUDY

This book asks how Italy attained the lowest birthrate in the world. The author finds answers in intensely personal dialogues with ordinary people ranging from sweater-makers to counts, and aging bachelors to doting mothers. Their life experiences reveal how a silent revolution against patriarchy reshapes social and sexual morality to create new imperatives for family-making. As one-child families become the norm, political and religious leaders engage in a futile attempt to resurrect the ideal of motherhood associated with the large families of past generations. Demographers fail to conceal their bias in sounding alarms about a newly defined problem of cultural decay that arises in the context of class conflict, immigration, and racial politics. The Italian case is indicative of a wider phenomenon of population decline in industrialized countries of Europe and Asia, and reminds us that governments care deeply about what people do in the privacy of their own bedrooms.

John A. Young
Series Editor
Department of Anthropology
Oregon State University
jyoung@oregonstate.edu

Preface

AN AUTHOR'S JOURNEY

> The starting-point of critical elaboration is the consciousness of what one really is, and in "knowing thyself" as a product of the historical process to date which has deposited in you an infinity of traces, without leaving an inventory.
>
> —Antonio Gramsci (1971[1935]:324)

A comment that my mother made to me before I left for two years of field research in Italy appears in a jotting notebook that I took to the field: "We just did what we did because that's what we thought we were supposed to do." She had made this remark in reference to why she spent most of her life as a housewife.

I feel awkward asking my students whether they plan to marry or have children. I am not sure why the question rattles me, since the topic interests me so much. I suppose it is because when I was in my early twenties, the thought of having a child never crossed my mind. I just did not want to think about it. I never imagined myself getting married or having kids. It just was not part of my identity. My mother was frustrated as a 1950s and 1960s housewife. The frustration penetrated even deeper as a 1970s housewife. The persistence of housewifery, you see, resulted in part from her and my father having had children over so many years: from age 19 to 43. They had my oldest sisters right after they got married, 15 months apart. They waited 9 years before having me, in 1962, and another 13 years before having my youngest sister. Of the four of us, my little sister was the only one who was actually planned. The rest of us came along due to malfunctioning birth control methods! It was only as a woman in my late thirties that I asked my mother these details about "family planning."

My mother raised four daughters with little day-to-day help from my father, for he was busy chasing the American dream. His father was an ethnic German who had served in, and had his fill of, the Prussian Army. An immigrant's son, my father wanted to be rich. As a young man out of high school he tried his luck as a taxicab driver, a pool shark, a door-to-door Fuller Brush salesman, and a poker player. None of those "career paths" panned out. But sales would. He landed a job in the industrial oil sector selling rust-proofing and other automotive and industrial lubricants. He eventually invented a special lubricant for the dye machines that punch out pull-tabs. "Tab-lube" was a specialized product for the aluminum soda, beer, and food can sector but one that made him good commissions. He worked for a small company whose owner granted him the large commission my father had the nerve to ask for. He has always bragged that he never would have invented tab-lube if he had earned a degree as a chemical engineer.

As time wore on, my parents expressed their love for us in part through things, and still do, only now they are bigger, though typically practical, things. They began spending their new money on collectibles, and my father became particularly fond of Oriental rugs, pocket watches, and Madame Alexander dolls. My parents were Depression-era kids. Consumer culture was a sure way to invest in class mobility.

When I was 21, I spent a semester studying abroad on an arts program in Florence and London. My parents came to visit me, and my mother was so taken by the art of Florence that she decided to enroll in art school back in St. Louis. She defied those "supposed to's" when she returned to college and at age 60 graduated with her bachelor's degree in fine arts, and now, 10 years later, she is an oil painter who exhibits her work in juried shows. She has used oil products from my father's business for the undercoatings of her paintings, which often include tree forms and wood nymphs and, most recently, re-interpretations of nursery rhymes. Her canvasses offer her outlets for working out a lifetime of frustration.

As a young woman I related much more to my mother's independent-minded side than to her maternal or spousal side. I never gave much thought to having children. I clung to a tomboy self-image. I thought about babies just enough to avoid getting pregnant. After graduating from the University of Missouri-Columbia with a degree in journalism, my editor introduced me to a friend of his who was a fiddler and a veterinary student. We ended up hitting it off, and within a little over a year, we got hitched and moved west: to Oregon. We never talked about having kids that I can recall. It seemed an impossible subject to breech. Then something strange happened. An old roommate of ours from Columbia called to tell me she was pregnant. Shortly after that, some local friends told us they were expecting. One evening around my 28th birthday, we threw caution to the wind. Three months later, I traveled to Micronesia as a technical assistant against the warnings of a friend who had gotten pregnant only after lengthy and painful infertility treatments. I thought of her after a bumpy boat ride on rough seas left me with pelvic ligaments so badly pulled that I could barely crawl the next morning. My roommates were shocked and insisted I go to the health clinic. I healed. At this writing, my daughter, born in December 1990, is 12 years old.

Life just happened to me. I got married and became a mother without really planning it. It happens to a lot of people that way. Then again, many people invest in education, get jobs, and never have children. Others decide they want kids but then learn they are infertile.

Italian women now have the lowest birthrate in the world. The average Italian family has one child. The average fertility rate is 1.2 births per woman. Fertility rate refers to the average number of children a given group of women is expected to have over the course of their childbearing years. It is not a measure of infertility, although as people delay having children the risk of sterility increases. I came to this topic in graduate school in a seminar on social memory. I had done some historical research on the Italian fascist demographic campaign of the 1920s. The fascists sought to increase the number of children Italians had. Benito Mussolini had the idea that he would use population to make a stronger Italy. Ultimately, he wanted to use many of those "extra" Italians to fight wars and overtake African countries, which he could then populate as Italian colonies.

Mussolini wanted to be like other European countries, such as France, Germany, and England, and show his nation's force through colonization of non-Western peoples. Neither his war program nor his birth plan enjoyed lasting success. But birth politics did not disappear.

When I learned of the record low birthrate of Italian women, it challenged the stereotype I held of the large Italian family. I had grown up in St. Louis, where the family-owned businesses of "The Hill" reinforce images of family-loving Italians. Furthermore, I had come of age on *Moonstruck,* a film that romanticizes the family-centered Italian culture. Growing up, it had never occurred to me to think about families and babies in relation to national politics. In graduate school, I began to grasp the connections; however, the courage to commit to the topic finally came to me early one morning at my campsite at a bluegrass and folk music festival in northern California. I decided to put the anthropological toolkit to the test and see what an ethnography of a low birthrate society might tell us.

What happens when a whole society's patterns of making families changes dramatically? What are the consequences of such a transformation on not only individuals but on the social fabric and political webs? How does the trend of people going from having large families to having small families play out at different levels of society? And how do these forces shape the behaviors of individuals in powerful ways that they may not recognize?

When I set out to do my fieldwork in Central Italy, I bought a supply of memo pads small enough to fit in a pocket. In my first notepad I wrote those words my mother told me right before leaving. I was sitting in her room in the world's most comfortable chair beside her dressing table. I think of that table as a shrine, bedecked as it is with anti-aging creams, jewelry, and crystals. Being there is like eating comfort food. It is a quiet space that cultivates intimate talk. On this occasion, she spoke about herself as a conditioned social being: "We just did what we did because that's what we thought we were supposed to do."

Her words and deeds have echoed through my work ever since. We all are conditioned in ways that stem from ideologies we grow up with related to gender, socioeconomic class, racial or ethnic identities, and uneven relationships of power (see Willis and Trondman 2000). The ways we come to make families are manifestations of ideas that shape who we are and what pressures we feel as we come into adulthood. This book tells a story of some of those pressures, what they have been and what they have become, and how Italians embrace and contest those pressures. This book also hits close to home. Beneath the telling of this story was my own struggle with the pressures and personal dilemmas related to family-making. As my daughter begged me for a sibling, I debated whether to stop with a healthy, only child or to confront the risks and joys of having another baby as an over 35-year-old woman. This project has allowed me the space to reflect on some of the important influences that shaped not only the future of Italy but my own.

The title of this book is intended to be ironic just as Eric Wolf intended his classic *Europe and the People without History* to be an ironic commentary on the common treatment of non-Europeans as though they had no history until the Europeans arrived. My title has two meanings. On the one hand, in the spirit of anthropology, it reflects the "indigenous" view. It echoes the words of the Pope and the dominant alarmist view of Italian demographers, officials, and journal-ists. On the other hand, it is intended as an ironic provocation. The crisis is also very much socially constructed and a result of these dominant representations. The crisis is very much a consequence of cultural politics. The realm of cultural politics, to paraphrase Glen Jordan and Chris Weedon, comes down to whose history will be remembered and whose forgotten, and which views of social life will be promoted and which silenced. In a quiet revolution such as the demo-graphic transition in Italy, many experiences have been and are being silenced. This book aims to give voice to those stories.

ACKNOWLEDGMENTS

The research on which this ethnography is based was made possible in part by the Council for European Studies Pre-Dissertation Grant (1995), U.S. Fulbright Grant and Renewal (1995–1997), Beth Wilder Dillingham Award, Central States Anthropological Society (1998), The University of Arizona Graduate College Fellowship (1998), Final Project Fund Award from The University of Arizona (1999), The UA Department of Anthropology William Shirley Fulton Scholarship (1999), and a Faculty Research Grant from the University of Massachusetts, Amherst (2002). Finally, my parents, Jack and Marian Krause, and my in-laws, Lee and Donice Brashear, lent a hand when unexpected finan-cial difficulties arose.

I am especially indebted to my field consultants, who in respect to their pri-vacy remain anonymous. Massimo Livi-Bacci, David Kertzer, Letizia Mencarini, Alessandro Pasquini, Luisa Passerini, and Alessandra Pescarolo openly shared their ideas, resources, and time with me. Marzio Barbagli of the Istituto Carlo Cattaneo in Bologna graciously provided me with my initial insti-tutional affiliation. Giuseppe Bocci, head of the bureau of records and staff in the Comune di Carmignano, once I received permission, allowed me open access to the Archivio Storico. Silvano Gelli offered priceless guidance in the archive, as well as historical insight. Sauro Lusini and staff of the Archivio Fotografico Toscana welcomed my use of the photography collection and library. Giovanni Michon Pecori, Franca Michon Pecori, and sisters gave generous access to the Archivio Privato as well as memories. Various assistance was offered by Cosimo Regina and Antonio Fortunato of the Biblioteca "A. Palazzeschi" in the Comune of Carmignano as well as of "Il Progetto." Sandra Carmagnini and Sandra Belluomini provided me with statistics from the Ufficio di Statistica in Prato. Tosca Masi, nurse-midwife, generously showed me the maternity ward of the Prato Hospital. Barbara Paulson, OBGYN of the Ospedale San Antonio, Fiesole, shared her views on low fertility.

For intellectual development and guidance on making initial sense of this research, I am grateful to my Ph.D. committee members Ana Alonso, Jane Hill, Mark Nichter, Susan Philips, and Hermann Rebel. Jane Schneider and Susan Greenhalgh offered inspiration, particularly in their roles as discussants on a panel for the American Anthropological Association, which I co-organized with David Kertzer. A number of scholars clued me in to specific references or images, and they are due my thanks: Massimo Bressan, Giovanni Contini, Luciana Fellin, Betsy Hartmann, Leslie King, and Teresa Picarazzi. I am grateful for transcription and translation assistance at various stages of the project from Antonella del Conte, Luciana Fellin, Ginevra Lombardi, and Matilde Zampi. Special thanks are due to Milena Marchesi, my research assistant during fall 2003, for sensitive translations, conscientious proofreading, and late-hour moral support. Colleagues in the Department of Anthropology at the University of Massachusetts, Amherst, offered ongoing gestures of support, such as Lynette Sievert, Oriol Pi-Sunyer, and Brooke Thomas for relevant articles or books they have slipped in my mailbox, and David Samuels, Alan Swedlund, and Jackie Urla for their many stimulating conversations and references. Several colleagues helped me puzzle through Chapter 7, including Julie Hemment and, in particular, Enoch Page. During a public presentation of that chapter a number of folks made stimulating comments, including Elizabeth Chilton, Bob Paynter, and Martin Wobst. Comments from readers outside of anthropology have also been invaluable, including Chris Brashear, Kate Hudson, and Marian Krause.

Graduate students of my Spring 2003 seminar on population and governmentality offered inspiration, insight, and reference materials: Broughton Anderson, Gordon Chase, Ge "Gladys" Jian, Cathy Dubois, Carla Hammar, Ioana Lixandru, Milena Marchesi, Lisa Modenos, Carlo Ruiz, Flavia Stanley, Shu Yang, and Angelina Zontine. The undergraduates from my Cultural Politics class that same semester are due thanks for their insightful essays related to the *60 Minutes* report of Italian *mammoni;* in particular, Elizabeth Boc, Maggie Gaw, Chelsea Goodchild, Jonathan Hitzges, and Sarah Young. My thanks for the video are due to Mary Deane Sorcinelli of the University of Massachusetts Center for Teaching and director of the 2002– 2003 Lilly Teaching Fellowship Program. My department chair, Ralph Faulkingham, deserves special thanks for nominating me for the fellowship, which granted me a semester leave and as such allowed me to devote myself to writing this book.

My daughter, Hollis, was a year-and-a-half old when I entered the Ph.D. program at Arizona. She turned 9 on the day I graduated, and at this writing she is 12. I joke that her childhood was lost to my dissertation. My husband, Chris, was my biggest supporter during my graduate studies, my fieldwork, my writing of the dissertation, and this book. I thank him for his infinite patience, inspiration, and love. He found the strength to believe in me when I had none. He also became a fabulous cook in Italy, and fed me countless meals as I wrote. His musical connections introduced me to numerous people; some found their way into my work. Having a daughter and partner with me in the field were of tremendous value for this study.

For her vision, my thanks are due to Wadsworth acquisitions editor, Lin Marshall, for copyediting Cheryl Hauser, and for technical assistance Mary Deeg. My editor, John Young, is deserving of special mention for inviting me to write this book. Throughout the process, he has shown himself to have dedication to clarity in prose and sensitivity to the non-specialist. May his policing of jargon make this a readable book!

I, of course, take complete responsibility for any shortcomings with the caveat that, as the late Daniel Nugent once said, any work is always "in progress."

Figure 0.1 Map of Province of Prato (Tuscany), Italy

1/Population Politics, Cultural Struggles

There is a serious threat that weighs on the future of this country. . . . I am referring to the crisis of births, to the demographic decline, and to the aging of the population.
— Pope John Paul II, addressing the Italian Parliament
La Nazione, November 15, 2002

Italians have roots like an oak tree; Americans have roots like moss. It's a lovely analogy—the *quercia,* or oak, with roots that penetrate deep and extend wide; moss with roots so fine, so delicate, so superficial you can lift a clump up, move it to another place, and keep the moss practically intact.
— Author's Fieldnotes, July 15, 1996

I was on the patio of a restored farmhouse in Tuscany when a dinner guest offered me the roots image to explain the difference between Italian and American experiences of life. I was well into my first year of field research, feeling confused about my work; I found myself in a muddle of complicated family relations. I had let people into my heart, and it left me vulnerable. The dinner guest's choice of metaphors energized me. She was handing me a clue for deciphering the meaning of the profound trend that I sought to grasp: Italian women in the 1990s attained the lowest birthrate in world history. The one-child family in Italy was becoming the statistical norm. But it was a very controversial norm.

The oak-moss analogy shed light on Italian culture. If Italians' sense of themselves was as deeply rooted as the dinner guest made it out to be, then I needed to search out people's relationship with the past to understand the meanings in the present. In newspapers, in scientific reports, in casual conversations, there was a great deal of fuss over the new Italian family. To some, the family was in the midst of a crisis. To others, it was undergoing a much-needed revolution. Perhaps these reactions were to be expected, given that the family is an icon of Italian culture. If Italians clung to their traditions, as the dinner guest suggested, then how could a society let such a thing happen?

Among Italian couples with children, most families as of 1996 were "small": 43.8 percent had only one child, 42.5 percent had two children, and only 13.7 percent had three or more children (Treves 1997:12, ISTAT 1996). By demographic calculations, Italian women had in the past decade on average 1.2 to 1.3 children (de Sandre 2000, Pérez Delgado and Livi-Bacci 1992, Population Reference Bureau 2002, ISTAT 2002). I wanted more than ever to know what motivated and constrained Italians to make such small families? How did Italians experience this profound change? What kinds of tensions was this trend producing? People's deeper motivations and experiences were absent from the statistics.

The small family has become an eloquent symbol of postwar, upwardly mobile Italy. It symbolizes modern motherhood. Some view it as a sign of a more thoughtful and empowered generation. But it also symbolizes a national problem, one that many demographers, politicians, and policymakers would like to fix.

A CRISIS OF BIRTHS

The profound changes in the Italian family have not gone unnoticed in Italy. As a nation, Italian society is bothered by this trend. The Italian government rates its nation's birthrate as too low as noted in the country reports of the Population Reference Bureau (2002). This grim mood is prevalent in demographers' scientific reports, which frame the trend as a problem. The dire warnings echo in the media as well. A woman's magazine spoke of "demographic desertification," a national daily described Italy as a nation that "is old and without babies," and another juxtaposed "empty cradles" with a growing "immigrant supply" (La Nazione 1997, La Stampa 1997). A cartoon appearing in a June 1997 issue of a newsmagazine offered social commentary on the trend: "Italians don't have children anymore. They want to be free to do whatever the hell they want without too many witnesses" (Figure 1.1).

In November 2002, the Pope put his mark on the problem during an historic and controversial address to the Italian Parliament, when he expressed concern over the "crisis of births" as a *"grave minaccia"*—serious threat—that weighs on the future of Italy (Drioli 2002).

The demographic situation across Europe has attracted similar attention. Spain's fertility rate reached 1.1, said to be the lowest national average in Western Europe. In Sweden, Germany, and Greece, the total fertility rate in 2001 was 1.4 births per woman on average, according to the World Health Organization (WHO). Pronatalist sentiments have popped up in popular culture. To wit, one image appearing on Swedish billboards and news media pages in 2001 pictured suit-wearing white men flanking several microphones, as though at a press conference, donning buttons on their lapels with the dictum, "FUCK FOR FUTURE." The circular layout of the words and the choice of yellow typography on a blue background mimicked the official flag of the European Union. The technocratic images suggested an official government campaign, which very political words reinforced. The print urged readers to procreate:

> Sex is no pleasure. It's business. And today it's bad business here in the Western world. There aren't enough babies being born. So, who will take care of us when we

L'Espresso

PER ESEMPIO   di Altan

GLI ITALIANI NON FANNO PIÚ
FIGLI. VOGLIONO ESSER LIBERI
DI FARE LE LORO CAZZATE
SENZA TROPPI TESTIMONI.

*Figure 1.1 Cartoonist Altan
captures the mood:
"Italians don't have
children anymore. They
want to be free to do whatever the hell they want without too many witnesses."
From the newsmagazine
L'Espresso (June 26, 1997).
© Altan/Quipos. Reprinted
with permission.*

are old? Who will work and pay for our pensions? Please. Don't just make love. Make babies. Or let's put it like this: drop your pants or drop dead.

On first glance, it appeared the Swedish government had sponsored a pro-natalist advertisement, but further investigation revealed the ad to be part of an ad campaign for Bjorn Borg fashion underwear. The only reference to underwear is "drop your pants or drop dead"; however, the ad includes the signature of the Swedish tennis star. That the people photographed were white and male serves as a reminder that population politics are simultaneously gender and racial politics. Images made clear the target population: white Europeans, not immigrants.

Europe's declining birthrates stand in contrast to a relatively robust, demographically speaking, U.S. total fertility rate of 2.1. Former presidential candidate Patrick Buchanan (2002:23–24) in his *New York Times* best-selling *Death of the West* uses the European case as a cautionary tale. "The death of the West is not a prediction of what is going to happen, it is a depiction of what is happening now. . . . Outside of Muslim Albania, no European nation is producing enough babies to replace its population. . . ." His political agenda strives to incite panic in his readers. He warns, "The First World has to turn this around, and soon, or it will be overwhelmed by a Third World that is five times as populous and will be ten times as populous in 2050." His project is very much concerned with preventing the decline of a white population—particularly those who are Christian, conservative, protectionist, and anti-immigration. He locates the heirs to a mythical, unified European legacy in his people, writing against the segments of society who are socially tolerant and secular. His enemies are the socialist state and women who have "given up on" bearing and raising children.

Similar panic smears the front pages of major newspapers. Declining birthrates have become newsworthy, and the trend receives consistent alarmist reportage. The low fertility is an "increasingly worrisome reality for Italy and other European countries whose fertility rates have plummeted over the last decades," wrote reporter Frank Bruni (2002) on the front page of the *New York Times*. He described a worsening situation in which the "slow-building consequences are coming into starker relief" as European countries "address the specter of sharply winnowed and less competitive work forces, surfeits of retirees and pension systems that will need to be cut back deeply." His descriptions reinforced the notion of Europe as a dying continent. At a playground in Ferrara, Italy, despite it being filled with children and adoring parents, Bruni nevertheless described there being "something wrong with the picture. Most of the parents were gazing at one, and only one, child."

Another doom-and-gloom report appeared in a *New York Times* article entitled "Population Implosion Worries a Graying Europe," which framed low fertility as an "epidemic." Reporter Michael Specter (1998) located the etiology of this epidemic in women's practice of "choosing work and education over having children." The article described birthrates in many countries as being "in a rapid, sustained decline. Never before—except in times of plague, war and deep economic depression—have birthrates fallen so low, for so long." Plague, war, and deep economic depression invoke disastrous moments in the history of populations and echo old Malthusian logics of the constraints that populations place on resources.

In light of the decades of global clamoring related to the "world population explosion," this mood of doom and gloom related to population decline would seem paradoxical. Globally, overpopulation has been depicted as *the* contemporary problem. Bottles of ink have been spilt to alarm people in wealthy countries about rapid population growth elsewhere. By the close of the 20th century, demographic analyst Nicholas Eberstadt (2001) notes that "a worldwide administrative apparatus . . . had been erected for the express purpose of 'stabilizing' world population. . . ." Foundations, ministries, and aid agencies vigorously pursued stringent family-planning policies as they focused on developing areas where birthrates were relatively high. A number of people questioned the wisdom of this crusade; it had liberating as well as oppressive dimensions. Family-planning workers used coercive measures to reduce births, often ignoring poor women's reproductive rights and viewing their reproductive health as secondary to preventing pregnancies. Sometimes, clinic workers forcibly sterilized women. At other times they pushed unwanted contraceptive devices or measures on them. India, for example, witnessed a brutal sterilization campaign in the late 1970s under Indira Gandhi. Furthermore, the population panic was often a case of misplaced blame. The 1992 UN Conference on Environment and Development, or Earth Summit, held in Rio de Janeiro, condemned explanations that blamed women's fertility rates for environmental degradation (Hartmann

1995:xiii). The document drafters called for identifying economic restructuring, militarism, as well as wasteful and unjust production and consumption patterns as key culprits in quality of life issues, not overpopulation. A move away from sounding tone-deaf population alarms was also witnessed at the UN Conference on Population and Development in Cairo in 1994, when delegates adopted an agenda of reproductive rights. Abandoned were contraceptive targets; embraced were improved education and health for women and children as well as voluntary contraceptive choices. The shift in political discourse has influenced policy, but the goals of women's empowerment have yet to be fully met. Many countries, including India, had recoiled against coercive policies. But in fall 2003 the *New York Times* reported a national mood that favored a hard-line renewal: "At least six states have laws mandating a two-child norm for members of village councils, and some are extending it to civil servants as well" (Waldman 2003). Policies also include incentives such as pay raises, and access to land or housing, for government servants who choose sterilization after one or two children. Women in India on average give birth to half as many children as they did 50 years ago, with a total fertility rate of 3.2 (Population Reference Bureau 2002), but with demographic predictions that India's population will surpass China's as the biggest in the world by mid-century, policymakers once again seek to regulate reproduction.

Global fertility decline is expected to be the big issue of the new millennium, so predicts world renowned demographer Jon Bongaarts (1998). Some of the major concerns will be related to "subreplacement" fertility regimes, aging of the world's population, and prolonged mortality crises such as HIV/AIDS. Some 83 countries now are showing signs of below-replacement fertility levels, according to Eberstadt, and these countries account for about 2.7 billion people, or 44 percent of the earth's population. So-called subreplacement fertility societies are not exclusive to Europe. One difference, however, is that countries such as Italy and Spain reached their record low levels without even trying in the sense that the governments did not run population limitation campaigns.

The dominant sentiment toward the low birthrate situation among European policymakers is trepidation. Italian demographers' reports, news media articles, and political as well as social commentary reveal that Italy does not find in low fertility cause to celebrate. Rather, it is something to fear. One demographer drew a parallel between teenage anorexics who refuse to eat food and Italians who exhibit a "hard refusal" to procreate (Livi-Bacci 1994:14). Similarly, Italy is repeatedly described as a dying nation. French sociologist Henri Medras writing in *Le Monde* described Italy's birthing trend as "collective suicide" and minced no words in blaming Italian women (Brunella 2002). "No people can support a trauma of that sort," wrote Medras, whose assessment was also published in the major daily *La Stampa*. This talk of national decay, as anthropologists Susan Gal and Gail Kligman point out, is "a recurrent theme of nationalist discourse all over Europe" (2000:27).

Indeed, the national social body appears to be suffering from an illness if a recent book by prominent Italian demographers is any indication: *Il malessere demografico in Italia*, or *Demographic Malaise*, draws on a metaphor usually reserved for bodily health. The term *malessere*, or malaise, implies that a demographic trend has become a national pathology. The authors speak of an "excess" of low fertility (Golini et al. 2000:7) and of pending "deformations" in the age structure (p. 98). They ponder the dangers that transmogrified generational ratios may pose to "adequate social cohesion" (p. 99). Such forecasts ooze with assumptions about a normal, healthy society—one based on a narrowly defined heterosexual, nuclear family of "white" Italian nationals whose composition should include two children.

WHY "CULTURE"?

I spent two years in central Italy, living and working with people to study the record-low birthrates of Italian women. When I tell people about this demographic distinction, the first question I always hear is "why?" The fact challenges people's stereotypes about the large, Catholic Italian family. A few years ago, I found myself in one of those "why" moments. I was sharing a table with my two older sisters and the platinum blonde president of a midsized Texas oil company, along with several of her associates. We were guests at a special event connected with my father's business association's annual meeting. Dinner was served at tables on the lawn of Marilyn Monroe's former house in Palm Desert, California, and lookalikes of Marilyn, Lucille Ball, and Clark Gable roamed the premises, creating a fantasy Hollywood mood. Meanwhile, the Texan woman told us of her rise to power in her firm, climbing 34 years ago from secretary to president, and marrying the president's son (10 years her junior). Attention then turned to me.

"So, what do you do?" one of the Texan women asked me. I'd been spending the last year in a cubicle writing and still had another year ahead of me before I finished the 440-page doctoral dissertation.

"I'm a nerd," I confessed. The *Dallas*-like life stories, not to mention the fantasy setting, made my life seem dull. Yet wearing a stylish black dress, I hardly looked the part. They cast expressions of part pity, part skepticism. Little did they know we had gone out and bought the get-up that morning just for the occasion. I dared to mention my research on Italy's low birthrate.

"What's the reason?" the Texans wanted to know.

"Culture" was my quick response. They looked puzzled. Wasn't the family central to Italian culture? Dinner talk lends itself to quick explanations, so I quipped, "coitus interruptus!"

One man at the dinner table had never heard the scientific term for withdrawal; he kept saying "cloitus interruptus." His gaffe brought chuckles, especially from the women at the table.

My research does make titillating dinner talk. Beyond that, my topic reaches deep into the meanings, desires, and tensions of life. Truth was Sicilian artisans in the 1930s learned about withdrawal from their French socialist comrades.[1] Anthropologists Jane and Peter Schneider (1996:163) learned that Sicilian artisans went from having about six children per family to two or three in the course

---

[1]Recent U.S. medical data have come around to viewing coitus interruptus as effective if practiced correctly. A chapter from *Contraceptive Technology* (Hatcher et al. 1994:341) argues: "Although coitus interruptus has often been criticized as an ineffective method, it probably confers a level of contraceptive protection similar to that provided by barrier methods. Effectiveness depends largely on the male's ability to withdraw prior to ejaculation. . . . Our best guess is that about 4 percent of perfect users would fail in the initial year."

SOCIETÀ

Provate a fare i conti: un padre, una madre, un unico bambino. Semplice? No: bisogna aggiungere l'ex marito della mamma, l'ex moglie di papà, i loro precedenti figli. Perché l'istituzione più solida d'Italia sta cambiando rapidissimamente. È la svolta ci riguarda tutti. Da vicino.

BRACCIA PER LA PATRIA... Un'immagine del 1935, quando la politica demografica del fascismo premiava le famiglie numerose. La foto ritrae un ufficiale dell'esercito con moglie e bimbi in posa. Davanti alla bandiera, le bambine vestono da Piccole italiane, il maschietto ha il fez dei Balilla.

La famiglia diventa mini (ma molto complicata)

DI RAFFAELLA PROCENZANO

Figure 1.2 A magazine contrasts the ideal family of the fascist era with the contemporary one. "Arms for the fatherland" was the imperative of the fascist demographic campaign, which rewarded large families. Circa 1935. Published in Epoca, *January 31, 1997 (p. 36). Reprinted with permission of Arnoldo Mondadori Editore S.p.A.*

of a decade or so.[2] They discovered that class position shaped people's outlooks and values. It also predicted when they joined the demographic transition as a way to attain respectability. How many children people had became an outward sign of their rationality. In a modernizing society whose members sought to distance themselves from the stigma of a rural and impoverished past, rational family-making was also a sign of morality, for women as well as men.

Given the extent of the public commentary on the subject of fertility rates, it is not surprising that social scientists as well as laypeople take a crack at explaining it. As many reasons circulate in Italian society about the cause of the low birthrate as there are pasta shapes at the local supermarket. Italians know well the status of their demographic profile (see Palomba et al. 1987). An article in a 1997 magazine supplement of the national daily *La Repubblica,* written by Laura Guglielmi, drew on a host of experts to attempt an explanation. I organized their explanations thematically:

- *Identity shifts.* Psychological motivations have changed as has the concept of family and of sacrifice. At one time, it was a duty to have children and to sacrifice oneself for them; now people think that parents have the right to have space and time for joy, happiness, and fun. Catholic social critics characterize

[2]Some 22 percent of fertile women interviewed in 1995 for Italy's national fertility survey said they had practiced coitus interruptus in the past four weeks. See Table 4.1 (p. 71).

...PERÒ IN TRE SI STA MEGLIO
Le cifre parlano chiaro: ormai la
coppia media italiana ha un solo figlio.
Così il legame è più stretto e anche
il lavoro della donna non ne risente.

Figure 1.3 "But it's better in three. By now, the average Italian couple has only one child. The links are stronger and even women's work is not impacted." Reprinted with permission of Epoca.

these new attitudes as self-centered and hedonistic, according to theologian Don Antonio Forte. He described values as "unhinged"—a reflection of a consumer society out of whack. Furthermore, he noted a fear about the future and a general negative outlook due to rampant insecurity about the economy and unemployment. On the other hand, socio-demographer Paolo Arvati, of the Comune of Genoa (the region has one of the lowest birthrates in the nation), attributed the low indexes of natality to people using "reason."

- *Gender roles.* Maternity is no longer the primary goal of women's existence. Researcher Alessandra Merozzi underscored the heavier workload of Italian women as compared to men—28 percent greater. Women lack time to dedicate to having babies, she reasoned, and they have found other projects to devote themselves to besides having children. They value their newfound autonomy and see no good reason to have children. Feminist Lidia Menapace said women do not want to replicate the triple roles of their own mothers: wife, mother, and worker. And despite a male identity crisis, men largely refuse to share in domestic tasks.

- *Social services.* The national government has been slow to provide social services and respond to working mothers' needs, according to Livia Turco, then minister of social affairs. She advocated a more flexible labor market with more part-time jobs. The structure of the labor market in the 1990s made it

TABLE 1.1 TOTAL FERTILITY RATES IN ITALY BY REGION

Region	1975	1980	1985	1990	Percent Change 1975–1990
Italy	2.18	1.66	1.41	1.31	−39.9
Abruzzi	2.10	1.74	1.47	1.30	−38.1
Basilicata	2.69	1.99	1.73	1.59	−40.9
Calabria	2.65	2.19	1.84	1.61	−39.2
Campania	2.82	2.29	1.94	1.70	−39.7
Emilia	1.74	1.18	1.00	0.99	−43.1
Friuli V.G.	1.81	1.24	1.05	0.99	−45.3
Lazio	2.12	1.58	1.32	1.24	−41.5
Liguria	1.65	1.11	0.99	0.98	−40.6
Lombardy	1.99	1.39	1.22	1.15	−42.2
Marches	1.94	1.51	1.28	1.17	−39.7
Molise	2.21	1.82	1.55	1.33	−39.8
Piedmont	1.91	1.33	1.16	1.11	−41.9
Puglia	2.78	2.19	1.71	1.56	−43.9
Sardinia	2.64	1.95	1.52	1.40	−47.0
Sicily	2.61	2.18	1.80	1.70	−34.9
Trentino A. A.	2.08	1.64	1.44	1.38	−33.7
Tuscany	1.82	1.31	1.11	1.04	−42.9
Umbria	1.90	1.48	1.26	1.10	−42.1
Veneto	2.02	1.82	1.23	1.13	−44.1

Source: Margarita Delgado Pérez and Massimo Livi-Bacci, "Fertility in Italy and Spain: The Lowest in the World," *Family Planning Perspectives* 24(4):162–171, 1992, p. 164. Reprinted with permission.

difficult for women to re-enter the workforce after maternity, if they took more than the year's leave or if they quit their job.

- *Demographic trends.* Late ages of marriage and children living at home ever longer also contribute to the low birthrate. Demographer Golini framed the birthrate as a "problem" that will result in an increasingly elderly population. Sociologist Maria Teresa Torti pointed to the trends of young people waiting ever longer to find work, to move out from their parents' home, and to marry than in other industrialized countries. Finally, gynecologist Sandra Morano maintained that there are increases in male sterility. She argued, however, that infertility is due more to psychological causes than to biological ones (Guglielmi 1997).

The above represent hypotheses, political hand-wringing, and demographic facts. They tell us little, however, about what led to the uprooting of the oak tree, to use the metaphor of the dinner guest, and its consequences. They tell us little about the adequacy of the uprooting metaphor for low fertility. Perhaps we might find an alternative.

My project seeks to shed light on how Italians are living this demographic shift (see Table 1.1). It places Italian culture at its center. The investigation takes place not on a demographic stage, where pie charts and tables predominate, but moves the spotlight behind the curtain of aggregate science to illuminate the players in this demographic dynamic. As such, I attend to the different ways in which people's lives are meaningful. I attempt to grasp what a swift demographic shift means to people. What explains and limits people's choices? How do Italians themselves explain their desire to have small families? To accomplish these tasks, I lived and worked with Italians to elicit their memories and to follow their day-to-day lives. I sought a strategy to get beneath aggregate statistics. I drew on a wide range of networks—including those made in a sweater factory, family finishing firm, at an elementary school, at community festivals, in a coffee group, and at a social club. My goal was to weave a story of changes in family-making, a term I use to emphasize that family forms have histories, too. My focus was people living in an industrial-agricultural province of Tuscany, a region Golini and his coauthors (2000:225) characterized as having "broad and diffuse demographic malaise."

As the researchers mapped the demographic health of the nation, they devised seven possible classifications (A–G). They assigned Tuscany to the second to last category (F): "new economic model in demographic crisis." On the one hand, they note, such areas are characterized by an equal percentage of workers employed in industry and in subcontracting; employment levels, whether male or female, are among the highest anywhere in the country, hence the economic structure appears vital. On the other hand, the demographic aspect is in crisis: the level of aging is elevated, the rate of fertility is very low, and the ratio of the population in the lower age range (0–14) is among the lowest. The conclusion: "intense malaise" (p. 81). The regional maps, however, show tremendous within-region variation. So that within Tuscany, hill towns and mountain towns are the most at risk. By contrast, the province of Prato where I positioned my research is rated as having only "moderate malaise," probably due in large part to its intensified industrial activity and the young workers it has historically and continuously attracted (pp. 224–235).

ENTERING THE FIELD

I arrived in Prato somewhat by accident, at minimum by coincidence. I had written to Carlo, an old friend whom I met during an art history study-abroad program in 1984. I told him of my desire to live in a working-class neighborhood of Florence and asked him whether he might have any leads. Carlo's mother had a friend, a widow, whom she had met through a mutual acquaintance: a psychiatrist whose house she cleaned and who treated the widow friend's daughter. The two women had met while doing some catering work for the psychiatrist—a sort of patron-client, favors-for-service relationship. It turned out this widow friend had an empty apartment and was looking for trustworthy tenants. She wanted to rent to someone who would leave when she was ready, who would respect her need for serenity, and who would not taint her reputation. She had formerly rented to a single man who had taken up with an ill-reputed young woman, and their domestic disputes finally ended in a police-enforced eviction. We came well recommended, so she agreed to host us for a month on a trial basis.

My appearance at the Florence Santa Maria Novella train station followed an orientation program that started in Rome and concluded on the Amalfi coast with the 30 or so other Fulbright scholars. I was the lone anthropologist. Most of my peers specialized in fields like art history, literary studies, classical music, sculpture—fields that lent themselves to spending time in prestigious archives, such as the Vatican in Rome and the Biblioteca Nazionale in Florence. They were studying Culture with a capital "C." I was headed to the "field" to study culture with a lower case "c." In particular, I was interested in the cultural practices of working-class people. I tried hard to shrug off my sense that, to some of my peers, my project lacked cultural capital.[3] My intention, after all, was to get to know working people to understand how a world-famous demographic shift was playing out on the ground. Somehow talking with and working with sweater-makers just did not seem as prestigious as fondling centuries-old documents. It would be some time before I really worked through my own insecurities about doing fieldwork. It turns out that fieldwork does not happen automatically. I knew going in that time and patience would be necessary, but knowing it in the abstract and living it in the concrete are as different as fantasizing about a lover and negotiating a relationship.

My friend, Carlo, met us at the train station. We headed north, leaving behind the urban periphery's boxlike high rises, where he lived with his parents and sister and two brothers in a two-bedroom apartment. We crossed the agricultural plain that extends to the northwest of Florence. The road traverses fields of grain and sunflowers, dye-saturated rivers, until the landscape gives way to rolling hills. Here, some 20 kilometers northwest of Florence, the province changes to Prato, sometimes referred to as "the Manchester of Tuscany." It is an industrial region, and many Italians here came into money through textiles: fabrics, clothes, sweaters bearing "MADE IN ITALY" tags. In the 19th century and early 20th century, it was native Pratese who wove the straw hats, sorted the old rags, and tended the textile machinery that was the basis of a rather stigmatized yet globally interconnected economy. Then there was the post–World War II economic boom, when the textile industry became known for producing not only affordable goods but also luxury fabrics. Its industrial artisans became known for their sense of innovation and style. During the 1960s, thousands upon thousands of Italian peasants migrated from Tuscany's countryside as well as from points South, such as Calabria and Sicily, to take part in the burgeoning economy. In the decades that followed, newcomers began arriving from other countries, and were known as *extracommunitari*, outside the European Union. The most numerous immigrant group in Prato has been, and remains, the Chinese. A development scheme planned for Prato resulted in an industrial district famous for its defiance of "typical" modernization patterns: rather than large-scale, centralized corporations, small- to medium-sized firms proliferated in Prato. This very diffuse industry has a history of subcontracting. The subcontracting has translated into increased autonomy for industrial artisans as well as exploitation of pieceworkers, especially women, who have worked in small shops in the hidden economy. In a countryside that seemed beyond the urban bustle, where olive trees and grapevines clung to hillsides interspersed with stone farm buildings, there too were housed noisy textile machinery. The small vans that speedily cruised the curves, loaded with sweater pieces to finish, interrupted the romantic image of Tuscany.

[3]The term "cultural capital," developed by French sociologist Pierre Bourdieu (1984), is useful because it allows us to see that prestige is not merely measured in economic capital, or how much money someone is worth. Important sources of prestige also derive from how much education people have, for example.

The neighborhood may have appeared at first to be a sleepy hamlet but the frenzy of activity proved otherwise. Car interiors burst with sweater pieces, and vans were loaded with giant spools of yarn. Trash bags were stuffed to the brim with partially woven discards. An ongoing dissonance of metal grinding against metal resonated from the mechanized looms. And the pungent and offensive odor of hot wool provided clues to the centrality of the sweater industry for this neighborhood's residents. In the province of Prato, textiles were king, and *lavoro nero,* hidden labor, was reputed to be the highest in all of central Italy. I came to learn that women did much of this hidden work. That particular history, it turns out, holds significance to this story of family change.

But I did not know any of this when, with Carlo, we pulled off the main drag and into a neighborhood. I only knew what I could see. The spiffy houses on the street were painted cream, white, or straw and topped with sienna-colored tile roofs. A smattering of large, centuries-old farmhouses reminded me of an agricultural past, though elaborate restorations pointed to newfound wealth. We passed a street named *Via Gramsci,* suggesting a fairly new—by Italian measures—neighborhood with left-leaning politics. After all, Antonio Gramsci was the communist intellectual from Sardinia whom the fascists imprisoned from 1926 to 1937 to "prevent this brain from functioning" (Crehan 2002:17, Gramsci 1971) but who nevertheless wrote a highly influential series of notebooks. Among anthropologists, he is most widely known for the concept of hegemony as a modern form of power that relies on consent with the ever-present threat of coercion.

Carlo introduced me, my husband, and soon-to-be 5-year-old daughter to Nicoletta, a widow who looked much older than her years: then in her mid-60s. She smiled tentatively as she invited us into her kitchen. It was spotless and orderly. She had prepared a hot meal, and my stomach, in knots from the travel, was grateful. The conversation flew by me; my Italian language skills were rusty and I lacked knowledge of the local dialect. Before long, we met her youngest daughter, Liliana, 38, who lived with Nicoletta in the main floor apartment. Carlo had warned me about Liliana's mental fragility. Liliana's face glowed, it was so heavily smeared with makeup. Her lipstick was overly pink for her stout body—likely a weight problem, I imagined, that resulted from years of psychiatric medication. Liliana squealed enthusiastically at my daughter. I detected discomfort on my little girl's face.

We soon met the other members of the household: Luisa, 41, struck me as upbeat, charismatic, and immediately likable. She lived with her broad-shouldered, soft-spoken yet friendly husband, Oliviero, in an apartment on the second floor of the house. They led us across the driveway to their workshop. Two textile machines clanked day and night, weaving threads into the basic parts for sweaters: the bodies and the sleeves. Piles of woven sweater pieces sat in stacks. Oliviero explained that they would soon be transported back to the *maglificio,* sweater company, to then be transferred to other workshops for finishing, and then back to the *maglificio* for their ultimate destinations: for sale internally, at local markets like the one at San Lorenzo in Florence, or distant markets well beyond the borders of Italy. This integration of work and domestic life fascinated me. I hoped to immerse myself in their world. Initially, though, the smell of burnt wool really bothered me, and I worried whether I would grow accustomed to it.

Next, Nicoletta showed us the apartment. My spirits fell. It was a dark and dank basement space, like a cave. It smelled of paint. It was small for three people and had no writing space. The kitchen lacked hot water, the bathroom lacked a tub. We had no control over the heat. In these parts of Italy, the heat was not left on in the winter. Rather, people used it a maximum of 8 hours per day, meaning the mornings could be quite damp and chilly in winter. Sweaters would certainly come in handy. The basement had originally been a workshop but then, after Luisa and Liliana's father died 8 years earlier, Nicoletta divided it into two and converted the street-facing half into an apartment. She intended the patio-facing half, with stairs to the main floor, the fireplace, and access to the garden, to be off limits to the new tenants. Access to this space would be a huge point of negotiation during the "trial" period.

The toughest aspect of this initial stage of fieldwork was my own sense of uncertainty. How would I spend my days? I had so many possibilities in terms of situating myself. How to choose in ways that minimized my potential to irritate people? I sensed in people's questions about my project a great deal of curiosity yet also confusion about having an anthropologist in their midst. These first few weeks—perhaps, months—indeed marked my own crisis of legitimacy. The people I met, including Luisa, generally were confused as to why I was not frequenting the University of Florence, a mere 12 miles away, rather than hanging around with sweater-makers. Luisa may have only had a middle-school education but she was smart enough to wonder why somebody like me was not hanging around other intellectual types. Her cousins, a few years younger than me (I was 33 at the time), went to university. She and others kept suggesting I, too, should be heading off to an institution of higher learning. What was I doing here?

> What a strange thing this idea of fieldwork. It is particularly strange, I think, to the people, the Italians, to whom I try to describe the nature of this work. I think of others in my Fulbright cohort, what they are doing, for example, focusing on a single archive. Their work has an air of scholarly pursuit that lends it legitimacy; my work, on the other hand, because it is more with the people, is somehow seen as more dubious. I like that feeling of being strange, of studying the everyday; and yet, at some level I sense people think it a strange way to do academic work. Particularly here in Italy, where there is such a huge division between the *dottore,* or elites with titles, and *il popolo,* or the common people. [*Fieldnotes,* October 6, 1995]

I could not stand it anymore. I started taking the half-hour bus ride into Florence, where I scoped out courses at the university, sat in on a lecture by a well-known British historian of Italy named Paul Ginsborg (1990), and where I finally secured a library card for the Biblioteca Nazionale after navigating a bureaucracy that seemed byzantine in its structure. This library was intimidating not only because of its stately structure and prime location along the bank of the Arno River in Florence, just down from the famous Uffizi Museum, but also for its operational mode that typically did not allow users into the stacks but rather enforced an elaborate system of requesting materials. I poked around there off and on for several weeks, until I finally realized that I had a decision to make:

either I was going to do a library-based project or a field-based project. My participation in a seminar at the exclusive European University Institute in Fiesole changed my mind. I arrived on December 6, 1995, to attend a seminar on oral history by Luisa Passerini, a scholar whose work on the experiences of Turinese workers under fascism I very much admired. One section of her book dealt with memories about resisting the fascist policies that sought to coerce men and women to make babies. Her work had strongly influenced my own eventual decision to study the experience and cultural politics of fertility decline (see Krause 1994, Passerini 1987). It was a thrill to meet Dr. Passerini herself, and to hear her speak in person about some of the challenges of doing oral history and making sense of people's narratives. The students nit-picked over whether the concept of "collective identity" was superior to that of "mentalities." How did these concerns connect with the way people right down the road were struggling with a changing world? At one point a snobby European student with a German accent cornered me in a corridor and grilled me about my project, then tried to examine me on my Italian speaking skills. I found this ironic since classes at the institute, despite its location in the heart of Italy, were conducted primarily in English or French—a sort of academic, linguistic hegemony.

"Well?" he pushed further. "I'm still waiting." I was incensed. Why should I suddenly perform Italian for him? Who was *he?* I loathed the posturing. I had not come to Italy to perform elite dog-sniffing rituals.

Around this period, now some 6 weeks into my stay, Nicoletta invited us along with some cousins to a Sunday meal. Our inclusion made me realize my relationships with these folks were becoming meaningful. I no longer felt that if I were hit by a car and hurled into a ditch that nobody there would notice.

In preparation for the feast, Nicoletta cooked for two days. She was proving herself to be the world's best cook! Was I the ideal Italian-daughter-in-training now, raving about my mother's cooking? The meal consisted of the following courses:

1. *Antipasto:* Crostini—slices of bread with olive and tuna spreads on top.
2. *Primo:* Lasagna—a most delicious sauce made from a mixture of finely chopped carrots, parsley, red onion, tomato sauce, and ground meats ladled onto fresh pasta sheets, then covered with a white sauce, in numerous layers.
3. *Secondi:* Roast pork and chicken.
4. *Contorni:* Rape (a green leafy vegetable in the broccoli family), roasted potatoes, and "twice-baked" eggplant (the eggplant filling was mixed with bread, parmesan, olive oil, eggs, parsley, and garlic, then stuffed into its own shell). The potatoes, chicken, and lasagna were baked in a brick wood-burning oven, located in the garage, because her gas oven lacked ample space for everything.
5. *Bevande:* Local white and red wines and water.
6. *Dolce:* Tiramisu (a delicious dessert, which means "pick me up") and caffé (which I made) and champagne and whiskey (which I skipped).

At one point during the meal, a middle-aged accountant cousin teased Oliviero about his sweater work. A normal day's work required that he "click" the computer keypad that controls the weaving machine. A hard day's work called on him to go "click, click." Everyone laughed. Then it was Luisa's turn.

Elizabeth L. Krause

Figure 1.4 The anthropologist's shadow cast on a workshop

The cousin teased her about how she would make such a good subject for me to study because she was close to the animals. I cringed, worrying, on some level, might they think this? And then he continued, saying I should *really* go to Calabria and study some of the kinfolk down there, especially a certain uncle because he was such an old goat! (I think "hillbilly" might be the closest translation for this moment of urban prejudice against rural folk.) I was growing increasingly uncomfortable with what I took to be a style of talking that disparaged the lower classes, making them out as primitive, lesser beings. I had come to Italy to practice European anthropology. I was not interested in repeating some old script in which the anthropologist was always tracking down things exotic. Rather, I wanted to study power relations in the modern world. As such, I was interested in ideology as well as history. Ideology was central given my understanding of it as the way people use ideas to manifest power, a notion inspired by anthropologist Eric Wolf (1999). The study of culture is ultimately an inquiry into ideology. Getting at manifestations of power called for historical perspectives on everyday life. But scripts are not easily rewritten. For Italians, as for many Americans, anthropology meant the study of non-Western, non-modern peoples. Hence, if I was an anthropologist, then these folks were the "natives." This conversation later generated ongoing jokes about Oliviero and Luisa being my anthropological subjects. They were the "native" couple who embodied the focus of my study: they had no children. They *were* practitioners of subreplacement fertility. They *were* zero-population growth.

There in the moment, I had to jump to the defense of anthropology. It had become, I argued, a cutting-edge discipline relevant to the modern world, to nation-states, to technology, to population dynamics. To which the cousin brilliantly replied, "Ah yes, sure," his hands gesturing just so, "but there *are* things that are more interesting." The implication was, *come on,* people who have strange and exotic characteristics are more interesting to study than "normal" people. I let it rest.

He and his wife, both professionals (she was a schoolteacher), had only one child, and my ears perked up when, he told me that one was all he wanted. He could not imagine the stresses another baby would bring.

Fieldwork, I suddenly realized, was happening.

NICOLETTA: SACRIFICES UNFULFILLED

Nicoletta embodied the quiet revolution: one of six children, she herself had two daughters, and neither of them had any children. She grew up in Calabria. In the early 1960s, she moved with her husband and two daughters to Tuscany, drawn there by the migration of her parents and other siblings. The postwar boom was in full swing in central Italy. In Calabria, Nicoletta and her husband left behind an agricultural life, working land they did not own. When they first arrived in the outskirts of Prato, they were hard-pressed to find a place to live. They were marked as Southerners, and they were discriminated against. Finally, they found an abandoned farmhouse to rent. The neighborhood was largely settled after the 1950s, as other migrants from Calabria, Sicily, and the Tuscan countryside came to take part in the postwar economic boom. Her husband was an artful iron-worker, and he kept busy crafting elegant iron gates and fences for the burgeon-ing new construction in the area. Within several years they built a house of their own. On the ground floor, Nicoletta set up a workshop finishing sweaters, and when her daughters finished middle school, they joined her full-time.

Nicoletta was a widow whose husband died 8 years before I met her in 1995. She was a salt-of-the-earth woman. She performed physically arduous labor: in fact, she refused to stop chopping her own firewood even when her health began to fail her; with great passion, she continued to make her own pasta and create multiple-course culinary feasts until she became so overcome with fatigue that she would end up bedridden for days.

One December evening, Nicoletta, my husband, and I were huddled close to the fire, in the ground-floor apartment we rented. My 5-year-old daughter was sleeping in a small bedroom. Dank air chilled the room. We wore layers of sweaters. These were gifts from her daughter and son-in-law, both sweater-makers. It was a convenient artisan-industry to work in come winter, though an uncomfortably hot one come summer. The joke in these parts was that sweaters just "happen" upon you.

The fireside space beckoned old memories for Nicoletta. She recalled with deep sadness what a beautiful family they had, a family of *toccare,* of love and affection. She and her husband had a way of communicating without words, only with their eyes. It ended suddenly. The family had driven to a restaurant in the mountains for a special New Year's Eve dinner, and her husband suffered a heart attack. The family has never forgotten the shock of that evening. Before the death of her husband, the family used this apartment for large family gatherings as well as for the sweater-finishing work. Festive celebrations there came to an abrupt halt after his death, and for 6 grueling years she rented the apartment to an unmarried, volatile couple whom she managed to force out only after a domestic dispute became so violent that the police had to break it up. "My life went from this to this," she told me, gesturing with her palm. Her youngest daughter's mental illness worsened, and she had to enslave herself to her daughter's psychiatrist, *la professoressa:* Nicoletta cooked specialty dishes for the psychiatrist's parties in exchange for professional psychiatric care for Liliana.

Only recently had she reclaimed the apartment and decided to rent it out to us. We lived in one half and shared the other half, so that she could use the staircase from her first-floor apartment to access her patio, wood oven, and vegetable plot, as well as flower garden. The sweetness of the flowers helped mask the pungent odors from raw sewage and burnt wool fiber that frequently infused the air in this neighborhood. Since we were foreigners, she was confident our stay would be temporary, a contrast with Italian tenants, whose legal rights were so strong that many property owners would leave apartments vacant rather than risk losing the space indefinitely to renters who refused to move.

Nicoletta sat on a folding wooden chair beside the fire, and she began to tell us about her life. I turned on my tape recorder, and she told me about the profound changes between her parents, herself, and her children. I had only been in the field for 6 weeks, and Nicoletta's way of talking presented a particular challenge to me: her own family spoke an Albanian dialect and, after she moved to Tuscany in 1962, she acquired aspects of the local dialect, one particular to Prato. Her painful experiences as a Southern migrant made her sensitive to my difficulties with language and culture. Since I did not understand everything, I tended to keep quiet and let her say what came to mind, planning later to transcribe and translate her story that so profoundly spoke to demographic changes.

"Our generation, we were the sort of people who were more understanding. I married and I entered—" Nicoletta paused and then proclaimed, *"suocera."* Mother-in-law. She uttered the word as though it were written in bold letters.

After marriage, Nicoletta moved in with her husband's family and assumed her "rightful" position beneath the mother-in-law. Her *suocera,* or mother-in-law, was a widow who wore black until the day she died. Nicoletta described her as a severe woman. Her husband had passed away when her children were small. The family did not own the land it worked and was always in debt to the wealthy landowners. The household consisted of an extended family: a married sister and brother-in-law with two children, two other unmarried brothers, and Nicoletta and her new husband. Each couple had a bedroom.

"How is it that we all got along and we ate one plate of pasta a day and that's it?" she asked. The implication was that young people today could not endure such a living arrangement. The question was perhaps also directed at me, a young woman, a member of this "new" generation.

Nicoletta's description of the household points to hierarchical relations that formerly existed between the generations under the patriarchal family form. This arrangement dictated social relations that shaped a person's everyday experiences and their social identity. The daughters-in-law had certain jobs to do, and they did them (allegedly) without complaint.

"Sometimes she'd say of the dirty clothes, 'No, no I'll wash them myself.' Instead, we—my sister-in-law (we were talking today)—we'd go rummage around and gather up all the dirty clothes. We'd wash them [by hand] until they were good and clean, and we'd put them away in the drawers. Because we were *nuore,* daughters-in-law; we had to make ourselves available to the ones who were of a certain age." Age implied status.

Living in a patriarchal household required its members to accept certain obligations and perform certain tasks. To behave otherwise would have been disrespectful.

"My sister-in-law and I did it." She then asked, "Why did I do it? Because I respected my husband."

Things have changed in her daughters' generation, born in the 1950s.

"Now they don't understand. If someone is 60, if they're 80, if they're 90 years old. It's as if these parents don't exist anymore for anybody. And like the daughters-in-law, there's no such thing as a parent. And why not?"

Her question signaled her sense that responsibility—manifested in the form of respect for elders—had eroded with the social transformations in the postwar society. I remember well how strongly she wanted me to understand this point about the patriarchal family and systems of respect. I remember then thinking, "Ah-ha! This is important. This is the crux of the whole issue in terms of changes in the family, changes in the economy, changes in consumerism, changes in senses of self." There was tremendous unraveling and redefining of the whole point of life. In Nicoletta's generation, rarely did anyone question the life course: when you reached a certain age, you married, started having sex, and then the children came along. Then you sacrificed for your children. You did all you could for them in terms of making their lives as good as possible. You never doubted that they would do the same thing: that they would marry and have kids. When you grew old, your children would take care of you, and their children would take care of them. And on and on, down through the generations. The intensity in Nicoletta's voice suggested that something in this chain of reciprocity had broken. Her experience was one of betrayal—betrayal, in fact, by a whole generation.

"Since when in the world has there existed a wife and a husband without parents? I beat my- myself here." Her hand had by this point formed into a fist and she hit herself on the chest, a gesture of a broken heart. "I'll make a real mess here. Because nobody is born without parents!"

"I see," I said.

"Mamma!" interrupted a voice from the top of the stairs. It was Liliana, the unmarried daughter. Liliana suffered from mental problems of an unnamed sort: sometimes manic, sometimes depressed, prone to outrageous storytelling and exhibitionist displays. It was somehow ironic, humorous, and tragic that just as Nicoletta's diatribes about family change was reaching its climax, her daughter was calling to her because she was jealous of us and wanted her mother's attention.

"And parents always have a right—"

"Mamma!"

"—to be appreciated." Nicoletta then added in staccato: *"As long as they're living."*

"MAMMA!"

"Love," she replied.

"Are you coming up?"

"Yes." Nicoletta laughed.

The fact that a grown woman was calling for her mother stood as one example, an extreme example but nevertheless one that Nicoletta had to contend with on a daily basis, of how the younger generation was not living up to their responsibilities. Nicoletta felt deeply that children were not honoring reciprocal obligations. Parents just were not getting the kind of respect that her generation had shown to their parents.

As I reflected on this story, Nicoletta's definition of family echoed in my mind: "A family is not a family without children." Several months later, I came to realize how my family's presence was bringing her joy but also pain.

> Nicoletta was cleaning out the basement storage room and called to me to come see something. A collection of clothing and accessories were spread out on the well-swept bricks of the patio. She lifted her wedding dress to her neckline. She recalled buying the material with her mother in a store in Calabria that stocked the finest of fabrics. An exceptional local tailor in her hometown cut and sewed the dress. She then held up Luisa and Liliana's First Communion dresses. Once stark white, the dresses were now stained and yellowed from sitting, stored and unused, for so many years, inside plastic bags and inside a zipped suitcase. Nicoletta also had spread out a collection of old, mildewed purses. They were once lovely, she said, and I believed her when she told me this.
>
> We spoke about the other night, when my daughter had a sleepover with her best friend, and Nicoletta was dying to see her. Nicoletta told me of her dream: "I was holding a *bambino* in my arms," she said. "He was small. I was filled with joy. Then, as I held him, he turned to stone." Cold. Lifeless. A memorial to desires unfulfilled.
>
> She wants so badly to be a grandmother. "When I'm gone, when my children are gone, where will all of these things end up?" she asked. "Everything we made, all of our sacrifices—there's no one to leave them to. Yes, there are nieces and nephews. But it's just not the same as having your own."
>
> The presence of a 5-year-old living in her household along with a "whole" family has perhaps made her desire for and absence of a grandchild even more stark, more painful, more pronounced. [*Fieldnotes,* May 18, 1996]

CULTURAL POLITICS AND THE QUIET REVOLUTION

Nicoletta's dream expressed a sense of loss and betrayal. It was painful for me to hear. I could not help but feel that our presence magnified her regret. It was easy to see her as the victim of this transformation in family-making practices. She felt cheated. Yet was she merely the victim of change? Or was she also one of its catalysts? Let us not forget that she also contributed to the quiet revolution. Recall, her parents had six children; she and her husband had only two. With those two kids in tow, she and her husband left their homeland in the South to cash in on the boom. The couple and their children became swept up in economic changes that fueled new ideologies, particularly in terms of gender and class relations. Nicoletta's sense of loss was the result of a clash between old and new values, attitudes, practices, and economies.

Nicoletta spoke of profound changes in the world of work and the related social milieu, which she said resulted in "another way of life that has been created, another society." These changes led to an imbalance of the sort that historical anthropologist Eric Wolf suggested long ago. He noted that social dislocations were brought about by a spreading market that had torn men and women "up by their roots, and shaken them loose from the social relationships into which they were born" (Wolf 1969:295). Nicoletta, I strongly sense, felt torn up by her roots. The new social relations she had to confront in the economically shifting context of central Italy was disorienting. Grasping the dominant values of an older way of life gave her a sense of security even while there was no way she would return to Calabria and the life she lived there.

Anthropologists might describe her experience of these profound changes as an example of *cultural politics*. I like this term because it moves away from notions of culture as a bundle of neutral habits, traits, values, and beliefs toward culture as practices implicated in unequal relations between people and social groups and, in fact, deeply connected to political processes, global economies, and identity formation. "Everything in social and cultural life has fundamentally to do with power," write Glenn Jordan and Chris Weedon (1995:11; Shore 2000). The connection of culture with politics is not likely to be found at the level of formal electoral events but rather at ideological as well as policy levels of the nation-state. In effect, the phrase *cultural politics* draws attention to the complex ways that people search for meaning, as well as make meaning, as they go about their ordinary lives, and how everyday life itself is about struggle as well as politics and power.

When I tell people about my work on Italy's record-low fertility rates, their interest is immediately piqued. "Why is it so low?" they want to know, just like those Texans at the fantasy-like convention dinner. This book is meant as an answer as well as antidote to the many casual conversations I have had about Italy's population paradox. That is, a paradox between a national context of emerging worries over low fertility, a graying population, and an immigrant presence, and a global context of persisting concerns over a population explosion that has long been portrayed as *the* demographic "problem." In contemporary Italy, I witnessed divergent ideas about what lifestyle choices were appropriate and respectable, and some of these fell out along lines of gender, class, ethnicity, and generation. Furthermore, generations differed over gender roles as well as behaviors related to love, sex, and reproduction. As cultural politics play out, rules of "normalization" become defined and codified through what people say, how people act, and what they do. In modern Italy in general, and postwar Prato in particular, a new world has been emerging, one that has brought new values, new possibilities, and new "necessities" for living life as well as for making families. Uprooting the oak has generated pain as well as liberation.

2/Family Tree, Revolutionary Roots

I would like to thank my parents in Vergaio, in a little village in Italy. They gave me their biggest gift, their poverty, and I want to thank [them] for the lesson of my life.
—Roberto Benigni, on accepting three Oscars for *Life Is Beautiful*, 1999

The whole history of Italy and Europe ends up in Prato—all of it in Prato, in rags.
—Curzio Malaparte, *Those Cursed Tuscans*, 1964[1956]

Native comic Roberto Benigni recalled easily Prato's history of poverty. The remark bemused the super-glam Hollywood audience as well as the fans who follow the glitzy, high-fashion displays of the Academy Awards stars. His family, friends, and fans watching him live—at 4 A.M.—on a big screen in the Casa del Popolo, a social club in Vergaio, certainly understood where he was coming from. Prato's history is in rags. And it is in straw. This reality marks a stark and grimy contrast to the glorious past of Renaissance gem Florence just 20 kilometers to the southeast. Prato is a new money place with new money desires. The *Pratese*, the people from Prato, remember well their history of poverty.

When I first conceived of my project in Tucson, while a graduate student in the Department of Anthropology at the University of Arizona, I imagined myself limiting the time frame to three decades: the 1970s through the 1990s. Once in the field, I realized I needed to extend my study to the postwar period—back to the 1950s, the boom period that Nicoletta, a widow and mother of two, remembered in her story about leaving her native land in the South and coming with her family to Tuscany. As time wore on, however, I kept running into reminders of a more distant past. The message was clear. The past was not so distant to the people whose lives were rooted there. I felt the need to grasp the interconnected meanings of those roots. Otherwise my project would be like trying to understand the acorn without having any knowledge of the life cycle of the oak tree.

A QUIET REVOLUTION

Large families have long been associated with rural life. Italian historian Denis Mack Smith tells us that "the great majority of Italians lived by agriculture" in the 1860s and 1870s (1959: 43–46). Agriculture continued to be the mainstay for Italians well into the 20th century. Yet by the 1920s, declines in fertility rates were notable—and for Mussolini's fascist government, troublesome. Mussolini pushed a campaign that idealized rural life as one of many strategies to entice women to have babies. He believed a larger population would be good for Italy. It would mean more men to serve in the military and more people to populate colonies in Africa. Mussolini wanted to make Italy modern, and he sought more bodies for his state. His dictatorial idea of being modern, however, did not jibe with that of most people's. His ploys and policies had little effect on overall family size (Table 2.1). Italians were already beginning to show declines in birth rates even though many still lived in rural areas. How to explain this conundrum? In central Italy the presence of diffuse industry and the emergence of a peasant protest are key elements to understanding the dynamics of family change.

Europe was the first world area to undergo the so-called demographic transition. This term describes a process of rapid and comprehensive fertility decline that began in the 19th and 20th centuries across Europe. It marked a stark break with the old patterns of births, deaths, and disease. A woman I call Carolina, who became crucial to my field research, gave me a genealogical chart mapped out by a local historian. Deaths of infants and youths were marked by a cross (†). Their numbers were striking. The effect on me was powerful and different from looking at aggregate statistics. Individual names and the frequency of the cross symbol impressed on me a sense of hardship these people endured. They lived during the old-regime demographic system in which pregnancies were many and life was short. Deadly infectious diseases were rampant. Infant mortality rates were high. One ancestor named Teresa (born in 1793) had nine babies, between 1820 and 1836. She would have been about 27 years old when her first child was born and 43 years old when her last was born. She had babies every one to three years, a so-called natural fertility cycle. Of her nine live births, five died as infants or toddlers: Angiolo (1823–24), Annunziata (1825–26), Rosa (1831), Florinda (1835–36), and Annunziata (1836–38). Two other children died as young women, one at 25, the other at 30. This cycle of life and death was not unusual under the old demographic regime. Under the new system, women began to stop having children before they entered menopause. Provinces across Europe, in the 1800s to early 1900s, began recording declines in birth rates. These decreases resulted from women's, as well as men's, conscious and purposeful limitation of family size.

Couples in Florence were apparently thinking about having fewer children for quite some time. David Kertzer (1993), a historical anthropologist, investigated infant abandonment in Italy for his book *Sacrificed for Honor*. The Catholic Church as well as the state supported institutions for orphans. Known as foundling homes, these buildings were constructed with a wheel by the front door. A person could anonymously leave a baby on the mechanism, pull a bell

TABLE 2.1 BIRTH RATES, BY REGION, PER 1,000 INHABITANTS, 1921–1945

	Italy	Northern Italy	Central Italy	Southern Italy	Islands
1921–1925	29.9	26.6	28.2	36.3	31.0
1926–1930	27.1	23.5	24.7	33.8	29.9
1931–1935	24.0	20.3	21.5	30.8	27.2
1936–1940	23.4	19.8	21.2	29.7	27.2
1941–1945	19.9	16.6	17.5	25.3	24.2

Source: Associazione per lo sviluppo dell'industria nel Mezzogiorno, un secolo di statistiche italiane Nord e Sud, 1861–1961 (Rome 1961), p. 79, table 77. Victoria de Grazia, *How Fascism Ruled Women* (Berkeley: University of California Press, 1992), p. 46.

string, and run away, with the confidence that an attendant inside would arrive, turn the wheel, and find the little bundle. Its future was not bright: hundreds upon thousands of infants crossed any given foundling home's threshold, and most would not live to walk back across it.

In the 1800s, the state and Church colluded to force unmarried women who became pregnant to give up their babies. The law required these women, typically from the poorer classes, to serve as a wet nurse and breastfeed a number of infants for up to one year as punishment for their dishonorable sexual behavior. As Kertzer details, the infants' biological fathers were not punished nor were they held responsible for their offspring. In most parts of Europe and Italy, abandoned infants were usually "illegitimate," meaning they were not born to a couple whose marriage was recognized by the state or Church. In north-central Italy, however, people abandoned "legitimate" children at surprisingly high rates.

Kertzer found that some 43 percent of all children baptized in Florence in the 1830s—meaning they *were* born to married couples—were abandoned at foundling homes. The most famous was the Hospital of the Innocents, located in the elegant Piazza SS. Annunziata, just down the street from Florence's famous Duomo (Figure 2.1). I studied the hospital structure's classic Renaissance architectural features as an undergraduate while on the study abroad program in 1984. The 15th-century building, designed by Filippo Brunelleschi and underwritten by the Florentine silk guild, is celebrated widely by art historians the likes of Frederick Hartt (1979) for its "clear-cut rationalism." The words of praise contrast with a tragedy that is all but forgotten. Hartt, for example, does not even mention the rates of death endured in these institutions, which resulted from a structure of patriarchy designed to protect legitimate heirs.

The timing for when married couples began to abandon their infants, Kertzer notes, "is intriguing." It was a sign, he argues, of what was to come in terms of efforts to control conception, pregnancies, and hence family size.

Poverty threatened people's sense of dignity and eventually led them to embrace small families as "normal" and morally right. Fertility patterns in Tuscany, Piedmonte, and Liguria had already begun to decline by 25 percent among the cohort of women making families in 1910–1912, according to demographer Massimo Livi-Bacci's *A History of Italian Fertility* (1977). These same regions through 1960–1962 showed the lowest marital fertility rates in Italian history. In the province of Florence, which until the early 1990s included

Figure 2.1 The Hospital of the Innocents, Florence, bears an inscription: This was for four centuries/Until 1875/The wheel of the Innocents/Secret refuge from shame, misery, and guilt/For those to whom charity/Never closed its door

Prato and Carmignano, dramatic declines from an average of 4 to 2.4 children per married woman occurred between 1911 and 1931. Livi-Bacci linked high fertility rates to agriculture. Agricultural families were also patriarchal families with rigid hierarchies, duties, and expectations. Agriculture as a category, however, becomes ambiguous in a context of diffuse industry. The rural women of Prato had life histories between 1920 and 1945 that spanned niches as share-croppers, rural-industrial straw weavers, and, later in the postwar era, as sweater-makers and housewives. Their husbands often worked both land and textiles. These couples were trendsetters in family-making.

The term "quiet revolution" describes the demographic transition (Tilly et al. 1992). The level of change in society was so profound as to be compared to the uprootings resulting from forceful overthrows of political regimes. It has been described as quiet because, unlike the explosive noises associated with militant uprisings, the demographic transition was relatively hushed. But it was equally profound in terms of long-lasting social, political, and personal effects.

A PEASANT PROTEST

Evidence of mounting tensions suggests a social revolt was unfolding against the rigid hierarchies of the patriarchal family. Giacomo Becattini (2001), an Italian social economist who has written extensively on Prato's industrial development, believes these tensions exploded into peasant protest. The key protesters were women and youth. They objected not to the countryside itself but to the rigid pecking order of the patriarchal family. They resented their close economic dependence on its older male members. You see, *la mezzadria,* or the share-cropping system of agriculture in which peasant tenants were required to give half of the crop to wealthy landowners, required top-down social arrangements. The powers of decision making and available income were inconsistent with individuals' workloads, capacities, and responsibilities. So, for example, the *capofamiglia,* or male head of household, had to answer to a count, or landowner, but within the family he held most of the power to make decisions, while the younger males, who perhaps did the most heavy labor, had little authority to make decisions. The younger women had it even worse, especially when they married in and hence were subject to the authority of senior males as well as the *suocere,* or mothers-in-law. Many of the women, dating back to the mid-1800s, worked for wages as straw weavers on an already globalized market, yet their work was materially and symbolically devalued. After the fall of fascism and the rise of the Italian Republic, the constitution of 1948 established moral and juridical equality between husband and wife with significant reforms related to comanagement of the family in 1975 (Sarogni 1995:152, 190). Prior to that, law vested power in the patriarch.

Peasant youth and women saw the patriarchal system as unfair. They objected to a social structure and ideology that permitted, even made necessary, an unjust distribution of duties and rights (Becattini 1998:83). They asserted themselves as individuals. Their self-assertion resulted increasingly in a turn away from agriculture and toward industry. For many decades agricultural and industrial activities were intensely intertwined.

RAGS AND HISTORY

Oliviero, the sweater-maker son-in-law of Nicoletta, gave me my first history lesson about the area's industrial origins. Industry was particularly diffuse in the province of Prato, and its diffusion meant that a society characterized as agrarian was not so purely agricultural. He painted vivid memories of Prato as a much poorer place. In his mid-40s when I met him, Oliviero recalled when he was 15 years old riding his bicycle in rain, wind, and heat to a textile factory. His shift started at 6 sharp, so he would set off at 5:30 each morning, riding 6 kilometers across river bottom flats distinctive of Prato. The city's name bespeaks of its landscape: a *prato* is a field. Oliviero was just out of middle school, and he and Luisa were dating. They would stay engaged for 10 years; when I met them they had been married for 15.

Compared with the women in his life, Oliviero was quiet. He tended his machines with the precision of a watchmaker: he kept each mechanism of the computerized looms running like clockwork. Initially, Oliviero kept his distance from us but, with time, he grew curious about us as a family: about Hollis as a *Toscanina,* little Tuscan, in the making; about Chris in his transition from bluegrass fiddler to Django-style violinist (since he could not practice veterinary medicine in Italy); and about me as an anthropologist. The places I went, the people I met, and the stories I brought home were often a source of amusement. I was learning on my own many things he had grown up with. The difference was my position as an outsider allowed me to cross boundaries that were hardly possible for locals. Class positions marked off different worlds.

Oliviero's connections in the community extended far and wide. When he was not tending his machines or delivering finished sweater pieces, he spent his evenings at the nearby Casa del Popolo, a collective known in local parlance as *il bar*. Much of his free time elapsed in a gender-segregated world, and I came to understand that it would be awkward for him to introduce me into that male realm. He was also protective of his reputation: he had told his friends that he had known us for 10 years. In a sense, he was merely stretching the truth. Marco was a family friend, and since he had known me since 1984—more than 10 years by 1995—by extension Oliviero had known me that long. I can only imagine this kind of logic because of the various ways that Italians lean toward a collective spirit. When I was 22, Marco invited me to come along with him to take an English exam. He told the instructor I was his cousin. The family connection legitimated my presence. I sat next to him during the exam, and he asked for my help. I worried that my help could get him into trouble but he assured me it was fine.

When I tell this story to Americans, they are deeply bothered because they view it as cheating. When I tell it to Italians, they shrug and laugh. One of my graduate students, native of Italy, recalled in high school in Milan passing her finished translations of Latin to the student next to her. It was part of a collaborative spirit. The ideal was to equalize, not to out-perform. According to this ethic, the sharing of knowledge is not really cheating but is working collectively. Similarly, I think Oliviero's claim that he had known us for a decade was not an outright lie and not even a stretching of the truth but another way of seeing relationships. His claim reveals the importance of social relations. It is not just who you know but how you are connected to them. If very close family friends were like family, then by association we were like family, too, and hence not a threat. It was an acceptable way to bring us into the fold.

With time, Oliviero began to share with me important details about local history. He knew I was deeply interested in this world of "impure capitalism." If pure capitalism is based on a crude sort of rationality in which bottom-line profit motives result in a free market culture where only big business can survive, Prato is far from pure. Its industrial district is well-known for unconventional economic development. As of the 1990s, Prato was situated in one of the top eight wealthiest countries in the world, and yet its economy was built on the backs of small- to medium-sized firms, many of whose workers consider themselves industrial artisans like Oliviero. He knew well how its style of development ran contrary to postwar models of the Marshall Plan, and he loved to tell me about this history:

> Over lunch, my mention of needing a new pillow led Oliviero to ask whether we'd ever heard of poly-*something-or-other*, some kind of synthetic stuffing used in pillows. The guy who invented it was from Prato, and he died about 10 days ago at age 83.
>
> This led Oliviero to provide an introductory oral history of the textile industry here. At the end of the 19th century, the industry took off because of specialization in recycling old clothes into fibers that were then used to make new clothes. Much of the old clothing came from the States. Before that, he says, Prato was just mostly *contadini,* peasants. He says Datini, the famous 14th-century Tuscan tycoon, is

Figure 2.2 A rag shop in Tavola (Prato)

known for inventing the bill of sale. The wool industry and textile industry really took form toward the end of the 19th century. (I was excited to hear him refer to a historical figure I read about the year before in Iris Origo's *Merchant of Prato* [1957].)

Early in the century, huge boats transported old clothing from the United States and elsewhere. The clothing was first heated or somehow cleaned so that infectious diseases were not shipped into Italy. There were certain people who were specialists in telling what clothes were made out of what fibers. In fact, some of these people still exist. They can touch a shirt or sweater or dress, and based on the feel of the fibers, they know what it is: cotton, wool, polyester, rayon, synthetic blend, etc.

After the clothes arrived, the fibers had to be broken down. The process was quite innovative. Oliviero says the Pratese are known for their innovation in industry. They're always trying something new, even now, trying a different color here, a different pattern there, etc. [*Fieldnotes,* November 10, 1995]

Rags seemed to touch everyone's lives in one way or another. The rag-trade industry was not particularly glorious, and for the Pratese this history conjures mixed feelings. The very rags that marked people from Prato in a negative way also offered them a source of wealth. This legacy makes Pratese proud, embarrassed, and defensive. They are proud because being a rag dealer stood for being resourceful. They are embarrassed because dealing in rags meant dealing in the throwaways from other, often wealthier countries. It was a dirty, smelly, unclean sort of endeavor. But it also made a lot of people a living.

There is a popular saying I heard people from Prato state with ironic pride: *"Io son di Prato, vo' esser rispettato,"* or, "I'm from Prato, I wanna be respected." The saying is often shouted with the comic flair of native son

Roberto Benigni. Locals poke fun at themselves for speaking loudly yet hearing loss is a casualty of working around weaving and textile machines. Feelings of inferiority drive them to ask for respect. Pratese often told me their dialect is *brutto*–ugly, vulgar. The "t" is typically uttered in an aspirated style as in "Pra*h*o" and "rispetta*h*o"; in local parlance, the "t" is *mangiata,* or eaten. This aspirated "t," particularly when it is uttered in an exaggerated style, points to a "low-class" socioeconomic status at the linguistic level of sound. There is irony at play. The style in which people speak the phrase calls attention to itself as low status just as the speaker asks for respect. Pratese, or people from Prato, sense other Tuscans look down on them for being industrialists, for coming from poor backgrounds, and, more recently, for having new money but little education and less taste. My Italian language teacher at the Università Popolare in Prato told the studetns about new moneyed Pratese who would buy books by the kilo once they came into money. Books marked a background in education. Such Pratese lacked the schooling, but they had the money to buy the signs of an education to lend an air of culture to their homes.

The experience of feeling disrespected has to do precisely with Prato's prox-imity and relationship to Florence, the Renaissance capital and fashion center of central Italy. Curzio Malaparte, an Italian journalist who was born in 1898 in Prato to a German father and Italian mother, recalled his boyhood visits to rag shops in his memoir *I Maledetti Toscani* 1964[1956], or *Those Cursed Tuscans* (1964). As an infant, Malaparte was sent to live with his wet nurse, Eugenia Baldi, and her family in a working-class neighborhood of Prato. His mother came to visit him occasionally at his wet nurse's family for the next five years. An excerpt, reprinted in the literary journal *Grand Street 64* with the title "The Little Hand" (Malaparte 1998), offers a sensory memory of the city of rags in the early 1900s:

> It was a world unto itself: the whole city of Prato was a mountainous landscape of rags, though few people, aside from the rag men and us boys, took the trouble to explore these mysterious continents. Occasionally Faliero, Baldino, and I would be joined by some of the other kids from our street, via Arcangeli, out beyond the Santa Trinità gate, and as soon as we crossed the threshold of the shop, that smell of rags— dry and dusty, yet strong and intoxicating as fermenting fruit—would go to our heads and trigger a kind of ecstatic snowblindness.
>
> The instant a bale was sliced open, the rags would pour out of the wound like yel-low-red-green-turquoise intestines, and we would thrust our arms inside this flesh the color of blood, the color of grass, the color of sky, rummaging through the swollen stomach, the hot viscera, of those bundles of rags—the eyes of our hands searching in that dark world for some luminous treasure: a pearl, a shell, a moonstone. Then we would plunge headfirst into those cloth mountains the way we might dive into the rapids of the Bisenzio on a summer's day, slowly dissolving in the deep, sweet swirling odor of incense, of musk, of clove, the perfumes of India, Ceylon, Sumatra, Java, Zanzibar, the fragrances of the South Seas.

Although the bales contained treasures, they also hid horrors. Among the finds that Malaparte and his buddies unearthed was a woman's hand, which he slipped into his pocket, took home, and hid under the pillow of the bed where he slept with his wet nurse (Eugenia), her husband (Mersiade), and their two sons.[1] Malaparte recalled a restless night's sleep as he obsessed over the hidden hand, finally dreaming that it had crawled out from under the pillow and was slithering along his shoulders, caressing his throat. Malaparte's recollection offers insight into the sentiment of fear, one which he depicts as rampant in the city of rags.

> I awoke with a shout and sat bolt upright, drenched in a cold sweat. Mersiade gave me a slap to chase away the fright, but when he saw the little hand, which had in fact come out from under the pillow, he turned as pale as wax. Eugenia, though, seized it with the tips of her fingers and jumped out of bed.
>
> "Calm down!" she said. "So much fear for a little hand!"
>
> It was the first time it occurred to me that Pratese are more afraid of hands of the living than hands of the dead, and that we might trust the dead but not the living. It was the first time I glimpsed that the dead may not be foolish, like the living, but prudent. And that while being alive exposes you to all sorts of dangers—forces you to sleep with your eyes open—if you are dead, in Prato,[2] you can rest peacefully with your eyes closed.
>
> Eugenia opened the window, ready to toss the hand outside. The warm, rich, sweet smell of tomatoes poured into the room.
>
> "Don't! It will shrivel up my vines," said Mersiade.
>
> "It's your brains that are shriveled up!" said Eugenia.
>
> And she flung the hand out into the garden, where we found it the next day, covered with ants. They were dragging it slowly through the tomato plants, toward the hedge of reeds.
>
> We let it go.
>
> It never came back.

Malaparte's story indicates that, in this context of poverty, those hands of the living were to be feared. Life was precarious.

DIFFUSE INDUSTRY AND THE FAMILY

Weaving was one stage in the production process that easily found its way into home workshops. Diffuse industry was constructed around the practice of subcontracting. Subcontracting is very different from a conventional system of capitalism, known as Fordism, in which wageworkers perform their tasks in a centralized factory with emphasis on efficiency and discipline. Subcontracting relied on middlemen who bought raw materials, such as rags or straw, on credit, and then distributed those materials to workers, often in home-based shops. As we will see, these diffuse practices have persisted despite a dominant, northern

[1]The *Grand Street 64* translation refers to Eugenia as the man's wife; the original, however, refers to her as "*la mia balia*," or the author's wet nurse (Malaparte 1964 [1956]:105) and I have aimed for a translation nearer to the original. That the translator of the 1998 reprinted version omitted this important term indicates either a lack of full appreciation of the significance of the historical role of the wet nurse in Italy in Malaparte's day or an assumption that without the context most readers would not understand the significance of a poor boy having a wet nurse.

[2]This reference to Prato was also deleted in the *Grand Street 64* translation.

Paul Scheuermeier

Figure 2.3 Straw weavers in Carmignano (Prato) circa 1925. Paul Scheuermeier Archive, Library of the Department of Linguistics and Literary Studies II and Jahberg Library, University of Bern. Reprinted with permission.

European and American model of industrial development that favored large factories.

The work of straw weavers was so widespread that it received mention in a 1904 tourism guidebook, *The Medici Balls: Seven Little Journeys in Tuscany.*[3] Authors Anna Sheldon and M. Newell Moyca (1904:46) wrote "Prato of today has of course its praiseworthy modern enterprise and industries: the women are picturesquely busy at every street corner with straw plaiting; there is a good trade in woolen cloths."

Why, I still have to wonder, might tourists see workers as "picturesque"? I eventually would find evidence in the archives as well as in other published accounts that would suggest a completely different story: one of long work days, of work devalued, and of workers struggling for rights and dignity.

The most extensive central Italian strikes of the 19th century involved non-urban weavers, mostly women, working out of their homes. Alessandra Pescarolo, a historian working at a research institute in Florence when I met her, discusses these massive labor strikes in a landmark chapter on the invisible proletariat. When massive labor strikes erupted in 1896 in the towns and rural hamlets that line the banks of the Arno River beyond the confines of Florence, few expected the strikers to reach some 40,000 workers the first year.

---

[3]My thanks to Tucson guitarist Peter McLaughlin for lending me this guidebook from his personal library.

Politicians, buyers, and merchants did not anticipate the intensity of the confrontations. Protestors yelled "bread and work," threw stones, and grabbed plaits from fellow workers (May 18, 1896). Still others lay themselves across the tracks and blocked the steam tram, which ran from Florence to Poggio A Caiano, to prevent the middlemen buyers from collecting finished plaits. Strikers set fire to finished straw strands to light a bonfire. They entered into homes, preventing women from working. Police squadrons hauled off demonstrators on horses. The next day, as the shopkeepers and intermediaries continued to distribute work to the women, guarded by the public security forces, a woman threatened a dealer who wanted to reduce her pay from 10 to 7 cents per meter of *treccia,* or woven straw. As the strike spread to the whole area, including Prato, the women invented slogans, carried the Italian tricolor, and constructed straw trophies. In the hamlet of Tavola, women with babies went to the *comune* threatening violence against the manufacturers and their fellow workers (Pescarolo 1991:42–43).

Pescarolo, in a separate study, examined industry reports and collected oral histories to reconstruct work activity related to the wool and rag industry in Prato and its environs at the turn of the century. In 1895, some 473 domicile handlooms were registered in the Pratese area, and by 1907 the number had increased to 2,400 units, only to fall to 1,000 units by 1911. Domicile workers were ubiquitous. Pescarolo found a 1907 report by the Office of Commerce and Arts of Florence that listed the industrial textile manufacturers of Prato. It noted that a few of the firms had in-house looms, "but for the most part they give work *a domicilio* to textile workers." Pescarolo recounted two crises in handloom weaving, one in 1901 and another in 1908, which led to the publication of vociferous testimonials about diffuse industry. One article published in a 1901 weekly complained of the "pathological relationship" between the *impannatore,* or a high-risk middleman investor on the prowl for new markets and the workers who refashioned them into usable fabrics. The middlemen bought wagons of rags on 6, 8, or 10 months of credit, and then paid those who reworked the rags into sellable fabric on a delayed cycle of 14, 16, or 18 months. This uneven payment cycle benefited the middlemen at the expense of the rag-regeneration workers, who had to wait months for their payment. When it came time to settle, the middlemen often found ways to renege, such as alleging defective workmanship. Such a system of conducting business, the report suggested, "impoverished industry and permitted a quantity of adventurers to throw themselves into commerce" (Pescarolo 1988:53, my translation).

Industrialists during the handloom crisis of 1908 blamed home-based weavers for unfair competition. This argument was designed to promote industrial upsizing. The hope was to prompt people to seek waged work instead of operating individual family firms. The industrialists took a moral tone, accusing those involved in subcontracting of immoral business practices. This kind of system threatened people in positions of authority. It also disturbed their ideals about a pristine countryside somehow beyond the reach of industry. Pescarolo found a letter to the police about labor agitation. An industrialist accused domicile workers who participated in the subcontracting phenomenon of ignoring "the best way to go about tending to their own economic exigencies, such as devoting to the countryside the arms that it clamors for, or helping the industrialist in his not-so-easy mission, instead they conduct themselves unwisely in reprehensible ways" (Pescarolo 1988:61). Subcontracting repre-sented a loss of control for the industrialists, and they sought to depict domicile work as assaulting the agricultural way of life.

The diffusion of rag regeneration and straw weaving in the countryside affected rural life. One historian in 1920 remarked, "New weavers and new looms are especially numerous among agricultural classes, who came onto the scene suddenly. They considered weaving a supplementary craft . . . , and this eventually led them to grow disenchanted with agriculture" (cited in Pescarolo 1988:54).

The evidence suggests that between 1895 and 1908 small firms multiplied in tandem with *tessitori a domicilio,* home-based weavers. Handloom weaving spread throughout the countryside surrounding Prato. "It was a particularly intense process in the villages of the plains," writes Pescarolo, "where often agri-cultural day laborers and youths from poor families were living off the most pre-carious of occupations; these same families in which women were weaving straw, others were participating part-time in weaving." The very fluid and risky character of the middlemen combined with the manufacture of low-quality wool made it possible for many peasant families—men and women—to get into the handloom business. These activities opened the way for the peasant protest that was to challenge the rigid hierarchies of the old-style patriarchal family. These shifts in how work was organized, who could do it, and at what cost, cracked open deep-seated family tensions that festered beneath a rigid pecking order. People were exposed to new possibilities.

THE LABYRINTH OF HISTORY

I felt eager to investigate this peasant protest. My initial foray into local history was through the Archivio Storico of Carmignano, or the historic archive. Most every *comune,* or county, has an archive that houses documents dating back sev-eral centuries. My motivation to dig around in the volumes of yellowed reports and records was as much about doing what I believed a researcher should be doing as it was about having a clear idea about what I might find there. Honestly, at the time, I had no clue what I was looking for. Little did I realize the impor-tance documents would hold for comprehending family and economic change. My desire to access the archive was largely motivated by a personal need to structure my days, to feel purposeful. It also meant carving myself out some much needed space.

The calendar had turned to January 1996, and the passing of the holiday eat-ing frenzy, along with the dreary mid-winter weather, colored life gray. The dra-mas of Nicoletta's family were wearing on me. One day, her daughter Luisa offered to drop me off in the piazza of Carmignano where I hoped to find the archive. Carmignano is both a town—it is the county seat—as well as a county. No one I knew could tell me exactly the location of the archive, and bus trans-portation from the house up to the town of Carmignano was indirect and infre-quent, so I was grateful for the offer.

The promise of a ride, however, seemed in jeopardy as the morning unfolded. The eldest daughter, Luisa, was supposed to drive her mother, Nicoletta, and sister, Liliana, into town for Liliana's weekly blood drawing. Liliana was taking new medication for her mental condition and needed to be monitored regularly. The health clinic offered blood tests only from 8:30 A.M. to 9 A.M. Nicoletta was standing by the door, bundled in her coat, at five minutes before the hour. Luisa had yet to come down from the upstairs apartment. Liliana had gotten up early and gorged herself. It was an obvious attempt to sabotage the blood test.

"What idiots I've brought into this world!" Nicoletta lamented.

"*Imbecille!*" Liliana called, insulting her mother as an idiot. "You never feed me!"

Nicoletta burst out laughing. Liliana was hopelessly overweight and we had seen her eat several helpings of her mother's perfectly prepared pasta the night before.

Luisa, the oldest sister, was still nowhere to be seen. Nicoletta's plans once again undermined, she handed me the keys.

I drove the narrow roads tentatively. I honked at each curve, as is local practice to avoid head-on collisions, and climbed the hill to Carmignano on my mission to find an archive or library. I parked in the quiet piazza. The labyrinthine town hall confounded me. Stairways and hallways led in perplexing directions. I found neither directory nor signage. I wondered whether my disorientation was the result of a current renovation project or of decades, even centuries, of remodeling. Seeing no indication of an archive and no obvious person to ask, and feeling intimidated by an unfamiliar bureaucracy that I had no clue how to navigate, I turned around and headed straight for the exit. I am ashamed to admit it, but my destination was a more familiar place: a boutique.

> I walked across the piazza to the store where I had bought my shoes under the pretense of seeing about a possible repair. Finally, I asked the salesperson, "Is there an archive or library here?"
>
> "No," she said, "but there's one in ———." [*Fieldnotes,* January 4, 1996]

Had she said Seano or Comeana? Names of unfamiliar places were still interchangeable to me. Later, I learned Seano was the most populous and industrial of the five main hamlets that comprise the Comune of Carmignano. Comeana, on the other hand, was a relatively quiet town surrounded by fields of olive trees, grapevines, sunflowers; it also was home to the last remaining sheep herd in the area. I gathered myself and headed to the town hall to try my luck again. I decided to ask for the office of the *anagrafe,* or vital statistics: births, deaths, migration. I was suddenly overcome with an uncomfortable feeling. Who was I to ask for access to such an office? I wandered into an economics office and asked about the archive. A woman replied that I could only enter if I had authorization; she pointed me to the office of cultural affairs downstairs. There, a friendly man told me indeed, to enter I would have to have permission from the *Sovrintendenza Archivistica per la Toscana,* or the superintendent of archives, located in an office of the Uffizi. The task of securing permission would have to wait until the next day, as that afternoon I was scheduled for an industrial-archaeological tour to the factory town of La Briglia, upriver from Prato, in the Bisenzio Valley. It is known as the birthplace of the rag industry when, in the 1880s, the town shifted from producing copper to wool. The street names bore witness to the wool and fiber regeneration process that enjoyed its heyday in the late 1800s: *via della Seta,* or Silk Road, *via del Carbonizzo,* Carbonized Road, *via del Lavaggini,* or Wash Process Road. We saw bundles of clothes before they had been processed. One man showed us fibers that had been carbonized and washed; another held a handful of rejuvenated fiber. I was struck by the historic connection between agriculture and the wool industry as evidenced in a local invention: a machine used by day for wool and by night for chestnuts.

The next day I took the bus to Florence with the goal of obtaining permission to access Carmignano's historic archive. The entrance to the superintendent of archive's office was just past the doors of the Uffizi, one of Europe's most renowned museums of fine art. To think that 12 years earlier, as an undergraduate, I had been seduced by the lectures of an art history professor, Janet Smith, who opened my eyes to Tuscan Gothic pathbreakers the likes of Giotto (1266–1337), whose naturalism allowed for an exploration of human emotion. In those corridors I also fell in love with *Quattrocento,* or 15th century painters, the heroes of the early Renaissance: the playful and naughty Fra Filippo Lippi, the sensual and pagan Botticelli. Their puzzling over perspective and geometry paved the way for Renaissance illusions of space and depth as represented in the works of masters Leonardo da Vinci, Michelangelo, and Raphael. To think that I had business to conduct inside such a historic building had multiple effects. The Uffizi was built as a suite of *uffizi,* or offices, along the Arno River during 1560 to 1580 for the administration of Cosimo I, the Grand Duke of Tuscany. I felt intimidated, humbled, yet important all at once. In retrospect this sense of grandeur was an illusion not unlike the trompe l'oeil, or deception of the eye, which Renaissance painters used to create perspective (see Metcalf 2002:105). State routines of authentication, after all, legitimize the power of the state. We often take the state for granted, yet states wield tremendous power in shaping who we are and who we are not.

I wrote a letter, in Italian, requesting permission to consult the archive. I left it with a staff member in the office:

> I am conducting a study on the experience of zero population growth in Italy with particular interest in the connections among family, work, and births. My research project, "Natalism and Nationalism: The Political Economy of Love and Labor in Italy," has been funded by a grant from the Commission for Cultural Exchange between Italy and the United States (the U.S. Fulbright Commission). I seek to conduct historical research in the state archive of Carmignano. In particular, I intend to look at vital statistics between 1860 and 1959. I hope to find other historical references in this archive that can help me.
> Sincerely,
> Elizabeth L. Krause 1/5/96

I was instructed to return the following week. I worried whether my request for access would be granted. Upon my return, I was relieved to learn that the superintendent of history had approved my archival project—though only from 1860 to 1926. The law permitted access to materials only after 70 years. The idea was to protect the records of the living from the gaze of historians. The state was acting as protector.

The positive effects of the approval process, however, went beyond the permission and were much better than I could have imagined. I was introduced to one of the archivists, Elisabetta Insabato, who offered me helpful hints about navigating my way through the archive in Carmignano; she had actually published an inventory on the pre-unification portion—before 1860 (see Insabato and Pieri 1989). We talked casually about women and the family as well as the household division of labor. She mentioned a study that found of all women in the world, Italian women worked the most! Then she offered to introduce me to another staff archivist, Giovanni Contini. I immediately recognized the name. I had read one of his essays (Contini 1993) and had heard locals speak of him because he was one of six children of the famous Contini family, whose grandfather-patriarch had been the most powerful count in Carmignano. The grandson did not look the part. His hair grew in shoulder-length locks, true to his local reputation as a strong leftist. He dressed in corduroy rather than tweed, his desk was piled high with papers, and he chatted freely about history. He had been educated at Oxford and though he had a degree in history, he placed himself between history and anthropology. It turned out he was working on an oral history project in Carmignano. From the start he had been rather reluctant about it. His employer, the *Sovrintendenza Archivistica per la Toscana,* Tuscany's central archive office superintendent, had asked him to spearhead the project. Contini explained to me that his personal history, as the son of a former local count, brought into play patron-client power relations that could be awkward. He offered to share the videotapes of the oral histories with me. I departed with energies renewed.

DUST AND DOCUMENTS

I presented the official letter, stamped and signed, to the keeper of the keys at the town hall, and he directed me to the archive. Behind an unmarked, locked door was a single wooden table, covered with dust and some old equipment. Behind the table rose about six floor-to-ceiling shelves with bound volumes dating from the 1600s to the 1900s. The stacks ran the length of the room. I walked through the aisles and marveled at the volumes. What secrets might they contain? Would I be able to find something meaningful to my project? I was most interested in the post-1860s material, which unfortunately was not catalogued. The cultural affairs office staff provided me with a few mimeographed pages that offered vague indications of the archive's organization, but for me, a newcomer to archives in general and Italian archives in particular, this helped little. One day in mid-January, I found a distinguished, middle-aged man sitting at the table, poring over the contents of a volume with the kind of purpose that I so longed for. He introduced himself: Silvano Gelli, a biology teacher. His current project had little to do with biology. Rather, he had a newfound passion for epitaphs— the inscriptions made on gravestones. He was reading the old records of the cemetery of Poggio A Caiano, from when it was built, around 1880. Apparently up until this time most people and their children were buried in common graves, except for the elites, who had their own chapels and land. Signore Gelli (1996) had found a document that spelled out an unbelievable process for granting the contract to construct the cemetery: The bidding began with the lighting of a candle. It ended as the candle's flame burned out, and at that moment whoever had the lowest bid won the job!

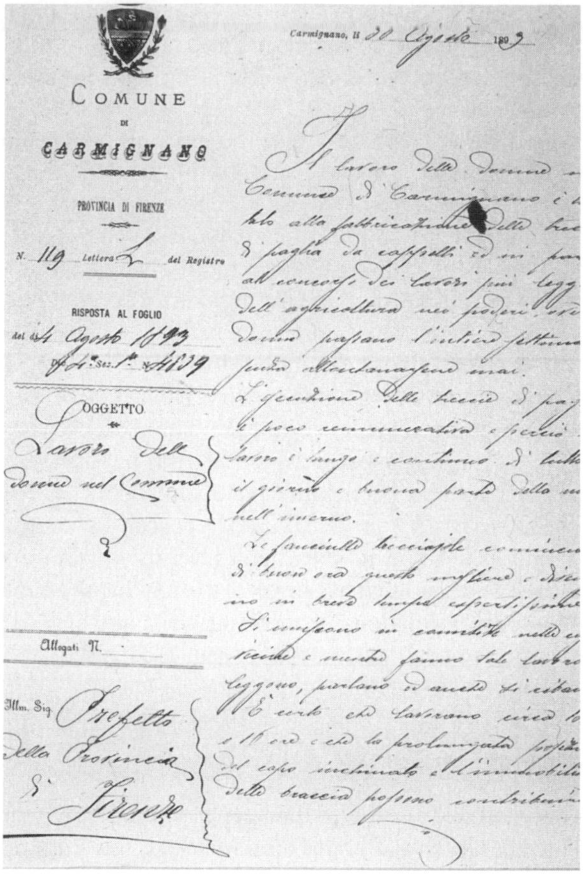

Carmignano, li 30 Agosto 1893

COMUNE
DI
CARMIGNANO
PROVINCIA DI FIRENZE

N. 119 Lettera L del Registro

RISPOSTA AL FOGLIO
del 24 Agosto 1893
... 4839

OGGETTO
Lavoro delle donne nel Comune

Allegati N.

Illm. Sig. Prefetto della Provincia di Firenze

Il lavoro delle donne n
Comune di Carmignano è
tato alla fabbricazione delle tre
di paglia da cappelli ed ai po
al concorso dei lavori più legg
dell'agricoltura nei poderi, ove
donne passano l'intiera settima
senza allontanarsene mai.
La condizione delle trecce di pag
è poco remunerativa e perciò
lavoro è lungo e continuo di tutto
il giorno e buona parte della n
nell'inverno.
Le fanciulle trecciaiole comincia
di buon ora questo mestiere e dive
ino in breve tempo espertissime
Si uniscono in comitive nelle c
ecc. e mentre fanno tale lavoro
leggono, parlano ed anche si ciban
È certo che lavorano circa 1
e 16 ore e che la prolungata posizi
del capo inclinato e l'immobilità
delle braccia possono contribui

Figure 2.4 An 1893 report on women's labor. Archivio Storico del Comune di Carmignano.

Several weeks later, I visited the cemetery of Carmignano with a new friend from the Casa del Popolo. Amelia showed me the section that was formerly reserved only for infants. Over the past few years, this section for the *angeli,* or angels, had been removed and replaced with ordinary plots. Memories persist of a time when infant mortality was much more common. Even Amelia's husband shared the name with a brother born before him who lived only one year. She took me to horizontal plots that created a wall: their facades were cement rectangles about two feet wide and tall. She showed me the stone that memorialized her sister, who died at 40, leaving behind two children and a husband. It was hard for all of them.

"Life is short," I attempted.

"Short and at times *brutta,* ugly." Amelia did not try to mask her pain. I later learned that she and her husband were unable to have children.

The next stop was her house. She wanted to lend me a thesis by a local man. Amelia offered me a glass of *limoncello,* a homemade lemon liquor, and we drank the sweet, potent drink together. Her house was filled with local things. It communicated to me a sense of local pride: a beautifully illustrated map of Carmignano; an oil painting and pencil sketch by a local artist, talented but not well known. From a poor *contadina,* or peasant, family, the artist was illiterate and not well connected in the art world. In the hallway were photos of wild-flowers—her mother-in-law took these. "Do you get along with her?" I asked. "Yes, just that sometimes she is possessive." Amelia tried not to create trouble that could fester like a boil. She then showed me outside to take in the view of the hills. Olive trees clung to the rugged yet well tended land. New homes clustered on some of the hills, and I asked about their construction. She expressed concern that the *paese* was changing too rapidly, too many people from outside. She acknowledged that it is a complicated and touchy *discorso,* subject. "Of course, it's important to be open, but too many outsiders risk turning the community into a *dormitorio,* a bedroom community with no sense of identity." She recalled the migration of people from the south of Italy, particularly in the 1950s and 1960s, and she respected their desire to keep their language. The 1990s brought a new kind of migration and new uncertainties.

WEAVERS AND WET NURSES

In the archive, I located information from a 1901 census: *Censimento Generale della Popolazione del Regno D'Italia, Provincia di Firenze, Comune di Carmignano, Frazione Poggio A Caiano.* I made notes from 111 households: occupations, number in household, relationship to the head of family. About 68 percent of the households had between three and seven members. Just over 10 percent had more than eight members. Typically these larger households consisted of extended families, that is, married children whose children were the grandchildren of the household head. What struck me was the number of people —men *and* women—whose occupation connected to the straw weaving industry: more than half of the households (about 60 of 120) had at least one woman listed as *trecciaiola,* straw weaver; other related occupations noted were *fabbricante di trecce,* a manufacturer of straw; *paglino,* a small-scale distributor of straw; *imbianchino di paglio,* a dyer of straw; *cappellano,* a seller and/or maker of hats; and *fattorino di treccia*, a middleman between the weaver and hat maker.

Under the dual systems of well-worn patriarchy and nascent capitalism, women's work counted for less than men's work. I found a clear piece of evidence of the way these uneven systems reinforced one another in a dusty volume in the archive of Carmignano. An 1893 report on women's labor, signed by the mayor, noted that women's work was "limited to the fabrication of straw plaits for hats."[4] The straw weaving connected these women to the global economy, for these hats were destined for sale in faraway places such as Great Britain, the United States, and Argentina. Certain words in the handwritten report were difficult for me to decipher. I was lucky to have Silvano Gelli there to offer me a hand. He helped me understand the content and significance of the document.

According to the report (Figure 2.4), the women's pay was low so they had to work long hours: 14 to 16 per day. Even in summer their weaving continued well into the evenings. It meant that women worked for prolonged periods in a position with heads inclined and arms immobile as nimble fingers raced. Such

---

[4]Archivio Storico del Comune di Carmignano, Categoria III, No. 93; Fascicolo No. 13, Filza 2, Agosto 30 1893.

work habits, the report suggested, "can contribute to more difficult functioning of the lungs and more sterile development of adolescents." In addition to the straw weaving, the report noted that "in the countryside, the women of the *coloni,* farms, do very little meddling; they provide food for the stall animals, gather the fruit, the olives, harvest the grain, and supply service to the family." With their earnings from the weaving, the women provided various utensils that were important for the household. Nevertheless, the report concluded of the women, "They are viewed as not very useful by the men."

The daughter-in-law within the patriarchal family lacked the autonomy to make her own decisions. Like other junior members of the household, she also was typically not permitted to keep her earnings. She was beneath not only her husband and father-in-law but also her mother-in-law. Birthing was historically not the sole business of the individual woman. It was family business. As such, it could also provide an opportunity for a family to convert a daughter-in-law's reproductive failure into a productive success. The mother-in-law could pressure the lactating daughter-in-law to become a wet nurse. A young woman might take someone else's baby to feed with her milk or she might leave her baby behind with relatives or a lower-paid wet nurse and take up residence in an elite household elsewhere. Adriana Dadà (1999) documents this little-known history in her monograph *Il lavoro di balia,* or *Wetnurse Work,* a project that involved middle-school children in collecting memories related to female emigration in the 1900s in the small Tuscan town of Ponte Buggianese. The earned income of the wet nurse who took a baby into her home was destined for the family fund; the higher paid emigrant wet nurse sent home a good part of her earnings.

In central Italy, as in many places historically, at least two different types of wet nurses existed in the early 1900s: those who served the rich and those who worked for the poor. For example, elite women from the nobility did not typically nurse their own babies but rather hired professionally trained live-in wet nurses. Having a wet nurse was a status symbol and was seen as the modern thing to do, just as feeding infants formula rather than breast milk was viewed as "modern" among U.S. housewives of the 1950s.

One day in the archive Gelli brought to my attention the existence of *Baliatici,* registries of wet nurse subsidies. These turned out to be a gold mine of sorts, for they revealed in striking terms the close-knit relationship between a global economy and local reproductive practices.

Poor women in Tuscany in the late 1800s and early 1900s might send their newborns off to a local wet nurse whose services were subsidized by the state. In the registries, I found evidence that the straw weavers often sent their infants to a wet nurse. A doctor certified that the new mother was *"dipriva di latte,"* or "lacking milk," at which point the woman was eligible to receive a subsidy designated as payment for a wet nurse.

Gelli and I argued about the meaning of these certifications. The biology teacher believed that women physiologically could not nurse because they lacked proper nutrition. I pointed out the work of physical anthropologists who have found that even very malnourished populations of women are able to produce sufficient milk for their infants (see Small 1998:177–197).

"Do you think it's possible that the women were not motivated to nurse," I asked him, "that they believed they couldn't so they didn't try?"

"No, absolutely not." He did not buy my suggestion since it was to their advantage to nurse. By nursing their children up to 2 years of age, they could prevent other pregnancies. Hormonal production induces what is called lactational amenorrhea, which stops a lactating woman from ovulating. The exact period of time varies and depends on frequency and duration of nursing.

But then Gelli said something that piqued my interest. "The fact is, even if these women had a decent diet, they expended a tremendous amount of their energy working in the fields or working as *trecciaiole*, or weavers."

In the Carmignano archive, I found a ledger of a charity organization, *Congregazione di Carità*, which between 1883 and 1902 reviewed 400 cases of women seeking assistance. Nearly all of the women were listed as *trecciaiole*, or weavers (390 of 405 cases, or 96 percent).

So-called insufficient milk syndrome, according to Meredith Small, is an example of an "invented" disease in that its occurrence results largely from how culture elaborates on biological processes. "In only about 5 percent of the cases is there something making it physically impossible for a woman to breastfeed," writes Small (1998:209). Aware of this cross-cultural research, I doubted that so many women lacked sufficient milk to nurse their own babies. Except for extreme cases of malnutrition, the female body is amazingly capable of producing milk to meet an infant's needs. Cultural practices, however, were and are very powerful in their ability to undermine the biological capacity to nurse one's child. At the turn of the last century, most likely the straw weavers could not afford to lose time working, hence they turned to the state for assistance. If they were trying to continue nursing their baby while working long days, indeed, this would very likely affect their milk production. Several factors are known to influence milk production: supply and demand, contact, and stress. How often were the weavers nursing and how long did they nurse? How much skin-to-skin contact did they have? Did the straw weavers co-sleep with their infants?

Contemporary researchers on sleep and breastfeeding have found that co-sleeping mothers are known to be more successful nursers since night nursing stimulates milk production. Co-sleeping habits are particularly important for mothers who hold full-time jobs but wish to keep a robust milk supply so as to have the ability to nurse their baby until both are ready to wean. James McKenna's (1996) groundbreaking research on co-sleeping often falls on deaf ears because of dominant notions about right and wrong as well as fearful messages from powerful entities, such as when the U.S. Consumer Product Safety Commission in 1999 issued a warning against co-sleeping—a move that met with harsh criticism from co-sleeping advocate and *Mothering* magazine editor Peggy O'Mara (1999). The commission's report lacked detail about alleged deaths of babies sleeping with adults and did not distinguish between safe and unsafe co-sleeping practices—as when a parent is drugged or drunk. McKenna, who advocates safe co-sleeping, has demonstrated that co-sleeping mothers get more sleep than mothers whose infants sleep in cribs. An additional benefit is that co-sleeping stimulates milk production. It extends nursing on demand to the night hours, thereby heightening the mother's chances for successful nursing due to increased mother-infant contact (see Small 1998:109–137).

Moreover, stress detracts from milk production. Working women who pump their milk commonly report reductions in their milk supply during stressful periods. Women whose partners contribute generously to domestic tasks and hence have lower levels of stress also report higher degrees of success. If those Italian weavers really did lack milk, it likely resulted from a particular lifestyle and a necessity to continue working—a necessity they realized swiftly by handing their infant over to a wet nurse.

Despite evidence that "breast is best," surprisingly few women in industrialized as well as developing countries breastfeed. As of 1998, 64 percent of U.S. mothers initiated breastfeeding, 29 percent were breastfeeding at 6 months, and 16 percent were still breastfeeding at 12 months. Factors such as ethnicity, age, class, educational level, family as well as peer influence, hospital policies, and formula advertising also affect and undermine breastfeeding efforts.[5] Women with less education and with lower incomes also tend to breastfeed less frequently and for shorter periods than do women with more education and higher income levels (Weimer 1998:1). Demands of work and home may be partly to blame as well. In the United States, insufficient maternity leave only partly explains why some women do not nurse.[6] After all, women can rent or buy electric pumps and express milk when away from their babies, and new models even include trendy cases designed to look like computer bags or backpacks. Nonetheless, few women arrive at the American Academy of Pediatrics' recommendation to breastfeed for at least 12 months, and thereafter for as long as mother and baby desire, not to mention the World Health Organization's recommendation to breastfeed for up to 2 years of age or beyond.

In Italy, a recent study found that upward of 85 percent of women initiated breastfeeding but most stopped far earlier than medically recommended. Of 1,601 mothers randomly selected the study found breastfeeding fell off steadily to 42 percent at 3 months, 19 percent at 6 months, 10 percent at 9 months, to only 4 percent at 12 months (Riva et al. 1999). This trend minimally mirrors the time frame of parental leave in Italy. The law of March 8, 2000, modified an existing policy, offering strong incentives to fathers wanting to take parental leave. The law grants 100 percent paid leave for 30 days and 30 percent paid leave for the next 5 months (see Krause 2003:347). What accounts for such low rates of breastfeeding?

Italian notions about breastfeeding appear to have been profoundly shaped during the fascist period, from 1922 to 1944, when the medicalization of motherhood resulted in stringent feeding regimens and in regularized weighing practices. Pediatric "experts" told women to nurse only six times per day—with no night nursing advised—and instructed them to weigh their babies before and after each feeding, and then record the amount of grams the infant had ingested. If the total grams were insufficient to the guidelines, the experts instructed the new nursing mothers to "top it off" with formula. This fascist history is outlined in Elizabeth Whitaker's *Measuring Mamma's Milk* (2000). Whitaker suggests that these regimens of 3-hour nursing intervals, weighing the baby before and

---

[5]These data appear on the Centers for Disease Control and Prevention website, http://www.cdc.gov/breastfeeding/faq.htm, accessed March 18, 2003.

[6]California workers were granted the most expansive family benefit in the country in fall 2002. The law guarantees 6 weeks of paid leave to care for a new child or ailing relative. It broadens the federal Family and Medical Leave Act, signed in 1993 by President Bill Clinton, which offered unpaid leave. John M. Broder, "Family Leave In California Now Includes Pay Benefit," *The New York Times,* September 24, 2002, p. A18.

after each feeding, and topping off with formula when the intake quantity did not "measure up," are still prevalent in Italy and undermine women's efforts to nurse their babies long term. Similarly, advice to U.S. mothers from "expert" pediatricians undermined breastfeeding efforts historically (Millard 1990). Lactation specialists and successful nursing mothers now understand well the reciprocal relationship between mother and baby: the mother's milk supply will meet the baby's demand—if given the chance. Many cultural practices and beliefs rob the infant of its chances to stimulate its mother's milk production. Rigid feeding schedules, formula supplements, prohibitions on night nursing, crib sleeping, and even high use of pacifiers and baby strollers can undermine milk supply. By contrast, practices that encourage mother-infant contact—such as nursing on demand, wearing one's baby, and co-sleeping—are key to stimulating the maternal body's ability to make enough milk to meet her baby's hunger, nutritional, and comfort needs. For the straw weavers, the possibility to hand their infant over to a wet nurse was likely a necessity just as the seduction of a scientifically manufactured product advertised as convenient has become a modern "necessity" for many contemporary women. Then as now, for a woman to breastfeed her own baby long term was and is a rarity.

State and institutional policies have also undermined women's efforts to breastfeed even as experts preached its health and moral benefits. As for the state's subsidies for wet nurses, this practice largely disappeared toward the end of the 1920s, but wet-nursing continued in unsanctioned forms.

The experiences of one wet nurse were documented in two separate interviews recorded on videotape as part of the Carmignano oral history project. The tapes were supposed to be housed in a video archive but the archive had yet to be set up. Eventually, the oral historian Giovanni Contini duplicated a master tape and gave it to Carolina who passed it on to me. I located a TV and VCR at the town hall and set them up on the table in the archive. I wanted a precise script of the interview. Nicoletta's niece Nicolina helped me transcribe. It was a time consuming, and eventually controversial, process.

A SOLD WOMAN

Iolanda Drovandi's family convinced her to become a wet nurse. It was a way to transform a birth crisis and a lactating body into cash for a household coffer. In two separate interviews for the video/oral history project of Carmignano, in 1991, Iolanda recounted her experience from the early 1930s as a "sold woman." Iolanda was born June 6, 1906. As she told Giovanni Contini, she became a wet nurse in 1932 after traumatically losing her first born.

"One evening, like every evening, we were gathered together, all of us. And I was sitting, like I was there, the first one. There was a knock at the front door."

"Who'll go open it?" someone asked. Iolanda went, and beyond the threshold stood two carnival masqueraders. "They were dressed up in the white cloak of death," she said. "I was so frightened. And from that fear it boiled my blood and the creature died on me at 8 months."

Twenty days later, she gave birth. She recalled that the midwife took the baby and went to light a candle to the Madonna.

"What's wrong?" Iolanda remembered asking, frightened and confused. "What does the baby have?"

"The baby was born dead," the midwife responded. "She's missing all her nails."

Iolanda was shocked and overcome with fear. The baby, Iolanda recalled, was buried outside the cemetery; it had not been baptized so, she was told, was forbidden from being buried in a grave on consecrated land. The details, that she never was allowed to see the baby and that it was never baptized, raise suspicions about the midwife's account.

After the death of her firstborn, Iolanda's mother-in-law pressured her to work as a wet nurse.

"To make a long story short, there was this man, Paolo, that lived here. His wife was ahead of me [in weeks of gestation] and she had hers a month and a half after I gave birth to the dead baby girl. So they start to say, even my mother-in-law was saying, 'What?' she says, 'you have a little milk. What,' she says, 'if you send it away then if you have another child who knows if it will come back.' Lots of things, you know how it goes. We used to listen to everybody, and so I took the child."

Iolanda admitted that she was easily coerced into becoming a wet nurse. She described her generation of women as subordinate to the senior members of the household. They did not question authority. Women accepted their place in the hierarchy like a station in life even when it meant agreeing to their own exploitation.

While Iolanda waited for her neighbor's child to be born, she nursed her niece's baby. Its mother did not have much milk. A month and a half later, the neighbor's baby was born and she began her work as a wet nurse. Shortly thereafter she learned of her reputation as a sold woman.

"This man used to always say, 'You shouldn't go in the fields.' He used to say, 'You, you're sold!'" She laughed as she recalled the details.

"He used to say, 'You have a pension,' like that. 'You have a pension and I pay you. You're sold.'"

"Why?" asked Contini, confused about the restriction. "If you'd go into the fields what would happen?"

She performed hard physical labor in the fields: wood cutting, corn and sorghum harvesting, grass cutting for the animals. "We'd go do everything. And every once in a while I was going and he would say, 'You're sold and you know it. You have to give milk to the baby. You give it to her sweaty.' He was right."

"And so if you gave it sweaty, what was so bad about that?" Contini wanted to know.

"It made the baby sick," Iolanda replied.

"It made it sick?" Contini asked.

"Sure!" she said. "Milk tainted with sweat made them sick."

"But is it true or not?" Contini continued.

"It's true. But I didn't nurse her as soon as I got back. I'd get back before the others and sit still for a little bit," she explained.

"Uh-huh," he nodded.

"And so he paid me monthly," Iolanda said, laughter again punctuating her story. "When he paid me each month I, there was my mother-in-law."

The year was 1932. She couldn't recall how much he paid her.

"Do you remember whether in the house this income was important?" Contini asked. "Did this money make a big difference?"

"The difference was this: that when he paid me each month my mother-in-law took it."

"Ah-ha!" Contini said. "Your mother-in-law would take it?"

"In 13 months that I nursed her I never saw a cent," Iolanda said.

"Never? Not even a lira?"

"Never, not even a lira. That money was hers. We ate that money, I mean, it was eaten."

Iolanda never saw the money. "Not for working the fields, nor as a wet nurse, I never saw it."

Contini wondered what kind of relationship she had with her mother-in-law. Did they get along? Did they argue?

"By necessity we got along because it was as though I wasn't there," Iolanda chuckled. "You did what you did."

Contini laughed, sympathetically. They both knew how much things had changed.

"Understand? Now I wouldn't do it. When the last of the 13 months came along, Paolo said to me, 'Look,' he says, 'what do you want?' He says it would be the month to pay me double. 'Do you want the money or a dress?' he says. Then he came back and he says, "So have you decided?" I told him, "Make me, you make me the dress. At least I'll have that!"

She laughed. So did Contini. A young woman of today's generation would not stand for such a system. Nor would she be expected to.

"It seems like a song," Iolanda said, "but it's actually a true story."

THE LAST LAUGH

The laughter in this story was pervasive. Iolanda laughed where she first admitted to having taken a child as a wet nurse. She laughed when she recounted the neighbor telling her she was "sold." She laughed at her monthly "payments." When she affirmed that she and her mother-in-law got along, she laughed—the implication being that she kept quiet. She laughed at her decision to take a dress over money as payment. Taken together, laughter pointed to how her location within the family enabled her to become a "sold" woman, that is, a woman lacking in autonomy and lacking in dignity. It was the laughter of recognition, of embarrassment, and of outrage. It was also the laughter of sitting between two worlds, each with its separate yet interconnected ideologies about gender and kinship relations. In a sense, it was the laughter of peasant protest.

Iolanda had the last laugh. She recognized that society and women had changed. She was talking to a male interviewer nearly half her age and hence from a different generation. Surely she imagined that he had a hard time understanding how little power she had, and yet the rigid hierarchy that shaped family relations and limited individual autonomy now seemed so ridiculous as to be laughable.

Iolanda viewed her situation as exploitative and recognized that changes have occurred in women's work. Iolanda also revealed her own ability to act in her own self-interest. Within her limited options, she resisted exploitation when she chose the dress over the money. That decision assured that her mother-in-law would not take away her "pay." She finally got something for herself from her months working as a wet nurse. Later (not reproduced above) she would put the dress away in a trunk and use its cloth to sew pants and a jacket for the first communion of the son she eventually had.

Iolanda described herself in another segment as *grulla,* or stupid. Clearly she was referring to her younger self, for later she refused to take anymore children as a wet nurse. Apart from the lack of direct remuneration, she became attached to the child she nursed, and it was a painful separation when the child went back to its own mother. "If my milk goes away for good," she said, "*pazienza,* patience. Too bad." No longer would she "listen to everyone," so to speak.

Her story reveals the roots of the peasant protest. Women's contributions to the household economy often entailed exploitative arrangements. The history of women's work in the context of patriarchal kin and capitalist market systems required the rights of certain family members, perhaps even their children, to be sacrificed for the family whole. The hierarchical family structure justified that Iolanda never saw her earnings. Women and youth protested precisely this kind of rigid hierarchy, which led to the unraveling of the large, patriarchal family (see Becattini 1998).

The onset of low fertility was undoubtedly linked to trauma. One has only to recall the widespread experience of childhood mortality, as the family genealogy reminded. The matriarch named Teresa gave birth to nine babies, and only four of those children made it past their 3rd birthdays and into adulthood. Of the others, one died before its 1st birthday, three died as 1 year-olds, and one died at 2 years of age. Imagine the cycles of grief. Add to these high rates of mortality those connected with infant abandonment, a practice that reached just under half of all baptized, hence "legitimate," babies in Florence of the 1830s. If abandonment was a precursor to fertility decline, it suggests that couples were having a difficult time managing households as new babies came along. It was not as though most women had the luxury to "stay at home" with their babies. Like their menfolk, they too engaged in hard labor. As the 19th century wore on, rural Tuscany became increasingly industrialized, and many women in the environs of Prato found themselves working long hours as straw weavers.

These activities certainly opened the way for a peasant protest, which witnessed cultural politics related to family-making. The upcoming generations challenged the symbolic and material foundations that formerly sanctified the rigid hierarchies of the old-style patriarchal family. Shifts in how work was organized, who could do it, and at what cost, cracked open deep-seated family tensions that festered beneath a rigid pecking order. New possibilities for making a life and making a family meant the gradual eroding of the extended, patriarchal family. Having large families began to matter less and less as a reliance on an agricultural way of life diminished. Moreover, new money led to new class divisions, new possibilities for demonstrating status, and new forms of consumption.

3/Fieldwork, Sweater Work

"L'abbiama trovata l'America—We've found America!"

—A common Pratese saying

The first time somebody looked me in the eyes and told me they had found America, I thought they were talking about me. I figured since I was American they took me to stand for the whole of my country. I was vastly mistaken. The comment represented newfound wealth—not a reference to America as the destination for millions of Italians, especially a century earlier, who had made fortunes relative to the rural lives left behind. Rather, the remark referred to home: no longer was "America" across the vast Atlantic. It was right here. As a major site of the postwar "economic miracle," Prato was the place where many former peasants, rag workers, straw weavers, even ironworkers and bricklayers had come into money through participation in the woolens and knitwear industries.

Popular depictions of Tuscany do not show Italians working. Frances Mayes' best-selling book, *Under the Tuscan Sun* (1996), inspired a movie where there are no factories and no one seems to work, except to pick olives or remodel the villa. Calendars and picture books proliferate an idyllic and golden countryside untainted by industry.[1] Such images please American tourists. They confirm stereotypes of Italians as leisurely Mediterraneans and of Tuscany as a place of leisure. Nothing of a "manic devotion to hard work" that one reads in accounts of the miraculous economic metamorphosis such as occurred in postwar Prato (Becattini 2001:92). Rather, the endless and narrow representations of Italy fueled my curiosity about economic transformation on Italians' terms. Under the agricultural system, the household was the center of the economy. Family and market were intensely intertwined. How did the economic boom affect the family? I wanted to understand the meanings and textures of work in a context that continued to rely heavily on industrial artisans, subcontracting, and hidden labor.

---

[1]Mayes' book also inspired its own engagement calendar, and in the 2003 edition, the only person photographed was an elderly man shown cultivating roses in a sunshine-drenched country garden.

How did women and men experience this kind of economy? What did it mean in terms of family-making? I set out to integrate myself into the rhythms of daily life.

LOCATING DIFFUSE INDUSTRY

My sense of what the term "diffuse industry" meant in practice had evolved from watching small cars and compact vans loaded down with sweaters and sweater pieces dash through neighborhoods and along country roads. These vehicles carried the woven fabrics to and from small workshops and to *maglifici,* or sweater firms, that served as central points of yarn and sweater distribution. They cruised past the local bars where mostly men spilled out onto the streets, along the busy roads that led to Prato, Florence, and Pistoia. Once the fiber was spooled and ready to be woven, before the articles were shipped to the buyers, in Italy as well as Europe and beyond, any given sweater may have passed through well over a dozen hands.

Prato's industrial district has ironically become an archetype for development in Italy—ironically because it built its economic success on the backs of small- and medium-sized firms, comprised of networks of subcontractors, small manufacturers, craftsmen, and independent finishers. The success of such an anomalous organizational structure long mystified economists who maintained that large scale was the key to postwar market success well into the 21st century. This view left uncertain Prato's status, given its dependence on relatively small firms. To use economist Giacomo Becattini's metaphor, had Prato really metamorphosed into an economic butterfly? Or was it an aging caterpillar, doomed to never expand its wings in full flight? The director of Tuscany's regional economic institute (IRPET) resolved the raging debate and released Prato from the shadows of development stigma at a forum in 1984 when he observed that "large-scale" was not merely "the scale of the firm" but "also the scale of the system" (cited in Becattini 2001:174). Suddenly the large-scale firm of Fiat and the large-scale system of Prato could be uttered in the same sentence.

I wanted an up close and personal, tactile understanding of this world of making a living. With the blooming of spring, I purchased a 16-year-old Fiat 127 from a local mechanic who came highly recommended. The car allowed me mobility around the area. I decided the best way to deepen my understanding of Prato and its environs was to immerse myself in the sweater economy. I dropped hints to Oliviero and Luisa, themselves industrial artisans. I suggested I might be interested in working in a sweater firm. They did not return gestures to take me into their family firm. I figured they had had enough of me. Perhaps my hints were lukewarm. After all, I was worried about relying too heavily on one family for my project.

I felt focusing exclusively on the lives and experiences of Nicoletta's family alone would be risky for several reasons. First, I worried about the potential harm to them. I worried whether focusing exclusively on one family could generate envy among friends, neighbors, or relatives. Second, despite my most sincere attempts to explain my project and future intentions, I questioned whether anyone, even me, could ever fully understand the implications of collaborating with an anthropologist. Some of the secrets they shared with me I will never tell,

Elizabeth L. Krause

Figure 3.1 An industrial artisan (circa 1996) operates a serger that overcasts the raw edges and finishes the seams of sweater pieces.

but would there be other stories that they would later regret reading in print? The use of pseudonyms provides limited protection of one's identity; some friends or neighbors would be able to see through the veil.

Third, I was uncomfortable with the idea that any one family might possibly feel they "owned" the project. In a worst-case scenario, what if our relationship soured? Might they then ask me not to use any information I gathered from them? The thought of focusing on one family made me feel vulnerable as the lines between work and personal relations became increasingly blurry. Fourth, I felt that as a social scientist I needed to cast my net wide to get a sense of the variety of people's experiences related to changes in family-making and Italy's population paradox.

This approach would mean extending my networks. The family did not seem particularly inclined or able to help me with networking. I say "seem" because in fact they *were* helping me; the problem was my own impatience. My sense of urgency clashed with their need to cultivate relations and to build trust. I only realized how much groundwork they were laying several months later. It would be Nicoletta's brother-in-law who would help me gain acceptance at a local Casa del Popolo, or social club, where Chris and I volunteered in the pizzeria every third weekend. There, known simply as *gli americani,* or the Americans, we made friends, including one man who I expect eventually eased my access to what began as a puzzlingly difficult entry to certain documents in the local archive. In addition, it would be Nicoletta's niece who would put me in touch with Carolina, a local mover and shaker. She had deep roots in the area though she had married a southern man, Leonello—Leo for short. Together, they had

had three children, who in 1996 were all in their twenties. Carolina was involved in an important oral history project and had extensive connections. She would land me an apprenticeship in a factory. Extending my networks, however, had a price.

JEALOUSY AND FIELDWORK

Cultivating other relationships meant spending less time with Nicoletta and her family. In doing so, I risked offending them. Relationships anywhere call for regular maintenance. I found my friendships in Italy, particularly those with people who had migrated from the South, required intense and regular maintenance. One historian friend of mine who had married an educated woman from Sicily empathized with me. He recalled the jealousy his wife's family used to have toward the couple when they would want to go out with friends: "*Amici, perché?*—Why friends?" To the parents' way of thinking, the couples' desire to go out was a sign that the family was not good enough. My friend laughed as he recalled how he and his wife would return from their night out to find all the relatives just sitting around, no one saying a word. It was as though it was enough just to be in each other's presence. Who needed friends?

I knew if I ventured further afield, I would have less time to spend with Nicoletta and her family, and their feelings might be hurt. They had become possessive of me. The potential to hurt them tore me apart. I had cultivated a close relationship with these folks. They had welcomed us into their home and their lives. They had practically adopted us, especially my daughter, as their own. I found in them a rich entry point into my project. They had been patient language teachers and superb consultants of local history. I owed much to their insights. But I needed to pursue other leads.

I began to cultivate a relationship with Carolina. She was a doer. She had organized a number of original initiatives in the community: children's festivals in the local sculpture park; outings to cultural events in Prato aimed at women who were not typical patrons of the arts; and a card tournament for women—an event normally dominated by men. Her initiatives always had a unique, intellectual, and community spirit. She was an organic intellectual of the left who believed the people were ultimately sovereign, even if they did not always show their ability to govern (see Crehan 2002:137–145). She grew visibly frustrated when narrow-minded causes marked local politics. In some circles, she had earned a reputation as a troublemaker, and she rather reveled in that image. I loved talking with her, and from the start, she showed enthusiasm for my project. She spoke no English, so I shared with her a summary of my proposal translated into Italian by my friend, whose doctor husband would later come to help out Carolina's ailing husband. Carolina seemed moved that a researcher would have come all the way from America to investigate the lives of Italians. I think she was particularly impressed by my interest in what had long been invisible in conventional history: the influence of women. She introduced me to journalists, and several newspaper articles were published about my project.

Little did I know then how slippery the slope would be from standing in her favor to falling out of it, and little could I imagine how painful the fall from her graces would be. All I could see then was that she held the key that opened many more. She recommended the local elementary school for my daughter, who the following fall would be entering first grade, and I found in that school a dynamic community of parents as well as teachers. She also landed me my first job as a sweater worker. For this, I was most grateful.

SWEATER WORK

One day in early March, Carolina took me to the end of a street lined with large, warehouse structures. She told me I needed to meet the owner, Pia. She had gone from a pieceworker to successful business owner, and I should hear her story. Being with Carolina gave me a sense of security and allayed my fears of rejection.

Pia was not in when we arrived; her husband, Martino, told us she had gone to take care of *his* aging mother, her mother-in-law. Could he be of help?

"Sorry, but Betsy is researching women, so she can't interview you," Carolina explained, a playful and proud tone to her voice.

"These days you can't tell women from men anyway!" he retorted.

Within several minutes, Pia returned. She referred to herself as the *capo-famiglia,* or head of the family, a gender-bending way to indicate she was boss. She was the mastermind of production; her husband, of design. They employed about 12 workers, including their eldest son, 29 (their daughter, 23, was study-ing to be an architect). Her gold jewelry, platinum blonde hair, and stylish dress set her off from the workers, who wore t-shirts and jeans. She was unmistakably the owner. The *maglificio,* or sweater firm, specialized in colorful, merino wool sweaters for men. Their primary buyer had its own label, attached within Pia's firm, and sold to high-end clients such as Saks Fifth Avenue. She walked us past boxes of sweaters ready to ship as well as other towering metal carts of woven pieces waiting to be cut and sewn. We entered the nave of the factory, where the woven pieces were first cut into two halves with a high-power cutting disk, then machine-cut into sleeve or body pieces, and next sewed with a serger. Sometimes the sewing was completed inside the factory. At other times the firm contracted with independent artisans to perform other aspects of production: machine weaving, some sewing, buttonhole sewing, button attaching, collar making, and sometimes ironing. They paid these domicile-based workers by the piece. Women performed most finishing work. There was a solid division of labor along gender lines.

"The work of women is very useful for this because men cannot do it," Pia asserted. "The sweaters have to be refinished by hand." Her explanation was a clear articulation of a gender ideology that shaped the possible jobs open to women and men.

Pia excused herself to measure sewn sweaters to ensure the sizes were pre-cise for the clients. These buyers came months earlier to help design the year's collection, see the samples, and place their orders. Her firm shipped most of its sweaters to New York.

When Pia returned, she acknowledged that it was cheaper to outsource some of the work. Keeping costs down was a major motive; however, outsourcing was risky. Laws required that every job taken outside the factory be accompanied by a *bolla da accompagnamento,* a receipt for tax purposes. Pia's son had been

Elizabeth L. Krause

Figure 3.2 Sample designs hang from boxes in a maglificio, *or sweater firm.*

caught several times transporting sweaters without a receipt and each time received a hefty fine. "The state, with all these laws, they have ruined women's work," said Pia.

We went into her office. An old handloom was hidden beneath spools of sample yarn. It sat like a museum piece, an icon of her modest roots. She had initiated her craft on this handloom when she graduated from middle school. It marked the end of her formal education and the beginning of her career. Numerous people in this industrial zone, including women who had worked from their homes in previous decades, viewed the laws that cracked down on *lavoro nero,* or hidden work, as well intended but impractical. As Pia put it in a taped interview in March 1996:

> Women were a little exploited, especially in the years of the *paglia,* or straw. There was a lot of poverty and women earned very little. But we've gone from very little (earnings) to too much (taxation). It doesn't just depend on the women but on the cost of workers; now they cost a lot. And a woman with a family—who can leave her family (and work outside the home)? Then with all these regulations, women have become increasingly unemployed. Everything's controlled and women's work has diminished. At one time women were working out of their homes—even if she was an old woman, even if she had small children. Women always earned money making sweaters. . . . Overtaxation of artisans has practically eliminated work done in the home. . . . And yet for a company to assume all these workers inside the firm becomes too great an expense.

As the cost of making an article has increased in Italy, many manufacturers began taking steps of production to less developed countries where labor was cheaper. The body of a sweater might be knitted in Albania or Tunisia but then finished in Italy. Around Florence, the primary workers churning out leather goods were Chinese who constituted the major immigrant group in the province of Prato. They also manufactured textiles, sweaters, and clothing. These realities recast the meaning of MADE IN ITALY labels. Just because the label said "Made in Italy" did not mean Italians made the article. Pia predicted:

> The moment these other countries become developed, they'll start taxing, and it will become like here. Twenty years ago, we were doing well. . . . There weren't all these taxes, all these contributions to pay. So sweaters cost a lot less to make. Now, on the other hand, you have to add up all the expenses. We are no longer competitive with these other places, so there's less work, much less.

Labor laws in Italy tended to be progressive; however, they were also often violated. Progressive laws designed to minimize the tension between demands of work and family, including maternity leave of up to 8 months of partially paid leave, in practice have had negative effects: such as when young women get fired under the guise of a layoff once managers learn they plan to marry, or when firms avoid hiring young women to escape the costs associated with maternity leave. These strategies in part may result from firms' sense that they cannot afford to pay the benefits mandated by law.

Small- and medium-sized firms have characterized Prato's economic development. Related to this, Prato has developed a unique code of ethics that guides business transactions: most subcontracting deals are based on verbal agreements and reciprocal trust as opposed to written contracts between the giver of work and the receiver.[2] This gives rise to an incredible social phenomenon in which nearly everyone finds themselves entangled in webs of obligations very much like what Marcel Mauss described in his classic work *The Gift*. And perhaps it is no mere coincidence considering that the subcontracting employer in Italy is referred to as the *datore di lavoro,* or giver of work. From the gift, Mauss noted, arises a social phenomenon that is total. In other words, gifts are not only about giving but the obligation to receive and, in turn, for the recipient to reciprocate. These ongoing obligations have significant economic, legal, cultural, and moral implications as they create whole new sets of relationships between objects, individuals, and groups. Long known for his critique of the free market, Mauss challenged the dominant notion in liberal, Western capitalist societies that humans were mere economic animals—brutish and calculating machines. He pointed to the gift economies of non-Westerners, such as Samoans, Maori, Trobriand Islanders, and Kwakiutl, to show how false was the prevailing belief

[2]Italian anthropologist Massimo Bressan conducted research into the cultural aspects of the textile district of Prato in the mid-1990s. He identified an important aspect of these trust relations to be a virtual ban on written contracts. One interviewee told Bressan, "With those from the north [including northern Italy] there are contracts; with those from Prato, there are verbal agreements and agreements of respect." Customers (or buyers) place their orders on faith, and as one machine warper told him: "They put trust in my words" (Bressan 1997:27).

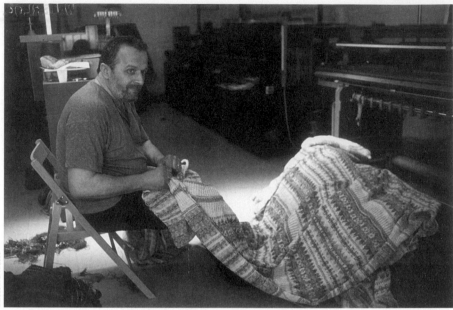

Elizabeth L. Krause

Figure 3.3 A sweater artisan in his workshop with computerized looms

that economic "man" was natural. Mauss sought an alternative to the icy values that a market economy of greed gave rise to. Free market culture, after all, leads producers to abandon local communities in favor of global markets and cheaper labor sources.[3] The forces of capitalism, here defined as the pursuit of financial profit as an end in itself, oppose the obligations and emotional ties that impregnate a gift economy. Modern Western societies, wrote Mauss, "have recently made man an 'economic animal.' But we are not yet all creatures of this genus" (Mauss 1990[1950]:76). Mauss suggested that principles very close to what he found in gift economies governed much of what people everywhere do. People just had to open their eyes and look for the evidence. In Prato, I observed that people experienced these two forces as deeply opposed. Trying to live up to economic efficiency and social obligations, many of which were connected to reciprocity, posed an ongoing source of stress yet also satisfaction in people's lives.

HIDDEN LABOR

In the townships of Carmignano, family firms multiplied as hand weaving of straw for the famous Leghorn hats gave way in the 1930s and 1940s to machine weaving of wool and synthetic fibers, first on handlooms and later on mechanical looms. The dominant economic sector after World War II became the *maglieria,* or sweater-making industry. A tremendous amount of women's labor went into sweater finishing. Firms specializing in various stages of sweater-making multiplied. By 1977, some 2,000 people in Carmignano and Poggio A Caiano (35 percent of the employed population) declared their occupation to be

[3]Jane Schneider (2002) discusses the implications of the free market culture.

sweater-making (Palumbo 1988). Official numbers do not, however, take into account the people working in the hidden labor economy. Many of these work- ers have been women, many of whom migrated from southern Italy or rural Tuscany after World War II, and more recently from outside of the European Union.

A common explanation I heard and read regarding the low birthrate was the idea that "before" women did not work, now they did; hence now women had little time to devote to motherhood. A 1998 *New York Times* article, "Population Implosion Worries a Graying Europe," described low fertility as an "epidemic." It seemed to blame women for "choosing work and education over having chil- dren" (Specter 1998). A handful of new historians has disputed the idea that "before" women did not work. Cycles of visibility and invisibility have shaped the interpretations of women's salaried work (Pescarolo 1995). Indeed, the fields of social and labor history have made huge strides in showing the biases of offi- cial sources such as census data. Domicile work, whether men's or women's, is typically hidden and viewed as "informal." In different historical moments, these data conceal in major ways women's participation in the labor market. For example, whereas at one point a woman working out of a home workshop might be classified as *trecciaiola,* or straw weaver, at a later point she might be classi- fied as *casalinga,* or housewife (Ortaggi Cammarosano 1991).

Nevertheless, official reports can be useful for big-picture trends. An annual report on the Pratese economic system noted the remarkable prevalence of arti- san firms in the counties of the province of Prato. Artisan firms as of 1997 com- prised at least 60 percent of total firms. In Carmignano, the rates were among the highest in terms of the proportion of artisan firms, with 83.4 percent of total firms classified as artisanal. The Comune of Prato proper had 62.5 percent of artisan firms (Balestri 1998). These numbers reflect the fact that industry was more diffuse in the countryside and more dominated by a model in which peo- ple had small workshops and in which family members participated.

THE APPRENTICESHIP

The next time I visited the sweater factory, Pia posed the question I was hoping to hear: "Do you want to talk or work?"

"Work," I replied, feigning confidence.

I had never been adept with needle and thread, but I soon learned this work had to do more with precise machine operation than with seamstress-like sewing. I followed Pia into the storage space of the firm, past the boxes filled with sweaters ready for export to the United States. The workers cut out sweater pieces, sewed pieces together with a serger, attached labels, ironed, folded, packaged, and shipped the merchandise. The workers received a set stipend, which in some cases was adjusted through a "family allowance" income sub- sidy.[4] Pia discussed with her husband, and then briefly her son, what I ought to

---

[4]This benefit is a monthly subsidy designed to help employees with total family earnings at low- income brackets. The amount varies, depending on income and number of family members, from a minimum of €10.30 to a maximum of €227.25. (The exchange rate for euros and dollars was nearly equal at this writing.) An employee from a family of four whose total income was only about €10,000 would receive an extra €250 per month; a family of six who made less than €29,000 would

Elizabeth L. Krause

Figure 3.4 Sweater making is a diffuse industry. Each sweater passes through many hands on its way to becoming a finished product.

do, and they decided to start me out shearing the *teli,* or sweater pieces, with a *taglierino disco,* or a cutting disk, whose phenomenal serge was powered by an air compressor.

> You take a big bundle of sweater pieces. You take the cutting tool. It's attached to a coil that connects to air pressure above. You cut the tie wrapped around the bundle. You take off the job order tag, then reach up and get another type of tag. You write the quantity, size, and order number on the new tag with a black marker, then set these aside. You lay out the sweater pieces on a large table, count them, make sure they match up with the quantity indicated on the order sheet, then separate sleeves from body pieces. With your left hand, you gently hold the left edge of the sweater piece; with your right, you take the razor-sharp cutting tool, press the handle that makes the disk whirl, and slice the pieces—not your fingers—into two halves.
>
> I was slow, very slow, and careful at first. I stopped, looked at Pia, and excused myself for my pace. *"Pazienza*—patience," I pleaded. Pia smiled and nodded: "It's fine to be slow. The important thing at this point is to be careful. It can be dangerous."
>
> I turned to the young women working next to me. They were in their late teens or early twenties and had begun as apprentices after middle school. They each worked on a machine that swallowed whole sweater pieces one by one and spit them out as arm and body shapes. I told them I was getting a little bit faster with the *taglierino disco.*

earn an additional €339. European Commission, Family Benefits and Family Policies in Europe, Italy, June 2002. See The European Observatory on the Social Situation, Demography and Family, http://europa.eu.int/comm/employment_social/eoss/index_en.html, accessed May 1, 2003.

"It seems to call for constant concentration," I said. "Otherwise, it could be dangerous."

"She tried to cut off her finger," one apprentice said to me of Gina, who was stationed next to me. Gina showed me the scar on the side of her index finger.

"I'm here for lots of reasons, but not that," I told her. "I'm not interested in that kind of pain."

"Oh, you don't feel the pain right away," Gina said, matter-of-fact. "It comes after."

I noticed about five other women were working at other stations. There was not much talking until around 11:30 A.M., when Pia's sister came in with her 6-month-old baby. (This woman, 37, was some 20 years younger than Pia.) Pia stopped working to visit her niece. She showed me the baby, and I felt permission to stop working. She took the little girl, blue eyes sparkling, a bow in her tufts of hair, over to the three women at the sergers. The women gathered around, and Pia's son came over to play a clapping game with the baby. It was a family moment. The message was that it was acceptable to bring a baby here. This was one of Pia's sister's regular visits; she used to work here, then took maternity leave. She did not expect to have another child.

Pia left at noon to prepare lunch. Before leaving, I noticed that Martino was checking a sweater that did not match the original sample very closely. He looked irritated, concerned. I entered the office, and the payroll manager freely provided me with the monthly pay receipts for three types of workers. The information was not secret: a union negotiated the pay rates by category of worker:

Type of Worker	Total in Lire	$US	After Taxes	$US
Apprentice	£1,137,293	710	£991,284	620
Single worker	1,826,246	1,140	1,398,714	870
Worker with dependents—child(ren) and spouse	1,937,469	1,210	1,603,669	1,000

I returned to my bundles. At 12:30 sharp, the workers headed out. One turned to me, "Aren't you leaving?"

"Do I just leave it like this?" I was in the middle of a bundle.

"Of course," they said, incredulous. So I picked up my coat and followed them, laughing at myself. I was accustomed to finishing things before I left, not working by a clock.

"You're always laughing," another of the women observed.

I realized that for me this was a temporary experience; for them it was life. [*Fieldnotes*, March 28, 1996]

FAMILY FIRMS, FAMILY OBLIGATIONS

I found Pia looking irritated when I next saw her. She had gone to take care of her aging mother-in-law. Her husband was an only son, so the task of caring for his mother fell on Pia, the *nuora,* or daughter-in-law, for she was the sole younger female kin in the family. I was struck by this dimension of demographic change: Pia was from a large family: nine children—eight girls, one boy. She and her husband had two children. Smaller families did not, however, mean the unraveling of values that associated women with healing and nurturing roles. Even this successful businesswoman was cast in the role of caretaker.[5]

"You know," Pia told me, "when we get old we smell. So she has to be bathed every day."

"It's sad," I said.

"Yes, it's sad, but especially for me. I've been doing this for 3 years now, and it's hard work. It would be one thing if she appreciated what I do. But she has a hard character. She doesn't appreciate what I do for her. In her eyes, it's my obligation. I can't do it anymore. I'm going to have to find someone to do this job."

Pia turned to measure, one by one, a pile of finished sweater vests. She looked frustrated. "Do those have some kind of problem?" I asked.

"Yes, one of the armholes is too small, so they'll have to be recut and resewn," Pia said. She wore a tense expression. She attributed it to a headache. "The work is stressful, there are lots of stresses."

She asked about my daughter, and then reflected on her experience as a parent: "As children get older, as they grow, so grow the worries, the stresses. Then you worry as they go out, alone, in the car. You worry that something will happen. Tensions, worries. Life is filled with stresses. . . . Life was better before, when families were bigger." Now, she told me, "*la vita costa troppo,* life costs too much."

One thing that impressed me about the family firms, including the *maglificio,* was the integration of work and family. By mid-April, Pia's sister had returned to work, her maternity leave completed. Occasionally, she brought her baby with her. I remember one day when the 6-month-old awoke, Aunt Pia picked her up and walked around the factory floor, coddling the baby and cooing at her. She perched her up on the table where her sister—the infant's mother—was folding finished sweaters and neatly inserting them into packets. The integration of family activities, such as child rearing, into the work space seemed easily achieved. Perhaps it was because family and work for income have long been integrated here. Pia raised her own children while sewing sweaters in a workshop with several other women, so integration seemed to come naturally. Pia's identity as head controller, as "head" of the family business, did not seem to conflict with her role as aunt or mother. The history of women in textile work was long. I later learned, however, that this kind of acceptance was not always extended to young workers who decided to marry.

IMPRESSIONS

When I returned home, Luisa was on the third story balcony hanging out laundry. She had angrily washed it by hand because both of the washing machines in the household were broken.

---

[5]A recent Eurobarometer survey (May 1999) asked, "Who has to bear the burden of looking after dependent old people?" Some 37 percent of Europeans replied that this responsibility fell to the children. By contrast, more than 60 percent of those interviewed in Greece, Spain, and Portugal, and over 48 percent of Italians gave this response. Only 2 percent of Italians think elderly parents should be cared for in a retirement home. Discussed in Sgritta 2001. See http://europa.eu.int/comm/employment_social/eoss/index_en.html.

"Where have you been?" she asked me in that brusque way of hers that carries with it a sense of envy, of betrayal.

"I've been working," I said.

"You were *working?* What do you mean you were working?"

"I was working at a *maglificio,* a sweater firm."

She cast a tilted glance my way. "A *maglificio?* Are you kidding?"

"No. Really, I was working as an apprentice."

"What good does this do you?"

I turned toward Chris. He was laughing and it got me started. Luisa joined in, somewhat confused. My husband was laughing because I had explained to her innumerable times my project and my desire to integrate myself better into the life of the community, but it did not resonate with her. I suppose it was too strange to imagine why on earth an American graduate student with a prestigious grant would choose to do sweater work. I began wondering if I had explained myself badly.

"I had told you I wanted to find an apprenticeship," I reminded her.

"I thought you were joking."

"Nope, I was serious."

She was flabbergasted. "*Sei una diavolina*—you're a little devil." [*Fieldnotes,* April 1, 1996]

My devilish trait was at times charming, but at other times it became the source of tension. I simply was not spending much time with Nicoletta and her daughters. They were starting to resent my absence. I felt the tension, and I knew the sentiment of possessiveness was not just in my imagination one day when things came to a head.

"Do you want to come this afternoon?" Liliana asked me.

"No, we can't," I said. "*Abbiamo un impegno*—we're busy."

"Where are you going?" she continued.

"Pistoia," I answered. (Pistoia is about 20 kilometers northwest of Prato.)

"*Pistoia?*" she accused. "Why Pistoia?"

"We're going to the antique market."

"With who?"

"*La* Carolina," I complied.

She was clearly offended. The message was one of family betrayal.

Later in the day, I ran into Nicoletta, walking down the steps. She looked my way so I stood up to greet her.

"*Siete tornati*—you've returned?" she asked.

"Yes. *Sei gelosa*—Are you jealous?" I took her cheeks between my fingers and tugged gently. It was a gesture that she had used often to show affection toward Hollis (my daughter, 5 years old).

She smiled sheepishly. "*Devo ammettere, sì, un po'*—I have to admit, yes, a little."

"At least you're honest," I said.

And she: "Better to be a little honest in these things." [*Fieldnotes,* April 14, 1996]

Several weeks later I received unexpected validation for my decision to immerse myself in the world of production when attending a conference on regional economics held at the nearby Villa of Artimino. Known as the villa of 100 chimneys, the structure was designed for the Grand Duke in 1594 as a

Elizabeth L. Krause

Figure 3.5 An artisan uses a special needle to fix a hole in a sweater.

country hunting retreat. I sat at a table with the well-known historian Alessandra Pescarolo. I was humbled to be sitting next to her. This must be proof that I am a nerd: I idolize certain intellectuals like most people idolize movie stars. Her work awed me so, I could barely talk. When she directed a question about my project right at me, I nearly choked on my pasta. I finally managed to mutter something about my work as an apprentice in the sweater factory.

"*Che colpo!*—What a coup!" she exclaimed.

I was taken aback. I did not expect such an enthusiastic response. In retrospect, I imagine that for an academic of her stature to enter a factory would not be easy. Barbara Ehrenreich (2001) managed to do it in the United States— though she is a journalist. Her book *Nickel and Dimed* is the result of her going undercover as a low-wage worker to expose the dismal conditions of America's full-time working poor and to generate empathy and change for this growing segment of the population. In Italy, class lines tend to be more rigid than in the United States, so I suppose that my crossing boundaries did seem like a feat.

Others, however, were not so impressed with the way I was spending my time. Most people thought the activity to be, at least, amusing and, at most, odd. A North American woman married to a local Italian man made disparaging comments about sweater-workers, describing their manual labor as "menial."

"Don't you find the work monotonous?" she asked, perplexed that I would dirty my hands doing such work.

Initially, monotony was not my sensation; having been accustomed for so many years at producing words and texts, my involvement in the global economy of commodities was initially exhilarating. I admittedly had a romanticized response to being involved in sweater production. All of my life I had related to

clothes only as things, fetishizing them as commodities, and now I was relating
to them through people. The writings of Karl Marx about modes of production
creating social relations now seemed concrete. Furthermore, the work was
embodied. My limbs and muscles were learning new movements, such as how
to hold my elbow close to my body so as to secure the *taglierino disco* in my
hand, to cut straight, not to let it slip.

The sweater-workers themselves had another reaction still. They told me I
was being exploited since I was not being paid for my work; I reminded them of
my income from an academic grant and of my concern that it would have been
illegal for the factory owners to pay me. Their concerns worried me. I feared my
presence was stirring up trouble.

> I'm having a conflict re: what to do about my work. My fellow workers think I'm
> being exploited if I don't get paid. Yet I entered the *maglificio* as a volunteer.
> Carolina did me a favor. Perhaps I should talk to her to see about other possibilities.
> [*Fieldnotes*, May 6, 1996]

BUTTONS AND A FAMILY FIRM

One day in May, I stopped by Carolina and Leo's house for a visit. They had me
stay for lunch. Leo, the family cook, had prepared *fagioli all'uccelletto,* a savory
dish made with cannellini beans, tomatoes, olive oil, sage, and salt. We watched
the 1 o'clock news and talked politics as we ate. Their part-time worker had quit.
They invited me to try my hand at sewing buttons on sweaters. It was the third
step of the process. Leo's job was the first step: he pressed a foot-pedal that triggered the machine to mark a row of chalk dots on the sweaters to ensure evenly
spaced and aligned buttonholes and buttons. Carolina performed the second step:
she made buttonholes with a machine whose motor growled. My job was the
third step: operating a machine to attach buttons. The task required that I slide a
button into an adjustable clip, position the sweater under the needle, press a lever
with my foot, and let the machine rip.

> "How do you like the work?" Carolina asked.
> Using the special machine to sew on the buttons was initially entertaining. It was
> a marvel at first to see how the details—buttons and labels and tags—convert a thing
> into a commodity that becomes so easy to fetishize.
> "It's kind of fun to see the finished sweater. How do you feel about it?"
> "I hate the work," she snapped. "I don't like it at all."
> "Then how do you do it?"
> "I just do it."
> "But don't you feel just a tinge of satisfaction when you see all those beautifully
> finished sweaters, ready to wear?" (I was exaggerating a bit.)
> She and Leo laughed. "No, the only satisfaction we feel is at the end of the month
> when the check arrives." [*Fieldnotes*, May 3, 1996]

Carolina often spoke loudly over the serging noises. Her topics covered
themes such as U.S. cultural imperialism and neocolonialism—she resented
the U.S. manipulation of postwar Italian electoral politics that ensured the

hegemony of the center Christian Democrats and the marginalization of Italy's communist party.[6] She recalled the practice of confession—she was against it from an early age. She identified with and criticized feminism—she refused to sign a document that called for giving women "dignity. "Why do we need to be *given* dignity?" she asked, enraged. "What, men already have it and we don't?'"

She loved talking politics, whether related strictly to government or broadly to cultural matters. She frequently repeated singsong one phrase that rang like a women's mantra: "*Che colpa abbiamo noi?* —What fault do we have?" It was as though she was railing the practicing Catholics—namely women—who flailed their chests while repeating, "*mea culpa, mea culpa.*" I once attended a special memorial Mass that Nicoletta had arranged for her deceased husband at a small church in a hill town, and I watched with a mix of awe and dread while the four or so women present engaged in this ritual of self-blame. The uneven power of men and women manifested itself in the town as well, where men had more freedom to linger in public spaces such as the piazzas and the bars. Carolina told me that women's activities tended not to interest men: "Really, men don't care about women. They'd just as soon be left to their own devices."

Neither Carolina nor Leo's identities were bound up as sweater artisans. Leo was a retired state railroad employee. Carolina was a community activist and politician. Carolina was most interested in her roles as a city advisor, as park curator, as festival organizer. Sweater finishing was a necessary work activity to bring cash into the household. Her husband, Leo, was motivated by culinary and social pleasures of life: securing fresh vegetables from an old peasant, taking a spin to the piazza for some cigarettes, having a coffee and a chat with the men.

Carolina and Leo continued to ask me to work for them. I joked that my pay was hanging out with them and learning Italian and eating the delicious lunches. "I'll sew on a button for every bean I eat," I said. Before long they insisted on paying me an hourly wage—the going rate of about £4,500, or $2.50, an hour. So I quit my apprenticeship at the *maglificio*. I learned that one of the benefits of domicile work was that it offered workers more freedom. Discipline, however, was still required. The rhythm of work was driven by the time demands of the contractors and ultimately the buyers as well as the fashion seasons.

I learned that all sweater jobs were not equal. I arrived one evening to find an exhausted household; the parents and three adult children had not gone to bed until 4 A.M. The weekend had culminated in the *festa della battitura,* a festival inspired by the traditional grain threshing. Carolina had been a major force in organizing the dinner for several hundred people. But the festival had coincided with a busy time in the sweater-finishing season, and so the family members had risen early that morning at 7 A.M. to work on some 3,000 sweaters that had been delivered the week before. The sweaters had taken over their house: bags and boxes full of sweaters spilled out from the workroom onto the front patio as well as into the living room, concealing Carolina's heirloom antiques and competing with her late uncle's oil paintings that adorned the walls. The sweaters themselves were a nightmare. They were all the same color—undyed white—and they shed so much lint, you could taste it.

---

[6]For background on Italian politics, see Ginsborg 1990; Kertzer 1980, 1998; Shore 1990.

"Get this place straightened up!" Carolina yelled. "When you're this tired, you need to have some order in the work space otherwise it will drive us all crazy."

Everyone, including me, started to sort sweaters and clear them out of the way. I did some buttoning. At one point Carolina threw a sweater across the room. It hit a pile of other sweaters; the air became a cloud of sweater lint. We all grimaced and held our breath. I opened the door. [*Fieldnotes,* June 24, 1996]

There is a word for this kind of job: *lavoraccio,* or lousy work. The suffix *-accio* denotes something negative, despicable, unpleasant. Carolina and Leo had started the business for their youngest son, Iginio, who that summer was busy fulfilling his obligation to serve his country: instead of military service, the 21-year-old was serving two years as a conscientious objector, working with several other like-minded males in the town hall. Occasionally he would appear in the workshop and be asked to adjust the machine. I managed to break two needles in a row one day. The machine was apparently set incorrectly. Iginio showed his face, and Leo asked him to have a look at the button-attaching machine. Iginio got it going just right—as though it was his.

"Yeah, me and this machine, *io e lei,*" he said, "we'd spend long nights together." He used the female pronoun to refer to the machine.

"Oh, so the machine is a female?" I teased.

He cast a flirtatious glance. I suddenly felt self-conscious about our interaction.

So then Iginio had to run off, back to the *comune* for his conscientious objector service. Leo worried about his son's future. Iginio did not yet have a clear idea what he wanted to do, but he desired something he would like. He had already tried his hand as an upholstery artisan, but did not much care for it. Leo said the button firm could be his work, but he didn't like that either.

"At his age," Leo said, "it seems a reasonable request for him to want something he likes." [*Fieldnotes,* June 25, 1996]

When sweater work was slow and I spent days in the archive, Iginio occasionally helped me decipher hand-scrawled words in documents. Most dealt with council proceedings from 1901 about the conditions of women applying for wet-nurse subsidies. I sometimes gave Carolina a ride up the hill to the town hall, as she juggled her roles. Two days after the outrage over the wretched, linty sweaters, piles of sweaters from that job order awaited us, and Carolina laid into Leo.

"How much are we getting for each button?" Carolina demanded.

"100 lire," Leo told her.

"You've gotta be *scemo,* an idiot, to accept this job," she ranted.

Leo clarified the pay: 100 lire to take off the buttons, another 100 to put on the correct buttons. (The normal rate for a button and a buttonhole was 150 lire total.) Taking off the buttons was not only time consuming but painful. My thumb was numb. I must have damaged a nerve when I was removing the buttons. I figured I had removed two packs each of 39 sweaters, each with six buttons, making for nearly 240 buttons.

"This is a *lavoro bestiale,* a *lavoro di fame*—a bestial job, a job you'd do if you were dying of starvation."

"Why didn't they take this work to the people who did it in the first place?" Carolina demanded. She was fuming. "What's their number? I'm calling them."

"Non fare la matta," Leo warned. "Don't get crazy on me."

Carolina went ahead and called the *maglificio*. She told them what a horrible job it was, how time consuming it was, all the while keeping her cool. She realized then that only 200 of the sweaters required removing the old buttons. The rest needed one button added.

Later, I told Leo that I realized that you can't say "no" to the *maglificio*—though you can tell them many other things.

"Yes, many," he laughed. [*Fieldnotes,* June 26, 1996]

The sense of *furia,* or urgency, to the pace of the work became incessant by late July. The contractors had to ship off all orders before production more or less stopped for August vacation. One morning, I arrived at 9:30 to Leo's calling me a *"birbona,"* or a slacker, for not having worked the previous evening; I had given into the temptation to go with Chris to an open-air jazz concert in Florence in Piazza SS. Annunziata, there right in front of Brunelleschi's foundling hospital!

That day I worked nonstop, sewing pearly white buttons on 50/50 wool-acrylic white women's sweaters until the lunch break at 1 P.M. *"A tavola!"* Leo called us to eat. All the produce was fresh from the garden: green beans, cooked with a little garlic, a delicious salad of fresh tomatoes, red onion, cucumber, olive oil. The main course was canned tuna fish. The wine was from a box. With the urgent sweater work, there had not been time to pick up fresh local wine. I returned to my button machine at 2 P.M.

The phone rang. I overheard Leo talking to Angiolo, the contractor at the *maglificio.* Angiolo wanted the sweaters immediately.

"Well, I had to tell them that 'the boy' couldn't come today to sew on buttons," Leo said. He used the masculine term for guy probably as a way not to offend me, as there I was sewing on buttons.

The main reason none of the sweaters were ready was because Carolina had lost her glasses, and without them she could not sew the buttonholes. So she had gone out looking for replacements—and likely made other stops along the way related to her community work. The marked sweaters, ready for buttonholes, had piled up beside her machine in an ever-growing mound. Now, as she began working, they fell into her shoulder; at times she asked Leo to take them away.

"Ci vuole un po' di furbizia—you've got to be somewhat clever," he said. *"Si arrangia*—You make things work." Leo explained that he could not tell the *maglificio* that his wife had lost her glasses and that was why the sweaters were not ready. Such a truth would lead to harsher truths: lost face, lost trust, lost work.

In the South, Leo explained, people are really experts at the art of winging it, or getting by. In Naples they're really *furbi,* or clever. "You know," he continued, "lots of people wake up and they don't know how they will put food on the table. They have to *arrangiarsi,* make their way."

Carolina jumped in and began lashing out on the whole notion of *furbizia,* cleverness. "Those Neopolitans, they're not *furbi,* they're robbers and thieves. I hate southerners. I am a racist. Everybody's a racist. It's not that they don't have work, it's that they don't want to work." [*Fieldnotes,* July 30, 1996]

On another occasion months later, Carolina would stand up for southern Italians when a repairman insulted them as *marocchini,* a slur that derives from the word Moroccan and that implies southerners have Arab blood (see pp. 161–163).

I kept at the button machine until 6:30 P.M. I spent an hour or so buttoning the sweaters and packing them into the clear plastic bags, ready for pickup. I returned home to find Nicoletta, my landlady and by now quasi–Italian mother, asking after me.

"What have you done all day?" Nicoletta asked.

"I worked," I said.

"You've become a *grande lavoratrice*—a major worker," she said. *"In Toscana bisogna a lavorare."*

"'In Tuscany, you have to work.'" I repeated. I then typed her words into my lap-top. "I wrote it down."

"You're going to make one heck of a big book," she said.

I laughed.

"Dilenguente!" she replied. Delinquent.

"I'll write that too." And we both laughed. [*Fieldnotes*, July 30, 1996]

RUSHING TO RUSH

An advantage of working in a family firm was the greater freedom to talk and to observe, even participate in, the interactions between the workers, the contractors, repairmen, and others who dropped by. Carolina suggested we talked more than most people did while working. I believed her observation to be true though whenever I showed up at a workshop, people tended to talk with me, nearly always continuing to work while we chatted.

By late October 1996, Carolina had grown increasingly free to criticize me and my lot. Her criticisms at times included acute observations, such as contrasting attitudes toward work between Americans and Italians.

"Americans," she said, "they *schizzano*." The term literally means splash, but the figurative implication is that a person is rushing around so fast as to make a splash. "Italians *schizzano,* or rush, when they have to, when they work. But Americans are always rushing around even when they don't have to. It's a disease. Even you have a little bit of this disease."

"It's true." I had to agree. "It's because we're raised with such a strong sentiment to produce, produce, produce. We feel like we always have to be productive." I took care to point out some Americans completely resisted this value, people like my own little sister, at the time a post-hippie youth traveler of the generation born in the mid-1970s.

Her criticism made me reflect on the way that Italians in Prato rushed around like crazy when they had deadlines to meet. But somehow, they managed to retain another *mestiere,* or craft, that of coming together at the table to enjoy good food and good company. Even at the factory, the workers broke for lunch and headed home for a hot meal. At the family workshop, we came around the table and, most days, took time to enjoy a delicious cooked lunch. Carolina's accusation that I also suffered from the rushing-around disease made me reflect on my own upbringing. I felt I was a product of a society that, somewhere along the line, had all but lost a sense for the art of living.

SEARCHING FOR SELF-RESPECT

One day in September I arrived at Carolina and Leo's house to find only their daughter, Catrina, at home. After a few moments I got to work, putting little black buttons at the collar of a 50/50 wool-acrylic women's sweater. Shortly thereafter, the phone rang; it was the factory that had contracted the work, saying someone would be coming soon to pick up the sweaters. Soon, a woman arrived, one of the owners. The interaction with her made me realize profoundly the value of autonomy. Those who worked as subcontractors in central Italy did not get rich like the larger contracting firm owners; however, they had more defense against the humiliating and alienating strategies of the boss than did a factory worker inside a firm.

The owner-woman was short with an unpleasant sneer on her face and never looked us directly in the eye. She didn't smile but cranked and criticized. She asked a bunch of questions of Catrina and me: How many sweaters had we done? Where were Leo and Carolina?

"Obviously, my mother had an appointment that she couldn't cancel," replied Catrina in the confident tone that she had learned well from her mother.

The owner-woman looked irritated. "If Carolina were here she could do them faster," she said.

"Well, not necessarily," I said, trying to stick up for my work but also not be overly confrontational. "Even though these sweaters only have two buttons, they are slow to work. You lose a lot of time handling them, searching for the label. It's often all scrunched up."

The woman started looking at the sweaters, to quality "control" my work, and she noticed that I was putting the extra button on a side-seam tag but not always in the same place. "You need to put them in the same place," she said.

"Fine," I said, "where do you want them?"

"Here, in this little corner," she demanded.

"That's impossible. First, because the needle comes unthreaded—the machine doesn't like this material. And second, because the tags are scrunched up and to place the button in the corner you'd have to place your finger under the arm and risk sewing your finger."

She insisted her idea was possible.

"Well then," I challenged her, "you try."

And so she did. She took her place at the button-sewing machine. Lucky for her she didn't get her finger sewn. But lucky for me, the needle came unthreaded—proving my point. The machine could not work well with such a small and slippery piece of fabric.

She finally relented. "OK. Put them here on this angle, near the sweater seam, but not too close to the seam. And make sure to put them all in the same place."

After the owner-woman left, Catrina and I shared our disgust at how she had treated us: as though she were disgusted with our low intelligence and ignorance. But then we had a laugh. "She thinks she's so smart; she doesn't realize what she's dealing with—a future engineer and a future anthropologist!" [*Fieldnotes, September 13, 1996*]

The disrespect the owner had showed us was truly offensive. We had searched for ways to resist her authoritarian plays.

When Leo returned from the auto repair shop—a common outing given the age and condition of his car—we told him what she had suggested. "*Che scema,* what an idiot," he said. "Often those at the *maglificio* ask you to do things that are impossible, and then they would never think to pay us more for the extra time certain tasks require."

I later observed that those at the *maglifici* perhaps get frustrated because they want to be able to control the subcontractors. Before the economic crisis, *maglifici* were more like factories and had more workers in house. They could keep a close watch on their workers. Workers in a factory are not allowed to talk, as I noted at the factory where I had worked. Leo viewed this as a right of the employer—though a right that gets excessive when surveillance of workers includes counting the minutes a worker takes to go to the bathroom.

As the crisis in the sweater industry expanded, workers became too expensive. The factories saved a lot of money through subcontracting because they no longer had to pay benefits. The owners often forgot that those they subcontracted to were not their hired workers. People like Carolina and Leo refused to be treated like underlings. They wanted to be treated as equals, with respect.

Carolina viewed herself as an associate, though a financially unequal one. "At the end of the year, I'd like to go to them and ask for our share of the profits. They drive around in fancy new cars and we have these used second-, third-, and fourth-hand cars. And they think they pay us too much!"

Indeed, one day the owner's son scolded Carolina for her public service work and the time it required of her. "You should stay off the phone," he said. "You lose money talking on the phone. You make money working on the sweaters."

He could not believe someone would dedicate substantial time and interest to public projects at the expense of private earnings. He could not relate to her sense of civic commitment. His obsession was money for money's sake. Carolina's obsession was for the betterment of her community, for the welfare of those men, women, and children living in it.

INTEGRATED YET UNENDING OBLIGATIONS

Immersing myself in the sweater industry broadened my networks and provided invaluable insight into local meanings and experiences in terms of how people reconciled family work with money work. My apprenticeship as a worker in the sweater sector gave me insight into the rhythms and demands of paid work in the marketplace and unpaid work related to the care of one's family. Even a woman like Pia, who had attained success and autonomy, was not absolved of her duties as caretaker for her elderly mother-in-law. In the button firm, I witnessed diffuse industry in the area of Prato, which has its roots in rural industry of the 19th century. Subcontracting shaped the contemporary organization of work and the rhythms of daily life. In this context of verbal agreements, relationships of trust were essential. Leo and Carolina's autonomy came up against its limits when confronted with job orders. The contracting firm's offer of work carried an assumption that the recipient would accept. Leo and Carolina could not simply say "no" to work. They were hard-pressed to accept even bestial job orders, such as the one involving the scratchy white lint-tasting sweaters. Just as the recipient of a gift has an obligation to give back, so the recipient of a job order has an obligation to get the work done when promised.

Moreover, in Prato the sensibility toward social obligations and loyalties overlies former patron-client relations that came with a number of expectations on the part of both parties. The rural world of peasants that existed in decades hence depended on favors in times of need, not to mention everyday hospitality, practices familiar to southern Italians who migrated northward to participate in the postwar boom. In the firm, we broke each day from our sweater work to come around the table and partake in a hot meal that Leo had lovingly prepared. Work and family were deeply integrated.

These persistent sensibilities contrasted with the cold, calculating assumptions of a "rational marketplace." Such logics were simultaneously present. Just as the struggles with global competitiveness in Prato were assuring cycles of crisis, the Italian government cracked down on informal labor practices, such as those so common in sweater-making. Pia observed that an increasingly rigid labor market hit women domicile workers particularly hard. Women performed much work in the informal sector, a role that many of their female ancestors had long occupied. Workers who did hidden and untaxed work received no benefits and lower pay than factory workers, and hence they had to work long and diligently to make the work worth their while. This gender division of labor perpetuated the ongoing devaluation of women's work relative to men's work. I was reminded of the 19th-century straw weavers known to work long hours for *un tozzo di pane*, or a crust of bread. That crust of bread, however, was crucial in an economy where cash was sparse (Pescarolo 1991:27).

The speed of the global economy meant Italian firms' competitive edge confronted ever new challenges and temptations to move beyond national borders, severing the social relations and obligations on which their firms' wealth had been built. The icy relations that arise from capitalist relationships were exemplified in Catrina's and my confrontation with the pretentious owner who treated us like idiots only to realize how unrealistic her expectations were. Finally, I observed the time-constraining demands of the market when family members came together to work urgently around the clock to meet a deadline. When the deadline was missed, due to other priorities related to replacing eyeglasses or doing community work, the domicile setting empowered its workers with the autonomy to offer excuses that protected their reputation and saved face.

Economist Giacomo Becattini noted that the family and community, often seen as "reservoirs of conservatism, paradoxically ended up as the springboard for the very special form of modernization that happened in Prato" (2001:90). Becattini's comment is intended as a critique of those who equate "the family" with tradition, and hence an undermining force against economic development and innovation. Criticisms aside, what does Becattini's comment suggest for how the organization of work has influenced family-making? In the context of a story about demographic change, one could twist his statement to mean that the demographers got it right after all. That the motor of low fertility was modernization. That economic development pushed fertility to decline. Jumping to such a conclusion, however, ignores the cultural and historical evidence related to an economy that, although connected to the competitive demands of globalization, was not driven simply by big-scale factory models of wage labor but rather was deeply moored in relationships of trust and reciprocity.

Prato's economic context of small- to medium-sized firms meant that a number of these businesses were family operations. It meant that a vast majority of firms were engaged in subcontracting, or outsourcing work, and a number of those who output the work did so as hidden laborers. It has also meant an embrace of a worker-based politics that, like the Catholic Church, placed a premium on volunteer work. As a whole, this translates to people having countless obligations they must attend to. Changes in family-making are not simply automatic reflexes to economic modernization. Rather, these transformations are local cultural responses to an ever-changing and unpredictable global market— one that would eradicate the cycles of reciprocity so central to the rhythms of work and social life in Prato.

When I set out to integrate myself into local rhythms of work as a way to grasp the stresses of reconciling family work with wage work, I sensed I was betraying a relationship of trust that I had established with my host family. Ironically, I was living the very tension I sought to understand. The confusion I sensed then has now given way to a glimmer of clarity. My relationship with Nicoletta, my landlady, and her grown children occurred in the context of Prato, where people find themselves deeply entangled in webs of obligation. These webs are inseparable from the social relations and expectations that make up the very foundation of work. Humans are not mere economic animals, calculating their every move in cost-benefit balance sheets. They do calculate but they also feel the pressures of global restructuring that squeeze the space and time available for respecting different sorts of obligations. An ever-encroaching global order demands relationships be based on profit; it threatens an economic and social system, similar to what Mauss described as a gift economy, long based on trust and reciprocity. Italians' record-low fertility results from a century of adjustment to ever-changing global orders (see Wolf 1969:295). Each generation makes new adjustments so as to live their lives with dignity. Family-making is not merely about reproducing babies, but also about producing the material goods and wages, as well as the care and nurturing, that make for a viable family.

4/Displaying Class, Consuming Distinction

Nicoletta, Liliana, and I headed off to the attorney's office this morning. The attorney asked what brought me here. I barely had a chance to mention the project when he quipped, "The low birthrate is because the cost of living is too high."

—Author's Fieldnotes, November 9, 1995

This generation was born into too much gold.

—Elvira, March 12, 1997

The most common reason I heard people offer to explain Italian women's low birthrate was the cost of living. Many others during my field research echoed the attorney's explanation. The cost-of-living account rang true to people's experiences. It made sense to people who had literally and swiftly gone from rags to riches.

Italy's well-known demographer Massimo Livi-Bacci (2000:138) suggests in his book *The Population of Europe* that children cost more nowadays than they did when families lived in an agricultural society. Parents in contemporary societies, he writes, find themselves having to invest heavily in their children's education, health, and welfare. I take welfare to mean well being, or the costs that parents accrue to feed, house, clothe, as well as entertain their children.

This explanation appears straightforward enough. The assumption is that people are rational and that they only have as many children as they can afford. Potential parents engage in calculating cost-benefit analyses that result in the small families across much of the world, industrialized as well as developing. Nodding to the conquest of rational choice, Livi-Bacci writes, "since the 1960s and 1970s, the availability of reliable birth control methods has allowed for perfectly planned conceptions" (2000:188). This kind of rationalist logic, though well intended, has several drawbacks: First, it cannot explain the fact that the onset of fertility decline did not follow economic vectors. Second, it cannot account for recent findings that Italians practice unconventional birth control and

68

that even in a society with a super-low fertility rate plenty of births are imperfectly planned. And third, the path to worshipping rational choice easily leads to stigmatizing those who violate its norms.

So what explains the beginnings of fertility decline? Initially, modernization was believed to hold the explanatory key. Modernization theory enjoyed throne status among demographers in the second half of the 20th century. This theory proved to be a problem as it carried a load of baggage. Some of its assumptions were pretty disturbing, ethnocentric, and downright presumptuous. Especially offensive was the notion that this grand theory could explain revolutionary changes without attending to historical differences. It was the ultimate flattener of diverse human experiences.

Modernization theory provided the impetus for one of the biggest undertakings ever in historical demography. A group of bright demographers came together in the 1960s at Princeton University and launched the European Fertility Project. They sought to discover universal reasons for why women stopped having children before reaching menopause. Their hypothesis was that modernization caused fertility to decline. But like good scientists, they did not take their assumptions to be true. Rather, they sought proof. So, they mapped and calculated fertility rates in 600 European provinces and compared them with the Hutterites, an Anabaptist group whose women averaged 12 children each. As Ansley Coale and Roy Treadway (1986) explained in their introduction to *The Decline of Fertility in Europe,* this population was chosen because Hutterite women had the highest fertility rates on record. They achieved this rate through a strict gender ideology that celebrated male dominance. Indeed, divine order subscribed that men ruled over women (Hostetler and Huntington 1967). They prohibited contraception and abortion. Furthermore, the women practiced early weaning of infants, resulting in short interbirth intervals. None of the European populations equaled this level of prolific birthing, even at their height in the pre-transition era.

The European Fertility Project was an astonishing undertaking. Imagine the quantity of local records, such as church and city registers, this team of international researchers perused! In the end, they amassed unprecedented amounts of data; however, their results were ultimately disappointing. They failed to prove their hypothesis. They failed to discover a universal explanation for the onset of demographic transition. They dethroned modernization theory. It turned out that fertility rates began to decline under all sorts of diverse circumstances. Hungary and Germany showed declines in fertility about the same time, in 1890, when the vast majority of Hungarians worked in agriculture but their German counterparts droned to the rhythms of industrialization. The greatest exception was France, whose fertility pioneers initiated their demographic transition in 1780, when economies were rural, a century before England, which was well into the throes of the industrial revolution. The project's major conclusion was people who spoke the same language tended to partake in simultaneous fertility declines. It seemed communication and culture predicted something. People got to talking, new ideas started flowing, and new behaviors began taking hold. So much for modernization as the motor of fertility decline.[1]

The second limitation of explanations anchored in cost-benefit analyses is that they offer little in the way of explaining contraceptive patterns. A recent nationwide fertility study in Italy revealed Italian couples to have surprisingly diverse contraceptive practices (see Table 4.1). As Franco Bonarini puts it, "the first result that emerges is that 24 percent of married women who are at risk of conception have had unprotected sex in the considered period [the past four weeks before the interview]" (1999:400). Comparative data suggests much lower rates of unprotected sex in Belgium (15 percent), France (10 percent), and Spain (10 percent). Bonarini fathoms that some respondents who said they did not use contraceptives ("None") may rely on coitus interruptus or natural methods. Alternatively, some may have babies in mind. In contrast to Livi-Bacci's statement about "perfectly planned conceptions," a recent review of Italians' fertility behaviors cautioned against assuming that Italians "are the masters of their own fertility"; although unplanned births and abortions have declined between the early 1970s and mid-1990s, as of 1995, 37 percent of Italians' conceptions were unplanned, reaching 45 percent among women under 20 and over 35 years old! (Castiglioni, dalla Zuanna, and Loghi 2001). The authors take care to distinguish between those unplanned conceptions that are unwanted and those that are welcomed. In any case, it appears that spontaneity, desire, and reckless abandon are still alive and well even in a super-low fertility population.

The third drawback of attributing changes in family-making to rational choices is that the explanation invites observers to stigmatize those people who have more children than deemed affordable. Jane and Peter Schneider detail in their study *Festival of the Poor* (1996) how the gentry class in Sicily stigmatized the poor once small families became stylish and the poorest classes continued having numerous children. Their investigation squarely places attitudes about family size in the context of a capitalist society, complete with its hierarchical class relations and consumer practices designed to flaunt status. Ultimately, the cost-of-living thesis raises as many questions as it answers. What makes children affordable? Who sets the standards? Are they everyone's standards? Notions of "affordability" are not universal. They have histories. In contemporary Italy, outlooks that favor small families are not neutral but strongly middle class. Furthermore, if the cost of living leads people to have so few children, then why are overall fertility rates higher in certain regions, such as the south of Italy, where economic indicators like unemployment rates depict a much poorer population? Isn't life relatively more expensive for people who have less money? Or does life become more expensive as people become more wealthy? Accounting for this puzzling phenomenon, I believe, is the task at hand.

Instead of explaining away low fertility rates with "cost of living" tales, anthropologists may think in terms of cultural politics. Such an approach probes the struggles over the moral stakes connected with family and self in society. How do people exhibit to their family, friends, neighbors, and even strangers

[1]Even though this major undertaking in historical demography disproved its hypothesis, modernization-theory assumptions about demographic change persist: that it is progressive, that it follows European models, that it is desirable, that it is similar everywhere. Greenhalgh (1995) offers an excellent overview.

TABLE 4.1 USE OF CONTRACEPTIVE METHODS AMONG FERTILE ITALIAN WOMEN, AGES 20–49, INTERVIEWED FOR A NATIONAL FERTILITY STUDY, 1995

Method	In Married Couple		In Unmarried Couple		Not in a Couple		Total	
	Number	Percent	Number	Percent	Number	Percent	Number	Percent
None	521	24.3	14	18.9	42	8.0	576	21.1
Pill	391	18.2	20	27.0	226	43.6	636	23.2
IUD	163	7.6	3	4.6	15	2.9	181	6.6
Condom or diaphragm*	412	19.2	19	26.3	167	32.1	597	21.8
Coitus interruptus	542	25.2	8	10.3	58	11.2	608	22.2
Natural method	101	4.7	8	10.8	10	1.8	119	4.3
Other	14	0.6	2	2.1	2	0.3	17	0.6
Don't know or no response	3	0.1	0	0.0	0	0.0	3	0.1
Total	2,146	100	73	100	518	100	2,737	100

Source: Franco Bonarini, L'uso della contraccezione in Italia: dalla retrospezione del 1979 a quella del 1995–96 (de Sandre et al. 1999:400).

*Diaphragm use appears to be very low in Italy if a recent study among women in Milan is a reliable indication. The Milan study design separated out condoms from diaphragms and revealed diaphragms to be rarely used: Only 1.68 percent of married women used diaphragms as compared with 30.2 percent of women indicating men using condoms to prevent conception (de Sandre and Ongaro 2003:45).

their worth as a social being? Those struggles were, and continue to be, deeply rooted in economic transformations involving rural industry, agriculture, and the patriarchal family. Cultural meanings became tangled in newly emerging class ideologies in the postwar era of the late 1940s. The economic miracle gave way to a burgeoning consumer society. Peasant classes became working classes. In Prato, a strongly identified leftist workers' culture thrived in the radical years of the 1950s to the 1970s.[2] By the 1990s, I frequently heard people lament "there is nothing left of the left." The rising tide of individualistic, middle-class desires was a force to be reckoned with particularly in light of the fall of the Berlin Wall in 1989. The post-socialist era threw Italy's leftist culture and political parties into crisis. The forces of change unleashed a new age of global consumer culture that affected central Italy in particularly fierce ways.

Prato's excesses are the stuff of legend. Recall, former peasants or agricultural workers who quickly came into money are said to have bought books by the kilo. They had little intention of reading them. Their purpose was to display the volumes on bookshelves as a sign of culture. People from old money had acquired books through education. New-money people bought books for show. Practices of displaying status became rampant in the postwar era.

Ideas about what one needed to show status were not arbitrary but rather the result of historical contact between social classes. This contact served as a reminder of uneven worlds. Landed nobility and tenant peasants were intimately connected through the sharecropping system, whose contracts spelled out tasks. I came across one contract, for example, that called for peasant families to deliver specific foods once per year: one freshly cured *prosciutto* ham, six new brooms, two capons (castrated roosters), six chickens, four young cocks, eight dozen eggs, as well as a specified quantity of straw and hay. The contract also spelled out peasants' obligation to wash the sheets of the nobility on a rotating basis, and former peasant women recalled the intense laundering process involving boiling sheets in ash and rinsing them in the river. Such arts were necessary to result in blindingly white linens.

The whiteness of whites continued to have meaning in the postwar context. I was instructed of its importance one day when I was doing laundry. Luisa, my landlady Nicoletta's oldest daughter, wore the signs of her obsessive laundering on her hands: her skin was often coated with a white chalky substance derived from the quantities of detergent she used for her athletic pre-scrubbing routines. One day she came walking down the cement steps that ran between the back of the house and her mother's flower garden. She caught a glimpse of me as I finished hanging out laundry on a drying rack on the patio.

---

[2]Pratese workers had a strong sense of local community, of "our Prato." The industrial city, along with *pane,* or bread, and *companatico,* or food that one eats with bread, defined people's sense of life, Becattini writes in his book *Il Bruco e la farfalla,* or *The Caterpillar and the Butterfly* (Firenze: Felice Le Monnier, 2000), 94–104. The book title refers to a much debated topic: did Prato's economic miracle metamorphose the ugly caterpillar (meaning the pre-boom economy) into the beautiful butterfly? Many criticize the metamorphosis, saying that a leftist agenda has moved squarely center. The leading concerns are now related not to collective interests but to personal and family ones: inheritance and vacations, in other words, issues of *benessere,* or well being. Some fear a gradual slippage from "political" to "private" interests.

Figure 4.1 Line drying means a lot of ironing.

"Did you finish *already?*" Luisa asked me.

"Well, yes. I have already finished," I said. "I'm that fast."

Nicoletta walked over to the drying rack to see for herself. She lifted up Hollis's damp white t-shirt. She noticed stains across the front. They ran across the row of three pink and turquoise teacups. The stains were months old. What did I care? At least the shirt was clean.

"I'll show you how to get them out," Nicoletta insisted. She took the shirt in her hand and headed into the basement laundry room. She stood at the granite washing sink and scrubbed the stains with a special bar of laundry soap.

"Like this," she said. "*Se no, non fa la figura*—If not, she won't make an impression. *I bambini italiani portano vestiti bianchi bianchi*—Italian children wear white, white clothes."

I tried it. The soap in my hand felt as slippery as a fish. Luisa entered the laundry room.

"Don't watch me," I pleaded. I took a sleeve of the shirt and rubbed it with soap. My hands felt awkward. I laughed. She laughed at me.

"Take the whole shirt!" Luisa instructed, somewhat bemused by my incompetence.

I started to jump around. "Let's do gymnastics!" I was much more comfortable moving my whole body than my wet hands. The soap slipped, the wet shirt moved against me. I lacked coordination in hands-on everyday laundering. What a curiosity

I surely was. A woman 33 years old who could hardly keep a bar of laundry soap under control and who could not get her child's shirt white.

Nicoletta could. When she was finished, the colors of the imprinted teacups were still vivid and the shirt was bright white. She became the laundry magician, a legend in my daughter's memory. [*Fieldnotes,* December 9, 1995]

A great deal of effort went into the presentation of self on a number of fronts: acquiring appliances, designing and caring for the home, displaying taste through clothing, and participating in leisure activities.

Prato is a place where people keenly remember the postwar period, when buying a refrigerator was of major importance. More than a mere material acquisition, it symbolized wealth and social mobility. The refrigerator revealed to others that you were not a *poveraccio,* or a poor person. It distanced you from *genterella,* or low-class folk.

People living in the province of Prato joked that you lived for your house rather than having a house to live in. Culture and language teachers used words like *mania,* or mania, *fissazione,* or fixation, and *ossessione,* or obsession, to describe how people, especially women, had a habit of always thinking about their house.

Prato is a place where people follow fashion closely. They are the ones who make it. They literally know style inside and out.

In the summer of 1999, black was in and it seemed everyone was wearing it.

"It's worse than Maoist China," lamented Oliviero, the sweater-maker son-in-law of Nicoletta. I could not resist pointing out that he, too, was wearing a black t-shirt. He smiled and shrugged, only mildly embarrassed by his stylish conformity.

Prato is a place where former peasants recalled all too vividly the different possibilities for vacations available to them as opposed to the noble classes. There were only two ways a peasant family member prior to the boom was likely to end up at the beach: if one of them was called on to escort a noble family to the beach for a summer holiday, or if one of their sickly children was sent with subsidies to a seaside colony. I found evidence of such charitable funding between 1877 and 1928 in documents in the Carmignano archive. The sharecropping system unraveled in the postwar decades of the 1950s and 1960s, but in the meantime recollections of that hierarchical, patron-client system fueled the emerging consumer culture.

Nowadays, many couples with children viewed a 2- to 4-week vacation at the sea as a "necessity." It was commonplace that parents considered time spent at the ocean not only a symbol of having "made it," but also a sign of good parenting: the sea air, laden with natural iodine, boosted their children's immune system for the damp, winter season.

Together, leisure practices, displays of style, and material acquisitions distanced people from a past of poverty, of humble roots of rags and straw. Anthropologist Eric Wolf in his classic and ironically titled *Europe and the People Without History* (1982) reminds readers of a central tenant of capitalist ideology. All participants in the market are believed to be equal, regardless of whether they are industrial artisans, factory workers, factory owners, or hidden laborers. According to the logic of a consumer culture, the ability to acquire valued commodities becomes the yardstick by which people measure and demonstrate success. Wolf suggests that the "inability to consume signals social defeat" (1982:389–390). The reverse is also true: the ability to consume suggests social victory. Consumption becomes a moral warrant for individuals and for society. Those unable to consume become stigmatized as poor or backward; those unwilling become marked as misfits.

Life became more expensive as consumer society took hold. Having a small family ensured that couples could attain the kind of consumer activity considered virtuous. As one married 36-year-old sportswear designer, mother of one, told me of having children, "Better to only have one and do that well."

ORDER AS MORALITY

Italy's new-style consumer society produced tensions and contradictions. Many of my insights came as a result of doing fieldwork as a mother of a young child. Through my daughter, her friends, and their parents, I came to learn about the complex ways that the cost of consumption played out in people's lives.

One of the first friends my daughter, Hollis, made was a girl named Irene. She lived in a restored farmhouse down the street from us. One day while walking, we saw the girl standing in her yard, beyond a rock wall. Hollis was lonely and longed for a friend. She reached for a flower and extended her hand up toward the girl. Her parents were cautious of newcomers, and so for a while after that we did not see the girl. With time, the family warmed up to us. The girl's mother, Carlotta, invited Hollis over to play. The girls entered imaginary worlds in cardboard boxes and sweater scraps scattered in the family *maglificio,* a small sweater firm that specialized in upscale merchandise, located in half of the spacious restored farmhouse. They would play at Barbies in Irene's immaculate room or in the workshop. By the summer of 1996, she and Irene were close enough friends that the girl invited Hollis to her birthday party. Irene, about to turn 7, was a year and a half older than Hollis. The family held the festivities outside in the big yard.

> I immediately noticed how Hollis stood out as the American child. Most of the other girls were primped. They wore dresses with darling little collars, perfectly laundered and perfectly ironed. Hollis wore a faded, unironed cotton dress that was almost too small for her, and her hair, though brushed, already looked messy. I felt a twinge of embarrassment. It's so hard to keep up with a growing child, particularly here where the appearance of children functions as a sign of one's morality. Carlotta, Irene's mother, one day told me how she would buy her daughter clothes twice a year: spring and fall. There was such discipline to her approach. The order was reflected in her daughter's closet, where clothes were hung and folded so perfectly I felt like I had entered an upscale boutique.
>
> Carlotta opened the present we had brought. Why hadn't the birthday girl opened her gift? The Italian mother appears willing to do everything for her child. There is a constant struggle to keep things orderly. Just as I made a mental note of my thought, I caught sight of Irene and another nicely dressed girl purposefully smearing chocolate icing all around their mouths. With its ritual defiance of order, the moment seemed carnivalesque. [*Fieldnotes,* June 16, 1996]

Elizabeth L. Krause

Figure 4.2 Birthday party guests pose for photos.

The theme of order came up repeatedly among parents, especially mothers. Sometimes, even the children internalized this regime. One Saturday in September, Hollis was playing with Irene at the end of a dead-end street. I was teaching the girls to do a figure eight with their bikes, and from that they had invented rules of play. The game finished, Hollis headed on her little mountain bike toward the gravel parking lot of a soccer field.

"You shouldn't ride your bike there," Irene said. "It will ruin the tires."

I reasoned that the rocks should not cause a problem since the bike had big tires. Irene jabbed her finger deep into mud at the bottom of a rain puddle.

"*Io non sono come te*—I'm not like you," she proclaimed to Hollis. "*Io sono una bambina precisa*—I'm a careful child."

It was incredible to me that a 7-year-old had internalized this norm of precision—all the while sticking her finger into the mud. It seemed she was at once acting like a child yet speaking like a grown-up. In her world, where people were socialized to distance themselves from a history of poverty, being precise and exacting was fundamental. Irene's mother was very disciplined in all things. Her discipline revealed itself in the way she kept the house, the way she managed her daughter's room, the way she ordered Irene's hygienic practices: While basin and bidet washing were daily routines, Irene received a bath with regularity on Saturday evening around 7 P.M.—after her mother had caught up on sweater work but before serving the family dinner. A number of conversations and interactions made me think that, as an American born in the early 1960s and raised

in the Midwest—and still in graduate school in my 30s *and* a mother and wife—
I was comparatively *disinvolta*, or laid back, vis-à-vis the presentation of myself
and my daughter, as well as the care of the home. I thought back to conversations with several parents at the birthday party:

> Neve, a yoga teacher, remarked that the Italian economy is "screwed up" in the sense
> that the cost of things (houses, clothes, etc.) is way out of proportion with what peo-
> ple earn. Another difficulty for her was that she did not have relatives nearby, not
> even an aunt. And even if she did, she found it unfair to expect grandmothers to be
> the primary baby-sitter. It's better to hire someone. Grandmothers, they spoil kids,
> she said.
>
> According to another mother of one, a schoolteacher named Diana, an only child
> was becoming the norm for most people.
>
> "Sometimes I think about having another, in the abstract, but when I think about
> the concrete reality: No way! Also I have health problems," she said.
>
> "I don't know exactly what your health problems are," replied another mother,
> "but I can imagine that if you add heath problems to what is already a difficult situ-
> ation, indeed, to have a second would be really difficult."
>
> I made my way over to a couple. I sat on a rock wall near where their two children
> were playing. The man asked about my research. He was a truck driver, earned £2
> million, or $1,200, a month after taxes; she sewed sweaters, likely in the hidden
> economy, and earned another £800,000, or $480. (The total income for the couple
> was $1,680 per month in 1996.) They openly talked about how hard it was to have
> two, how wild they get. "The two kids are driving me crazy, turning my brain into
> mush," the man said. [*Fieldnotes*, June 16, 1996]

People offered rational reasons for having small families. Their talk unfolded
like ongoing social commentary. Adults frequently spoke with conviction about
the merits of stopping with one child. Their stances served as warnings to others. I sensed great importance placed on doing things *perbene*, or well. This
value seemed to apply to most every aspect of life, whether it involved acquiring food, preparing meals, making sweaters, or raising children. Having only
one child increased the odds that parents might succeed in doing it well, so the
thinking went. Those who had children displayed their own morality through
their children. The emphasis on order and on style was not merely a "choice" but
rather living out a particular class ideology. Stakes were high for performing
middle-class status in the context of postwar wealth.

GENTERELLA, OR LOW-CLASS FOLKS

One day in late June 1997 I chatted with Carlotta while she and her mother-in-
law basted sweater pieces to flatten the edges. The step in production facilitated
the work of the subcontractors, largely women, who finished the pieces on sergers. Carlotta spoke at great length of the frustrations she felt about raising a child
in a highly self-conscious consumer society.

"Italians are exhibitionists," she told me. "Everything has to be a name
brand. Last year Irene had a backpack that cost £30,000 [about $18.00]. All the
kids looked at her, so this year I spent £130,000 [about $78.00] and got her a
Sailor Moon backpack, the type used in middle school."

Irene was gearing up to start third grade.

"Otherwise you're looked upon as *genterella*—or low-class," she continued.

"Ah," her mother-in-law interjected, "they're all really *genterella*."

"Of course they are," said Carlotta. " But everybody wants to cover it up, to show the next person up."

The noun *gente* means people, and the suffix *-ella* indicates a negative, a lack. The slur was similar to calling someone white trash. In this particular context, it not only underscored material lack but pointed to a rural, peasant past— a past when certain consumer goods and education levels were scarce.

Carlotta grew interested in my project and toward the end of my stay permitted me to tape record our conversation, which I later transcribed and translated. At one point she reflected on the stress that the current context created.

"So you were saying," I asked, "it's good I'm going back to the States because life here is too stressful?"

"In America?" Carlotta asked.

"Yeah, you were saying—," I repeated.

"Yeah, too much," she said. "There are too many stresses here. Too much everything. Too much precision. Too much of that person looking at that other person. Of that person being envious of this one who bought a nice car. And the house, and going to the sea, and going to the mountains. And just everything. For example, you'll make few friends if you're at *terra terra*."

"Oh," I said, not sure I understood. The literal translation was "earth, earth." Did she mean down to earth?

"Understand, Betsy?" she asked.

"Uh-huh." I nodded, confused.

"Do you follow me?" Carlotta repeated the phrase. "*Terra terra*."

"Yeah, yeah," it clicked. She meant dirt poor. "If you don't have money, if you don't have—"

"So say if someone doesn't have a position," she explained.

"I get it," I said.

"If they don't have a good, a *respectable position*," she emphasized. "But if you are really so dirt poor that you can't afford to go to the sea. And you can only take a vacation every once in a while. And if you don't even have a nice car."

I laughed thinking about my 17-year-old little rusting, white Fiat.

"Or, or the house. Y'know the house, well. You'd better have something. If you don't have a nice house, or a car, then at least you'd better have a *mentalità*, an attitude."

In other words, I thought, an attitude that shows that you're modern. That shows you have class. French sociologist Pierre Bourdieu used the term "cultural capital," meaning you may not have money but you may have other signs of prestige, such as education.

"But if people don't tell you this it's because they don't want to admit it, Betsy."

"I bet," I said.

"But everybody senses some of this inside themselves," she confessed. "A tinge of envy or a desire to feel like you're better than somebody else. It's there, Betsy. The Italian is like this. I regret saying it. But then there's—sincerely and honestly there will always be fair and honest people."

"Of course," I offered. She clearly did not want to offer me stereotypes. Nor did she want me to feel inferior since in her world I had neither car nor house nor access to nice vacations.

"Just like there's bad in every part of the world. But normally if you're of a, of un ceto terra, a dirt-poor class, friends are not—let's just say there will be few, for example. If you are in a group in which there are couples, take for example me and Antonio, two or three other couples that are well off. And if there's one from a low class—"

She trailed off. The unfinished thought implied problems.

"If on the other hand they're all of high class then. Well, understand how it is?"

I understood, too, that these class tensions were hard to talk about.

"As for me," Carlotta continued, "these things—I'll tell you once more that I value honest people even if they don't have anything. Understand, Betsy?"

"Of course," I said.

"This is what I want to say," she concluded.

I felt in Carlotta a deep sense of being caught between two worlds with two opposing value systems. She felt caught between the old world of peasants and diffuse industry and the new values of an intense new-moneyed consumer society. Ultimately, she told me, the social obsession over distancing one's self from genterella, low-class folk, created so much pressure that she and her husband could not agree on having a second child.

PRAYING FOR A SIBLING

Carlotta spoke openly of her conflicts about being the mother of an only child and of stopping with one. Apparently, many Italian women shared this sentiment. Demographic surveys have shown a huge gap between the number of children Italian women want and the number they actually have. Most women say they want two children but tend to have only one (see Pérez Delgado and Livi-Bacci 1992). Not only adults have these feelings of desires unfulfilled. So, too, do children.

Carlotta's daughter sought divine intervention to manifest a sibling.

"Irene said to me, 'I have to go to the Madonnina,'" Carlotta recalled. "There's a Madonna shrine here. Have you seen it?" (See Figure 4.3.)

"Yes, yes," I said. Two roads met at the foot of their property and, like most intersections in the area, it bore a religious symbol of protection: inset into the stone wall was an enclave that held a small statue of the Virgin Mary, a burning candle, and fresh flowers.

" 'I have to do one thing,' " Carlotta quoted her daughter. "'I must go to the shrine to do one thing.' So she went to the shrine and this child knelt down. I tell you, the effect it had on me, Betsy. She was completely focused. So I said, 'Antonio, what on earth is that child doing?'"

"'Well! If you don't know!" says Antonio.'"

The girl returned to the house. "So I'm like, 'Irene! What on earth did you ask that Madonnina?'"

"She says, 'That—that my mamma would make me a little sister or a little brother.'"

Elizabeth L. Krause

Figure 4.3 A Madonnina,
or shrine to the Virgin Mary

I could relate to this pressure from a child. Even my daughter, barely 5, had started begging us for a sibling.

> Hollis is really pressuring us to have another child, to give her a brother or sister. Chris is warning her that the reality of a brother or sister may not be exactly how she imagines it.
>
> "Well, why can't we do one when I'm really big. Like when I'm 6, or 8, or 10?" she asks.
>
> "I have to admit you're awfully determined," says Chris.
>
> "But *please* do a baby," she insists. "Because I want to have a brother or sister."
>
> Who would have imagined the pressure a child can put upon you to have another child? [*Fieldnotes,* April 14, 1996]

These two children had similar sentiments about wanting a brother or sister, but their methods of realizing their wishes reflected different religious orientations. Catholicism continued to influence many Italians' worldviews even if church teachings hardly determined family size. Even as the Pope condemned birth control and abortion, Catholic women regulated their fertility to limit family size. Contraceptives, illegal under fascism, were legalized and made readily available in pharmacies in the mid-1970s, and abortion as well as divorce became legal in 1979 with reforms in family laws. On issues of family-making, one elderly local priest told me his view that it was "old fashioned" to expect people to have large families. For him, birth control was a nonissue. He concentrated on pragmatic issues, and he proudly took me on a tour of a small nursing home he had built adjacent to his parish. This reflected what he identified as relevant concerns: caring for the old and recruiting the young into the Church.

CATHOLICS AND COMMUNISTS

My view of possible worlds expanded as I learned about the significance of local cafés. Each hamlet had its church, which in turn had its community hangout, often referred to as the *bar di prete,* the priest's café. Each hamlet also had its leftist hangout, the *Casa del Popolo,* or *circolo,* the café historically affiliated with the Italian communist party, reconfigured in the 1990s into two parties. There was a great deal of tension in the postwar era between people affiliated with the Church and those affiliated with the communist party. Those on the left had been most strongly identified with the Resistance movement; they had been the staunchest critics and greatest victims of fascism. The Church was viewed as having collaborated (see Kertzer 2001). As the postwar boom wore on, however, communists and Catholics made an unlikely alliance: they both viewed consumerism as rampant and sought to counter the ills they believed it produced.

Changes in the economy triggered profound transformations in relationships. Carolina, whose family firm I worked at for some 6 months, one day in July 1996 reflected on how, before the economic boom, her family was well-off and others were much poorer. During the boom, her family's wealth declined after the death of her father, who had been a builder. Other families became arrogant as they came into money with a rapid pace never before seen or experienced. The arrogance became unbearable. Carolina changed friends. She searched for people who were interested in more than just making money and showing it off.

People recalled easily the flagrant consumerism of the 1980s and into the 1990s. A young local priest, in his twenties, lamented that what people really wanted from the Church was linked to consumerism. The Church became a site for flaunting wealth in the context of religious rites of passage: baptisms, first communions, marriages, even deaths. Local families simultaneously lamented and marveled at the extraordinary amounts of money people laid out for their children's first communions in terms of clothing, dinners, and gifts. One woman told me a first communion she attended cost the parents £21 million, or about $12,000. The church sought to combat such excesses by eliminating the choice of dress that children could wear for the ceremony. Plain white gowns had become the practice by the time I attended my first communion.

My friend Catia was all aglow when I arrived at her house one Sunday morning in May 1997. "I feel electrified," she said, flying down the stairs from where people were dressing. I then glimpsed a hidden mood as she mentioned her son's deceased twin brother, whom Catia had lost shortly after his birth. I thought about that lost infant and how rites of passage trigger one's memory of deep, tragic, and even secret losses.

All the family members, including the well-dressed fourth grader and his little sister, went outside to pose for videos. Then it was off to the church. Catia's mother-in-law rode with me into town. She described this as a momentous event. At the church, people gathered in the courtyard. People spilled out from the *bar di prete.* The atmosphere was abuzz. Catia's cell phone rang. It was her mother calling from the South; she spoke through tears because she was unable to make the trip to Tuscany for the big day.

The procession began. Parents flanked either side of their children. Each child, dressed uniformly in the standard-issue white gown, carried a calla lily into the crowded church.

> The sacred part of the mass began, and the priest asked even the official photographer and videographer to stop their filming to get everyone to concentrate.
>
> "We have been reduced to *animali di lusso,* or luxury mammals," the priest said.
>
> First communion was the most important moment in the life of a child—from the Church's point of view. "You can see the joy on their faces. They accept Jesus in their hearts. Hence they're allowed to take part in the communion, to take the host."
>
> The priest encouraged parents to bring children to church every Sunday as a way to renew their faith.
>
> "You see these relatives that came from faraway? And why did they come? Because this is such an important event," he continued.
>
> "We are human and we need signs. Hence Jesus gave us this bread. Eating this you become him."
>
> The message was straightforward. The Church offered something to lean on. "Without this *appoggiamento,* or support beam, life is empty. Health, school, play— these are important. But instilling in children a belief in Jesus, the Christian faith, this is the most important thing a parent can do." [*Fieldnotes,* May 23, 1997]

The vast majority of Italians had their children baptized and officially indoctrinated into church teachings. A local nun came to the school to teach religion as a subject. Parents could choose a nonreligion alternative for their children but most children participated in religion. In my daughter's first-grade level of 32 students (two classrooms with three teachers), only two children in 1996–97 did not participate in religion. My daughter went with the majority. I was not raised Catholic, but I believed this exposure to be an important part of her cultural experience. She found the habit-wearing nuns and the public religious iconography—at times, graphic, such as images of a woman stabbed in the heart with swords or of a man bleeding from a wreath of thorns—a grand curiosity. She asked to take the religion class. Moreover, I did not know of anyone, not even the most ardent communists, who refused to allow the priest to come to their house in spring for the annual benediction. Some of the more older and religious women spent days, even weeks, cleaning their house for this rite of purification: the priest entered each home, sprinkled holy water on the premises, and said a blessing.

A number of people, however, described themselves as culturally Catholic but not practicing. Others, who had been raised in Catholic homes but had politically left leanings, severely opposed a Catholic upbringing for their own children. At the *scuola materna,* or public preschool, which Hollis attended our first year in Italy, she found a friend in a girl named Giulia. The first weeks of the preschool experience in a foreign culture brought tears and feelings of loneliness for Hollis, then 4 and a half. She would return home with her pockets bulging with drawings. For several months she could not communicate because of the language barrier. The school offered no program to help a non-Italian speaker make the transition. It was pure immersion. What better way to spend her time than drawing? Giulia was a bright, witty, strong-willed yet sensitive girl the same age. Seven years later, Hollis still remembered how Giulia sought her out.

"She asked me if I wanted to play," Hollis told me in the summer of 2002, when I asked her to reflect back on when she and Giulia first met. "Of course, I didn't understand her. But she understood that I didn't understand her. She took me over to a corner of the playground. I think there were some pinecones there. We used to go to that corner a lot." In fact, one of the first phrases Hollis learned to say in Italian was, *"Vuoi giocare con me—*Do you want to play with me?" Within 4 months, she was communicating, and within a year she was speaking like a native. The language learning happened because she was young and because she found a social group of playmates who spoke no English yet reached out to her. Being educated Americans made certain people take interest in us.

The girl's parents, Marco and Gabriella, became our dear friends. We wanted Hollis and Giulia to be together for first grade in the fall even though we were not living in one of the school's feeder neighborhoods. We managed to receive permission—perhaps partly because of Carolina's influence in arranging for me a tour of the elementary school in question. Once there, Giulia did not take religion. Her parents were devoutly opposed to official church doctrine.

I was reminded of their deep and persistent conviction 2 years later, in June 1999, when we returned to Carmignano. Marco and Gabriella invited me along on a guided tour of the interior of the local church where I had attended that first communion mass 2 years before. As we walked and listened, Marco whispered to me that he found the decor to be *orpelli,* or cluttered, overly opulent, tinsel-like. I wondered whether he and Gabriella remained as strongly opposed to the Church as I had remembered. I asked whether Giulia was now taking religion in school.

"Absolutely not!" he replied. "It's the most degrading, humiliating thing a person can do: to instill a sense of sin in a child."

He believed that not doing religion was very instructive. "She thinks where others blindly accept." He recalled one time recently when a child told Giulia she had to go confess.

"What's a confession?" Giulia had asked. The child had to stop and explain.

"How can a child 8 or 10 years old know what a sin is?" Marco reasoned. "This kind of indoctrination is worse than pedophilia!" Marco's passionate point was clear: church teachings corrupted a young spirit.

ANTIDOTES TO CONSUMERISM

Marco and Gabriella had other ideas about what children needed: connections with community, cultivation of their creative spirit, and linkages to the land. They could have afforded an upscale apartment in the city and a fine private school for their daughter, but they wanted no part of the cosmopolitan quest for status. They both worked in the city of Prato yet had moved to a restored farmhouse in the hills of Carmignano—a landscape so rugged that our Fiat 127 on one occasion slid backward on the steep gravel incline as I transported visibly concerned in-laws to meet our friends. Marco and Gabriella had chosen this bucolic rural setting for making a life and raising their children: their 5-year-old

Elizabeth L. Krause

Figure 4.4 Local cuisine places a premium on fresh ingredients.

daughter and, eventually, the baby boy Gabriella gave birth to in spring 1996. They sought meaning in an alternative lifestyle. They revalued the countryside and the peasants who still lived there in a way particular to urban transplants not originally from the hill towns of Prato. Marco and Gabriella resented the noisy weaving machinery housed in at least one stone workshop along the gravel road that led to their house. Folks raised in those hills took as a given the integration of rural and industrial livelihoods.

As a couple, we shared much in common with Marco and Gabriella. Marco, flamboyant and passionate whether pontificating about hospital politics or pressing out his most perfect pizza dough, so engaged Chris in life that he brought into existence a man I hardly recognized. In the process of making a friend, Marco released Chris from an emotional yoke born in part from a southwest Missouri Baptist upbringing—though one traded in for the fiddle—and in part from a shy character. Chris's music had always been an outlet, but Marco introduced Chris to a new strategy for engaging life. It was transformative and lasting.

Parenting, however, was what initially drew Marco to Chris. I have heard Marco tell the story numerous times: At the preschool, he would watch this *Americano* interact so tenderly with his daughter—the calm way he spoke to her, the gracious manner in which he picked her up, the unselfconscious way he kissed her on the cheek in public. His style of interaction impressed Marco so much, he was moved to get to know this stranger. Apparently, he rarely saw such an affectionate way of interacting, at least in public, in relations between fathers and their children in Prato.

The two men bonded over a number of life's other passions. They talked shop connected to Marco's training as a doctor and Chris's as a veterinarian. They shared enthusiasm for music, and they swapped favorite artists: Marco's were classical pianists and Chris's jazz guitarists and bluegrass fiddlers. They both loved the land and what it potentially rendered. Chris beamed as he learned from Marco about Italian-style beekeeping and honey collecting as well as olive tree cultivation and olive harvesting and pressing. He delighted in surprising Marco with obscure words discovered in antiquated handbooks related to olive tree cultivation, such as *slupatura,* or decayed wood. Shared interests and a sense of connection kept Marco extending regular invitations to us.

At times I worried that Marco pushed a degree of socialization on Gabriella that she rather resented. Gabriella was given to moodiness. She was much less outgoing than her partner (they were not married when we met them); indeed, Marco used to lament that she behaved like a sea crab, but I came to admire her pensive and compassionate demeanor. The couple shared a love for the country, but they had contrary visions about how to inhabit a rural space. While Marco was drawn to live in the countryside because its setting fostered friendships due to fresh air and views that encouraged walks, exploration, eating, and projects, Gabriella loved living there because of the solitude it promised. I suppose Gabriella gave in to Marco's needs to socialize because, when we met her, she had an only daughter who also needed companionship. She just so happened to find a friend in Hollis.

Gabriella and I connected on a number of fronts. We had plenty to talk about regarding issues of juggling careers and families. Her work as a psychologist in the center of Prato fascinated me if only because she knew in-depth what I saw on the surface: visible madness in the urban setting and even the towns. I heard many stories that linked mental illness or outright madness to quick money. Having a psychologist friend to chat with enriched my understandings of the stresses of living in Prato and countered the cacophony of idyllic images of Tuscany that tempted my imagination. Even Nicoletta sought Gabriella's counsel, hoping for a solution for her daughter Liliana's psychological suffering. Furthermore, Gabriella had a deep and ongoing concern for immigrants and their children. My interest in the cultural politics of population led me to listen attentively to her stories related to Prato's immigrant population, about 11 percent of which, in the late 1990s, were of Chinese origin.

I found much to appreciate in the couple's style of day-to-day living. They rejected fruitless, flashy consumerism. They embraced the good things in life without doing it just to flaunt status or wealth. They introduced me to *la cucina povera,* literally poor cuisine. This translation does not render what I want it to say. The Italian phrase is loaded with local meaning. Peasant cuisine might be a better choice. *La cucina povera* is the kind of eating that New York City chefs only dream of when they post so-called market menus. Having acquired the prestige that "Mediterranean" had a few years back, these menus surged in popularity in the summer of 2002, when *New York Times* food critic Regina Schrambling exploded the truth behind restaurant claims of "market-based cuisine": that city chefs were advertising local products yet filling people's plates with the contents of FedEx boxes that arrived from distant lands. Their over-elaborated food combinations were a far cry from *la cucina povera* that was their source of inspiration. Practices of luxury consumption cannot help but grotesquely transform a rural cuisine, based on simplicity and freshness, into something unrecognizable and often overdone. I think this truth stems from a reality that Wendell Berry (2002) described in *The Progressive:* that modern society holds a "widespread prejudice against country people." This prejudice runs so deep and is so taken for granted that people rarely recognize it. Sophisticated urban people want to make selections from market menus and *feel* like they are close to the farm, but only if the plate set in front of them has cosmopolitan signifiers written all over it. Nothing *too* farm like. Nothing *too* rural. It might taint them for God's sake. After all, isn't being cosmopolitan distancing oneself from what is culturally inferior? Isn't it distancing oneself from simpletons, hillbillies, or rednecks? "We" want to be close to nature, close to local products, but not *so* close that we return to some primordial state on the evolutionary social ladder. Claims of authenticity amount to smoke screens for masking histories of social mobility.

LA CUCINA POVERA

Marco was dead set on introducing me to Elvira because of her legacy: she was tragically and famously connected to *la cucina povera,* or peasant cuisine. Central Italians feel about as mixed up about the peasant as Americans feel about the farmer. The range of emotions and the historical tracts are different, but the ambivalences are strikingly similar. On the one hand, the peasant symbolizes what is backward, unsophisticated, and humiliating. On the other hand, the peasant stands for what is pure, fresh, and healthy. There is nothing like having your "own" peasant to turn to for fresh eggs, fresh ricotta, or fresh olive oil, particularly for your child, niece or nephew, or grandchild. In a world of dioxin-tainted eggs, lead-contaminated olive oil, and mad cow disease, knowing where your food comes from is reassuring. It can make a mother, father, grandparent, or relative feel like they are doing their best to raise their child.

Elvira, an octogenarian when I met her, was locally famous for her renowned restaurant that specialized in upscale *cucina povera*—yes, upscale poor folk's food. What Tuscans fondly call *la cucina povera* has changed a great deal from what the children of poor peasant families ate. Elvira's story confirmed that.

I met Elvira at a family potluck in a field between a thousand-year-old abbey at San Martino nel Campo and a trailhead into Montalbano. The modest mountain was famous for its section of trail, the Via Francigena, which pilgrims followed from France to Rome during the Middle Ages. The forest has become the site for other pilgrims: those who combed its flora for wild asparagus in early spring, pine nuts in summer, and wild mushrooms come fall. Marco and Gabriella invited me to this feast-in-a-field. They were the unspoken guests of honor. The annual invitation was the host family's way of repaying the doctor, Marco, for his "favor" of looking after an ill loved one several years past.

Marco repeatedly urged me not to miss this invitation. The meal as promised was unforgettable: *panzanella,* a salad made with stale bread soaked in water, then shredded and mixed with tomatoes, basil, cucumber, lettuce and olive oil; *baccelli,* fava beans finished with olive oil; various pastas, fresh salads, local wines, and desserts—everything tasted powerfully fresh, indeed, everything exploded with the flavor of another era (see Seremetakis 1994). There was a history here, and that history was rooted in Elvira, the family matriarch and namesake of the locally successful restaurant.

When I first met her, Elvira was arguing with a man probably 30 years her junior over "the better sex." I scrawled notes from their spirited exchange into my 5 × 3 inch Mead memo pad I carried with me at all times.

"Women must observe," a man called Franco was saying. "They must observe so as to learn. And to learn so as to obey. . . . Men must carry the world forward."

Elvira did not waste a second. "What a wretched man you are! The woman must be in charge of the house because she has to pull the family forward."

"Women—when they speak nobody understands," he carried on. "Not even they know what they're saying."

Elvira would not be silenced: "It's easy to see why he's a *coglione*." The insult literally means testicle, figuratively, twit or idiot.

"Women are like flowers. They flower," Elvira continued. "Men are like wine because they last for a while and then, at a certain point, *si sciuppa,* they go bad."

Granted, flowers may also wilt, but in the Mediterranean the common blooms of geraniums have a way of outlasting an open flask of wine.

Elvira soon took her 16-month-old great-granddaughter to get a helping of *pappa col pomodoro* (pasta with tomato sauce). "*Vieni con la nonna, ti do la pappa*—come with grandma, I'll give you your din-din."

The toddler, a month younger than Marco and Gabriella's baby boy, weighed in at 11 kilos. "She's huge!" exclaimed Marco, the doctor. "She must be off the charts."

"Where is your baby?" someone asked him.

"In the car," Marco replied. "Sleeping."

"I'll go check on him," offered Gabriella, the psychologist and mother.

"No! No!" said Marco. "Leave him there. What an embarrassment, next to this girl."

Gabriella returned with her little guy. "Oh have I got a girl for you!" she teased.

The interaction between the restaurant owners and the doctor/psychologist couple suggested the robust (but not overweight) child was a sign not only of good health but of good parenting: this particular family gained social status through their well-nurtured youngest member, fed fresh, peasant-like ingredients yet amply distant from poverty.

Elvira was a daughter of poverty. Like many Tuscan women, she had a long engagement: 14 years. She did not marry a peasant or an agricultural day laborer but rather a man who worked as the hunting guard for Montalbano, formerly the Medici royal forest surrounding the villa of 100 chimneys. She cooked for guests staying in the luxurious villa as well as for groups of hunters. Later she began her own restaurant, which her son managed when I met her. The octogenarian still made a point of washing all the table linens herself and hanging them out to dry in the fresh country air.

Months after this potluck, I interviewed her. We sat on the sienna-colored stone porch of the restaurant overlooking the valley of Artimino in full March bloom. As she spoke, I hung on her every word, stretching my ears to make sense of phrases and inflections unfamiliar to me. She spoke with a "tight" Tuscan dialect. I would eventually listen to the tape numerous times to transcribe her story from audio to text on the computer. I would enlist the expertise of two native Italian speakers to perfect the transcription. Elvira was raised one of seven children but herself had only two. She told me of her regrets.

"Your generation, you, you decided to stop—." I began to ask her about family change.

"Yes, it had already changed, but it was a mistake," she said.

I was surprised to hear her express such a strong, negative view on family change. I wondered whether her story would explain this stance.

"Look, up to a certain age, children bring joy to the family," Elvira said. "They're *so* darling."

"So would you have liked to have had three, four, or seven kids?" I asked, somewhat jokingly.

"Oh sure," she laughed. "No, no, I don't know how they did it before. You've got to understand that when my dad—" she hesitated. "Before, they used to go buy animals far away from peasants. Always by foot, poor things."

"Ah," I said, offering a cue that I was listening.

"And so when he went this time, well, he went and left mamma a sack of chestnuts. That was it in the house. With seven children. *Capito?* Understand? He goes, 'If they get hungry cook 'em a few chestnuts.' *Capito?* He left Tuesday. Tuesday morning. He says, 'if I don't return tonight, it means I'm out for the animals and that I'm sleeping out, at a peasant's place. My mom's like: 'OK, so he's not coming back,' my dad, her husband. She wasn't worried about it."

"Oh," I said, trying to follow her story.

"Tuesday morning, one of my brothers saw— He was always hanging out down there. They saw a couple animals nearby coming down. 'There's Dad! There's Dad! Let's all go meet him.' But instead of Dad, it was the peasant where he had bought the animals, it was him coming. He thought that evening they'd meet each other midway. Understand?"

"Yes," I answered.

"Well, this guy didn't find him. He came all the way to our house to bring the animals. 'What?' he says, 'He took off at eight. He bought them at Nobel.' You know where Nobel is? Down below Comeana on the way to Signa. So in a half-hour he should have been home. And he didn't return. He passed the Carmignano station. He saw a train arriving, with the lights. He was on a little road near the Arno. He fell and ended up in the water. And he died."

"Your father? No." I said, shocked that my question about family size would lead her to tell a story about her father's tragic death. This seemed to be the nature of my research. Ask for a simple explanation, get a complex and tragic tale.

"So Wednesday we looked for Dad but didn't find him. In the water, there was only a bit of his jacket sticking out. Nothing. Wednesday we went to bed but this man had not been found. I was little, 6 years old."

"Oh," I said.

"Thursday would have been Holy Thursday," Elvira continued. "If you can imagine, it was Easter. The chestnuts were already sprouting. So there was my brother, who was 17, 18 years old. My oldest sister she was, yeah, 18. What am I saying, 19. She says, 'Let's trace the path of the Arno, along the cane. Let's follow the path where Dad went." When he was on his way back he would have gone by there. Then when we got to the station. Oh! I didn't see his jacket. Understand? What sadness."

"Oh for sure," I said.

"So they pulled him up. 'Look out!' He had a hole in his head," she said.

"And nobody knows how it happened?" I asked.

"Precisely, no. No one knows 'cause back then they umm, they didn't do— not even the police, mm, mmm—Well, they imagine from the body that he slipped down and hit his head on a rock. Mamma, to see her now. Three days unconscious, with no way to revive her. Seven children starving to death, can you imagine?"

"No," I said. I really could not imagine such a fate.

"If it were to happen now—" she said.

"Now people don't know what hunger is," I said.

"Exactly. That's what I say to those young kids: 'Well in my view, I'm sorry, but if you were to spend two months of the life that we lived before.' We had this card (a rations card), they would give us that basket of ugly bread, we were so hungry we'd eat it along the street when we'd go to pick it up. The youth of today would not be able to stand it."

"No way," I agreed.

"This generation was born into too much gold," Elvira said. "They've had everything and they have everything. And we didn't even have any shoes. Not in winter, nor in summer."

Why had Elvira answered my question about shifts toward having smaller families with a long story about her own father's tragic death? These two top-ics—family size and a tragic death—were linked in ways that informed the choices about family-making Elvira and her generation made. Elvira's narrative gave voice to the quiet revolution of fertility decline. It underscored the precar-ious economic conditions of peasants and day laborers. I believe she told me about her father's death because she was trying to illustrate how on the edge life could be. Not all parents managed well in this era, when even a peasant was bet-ter off than a day laborer like her father.

The detail of the already-sprouting chestnuts, a sign of fruit so fecund as to "rot" and no longer be good to eat, brought into focus the absence of other foods in the house. It was the moment in the narrative in which the children took it on themselves to search for their missing father. They eventually witnessed his body lifted from the river, a hole in his head. Elvira's reminder that the seven children "were starving to death" makes the overripe chestnuts, the death of her father, and the fainting of her mother even more powerful because it suggested this family form was not functioning well.

The world Elvira evoked was not the nostalgic peasant past associated with fertile fields and endless crops and, today, *la cucina povera*. Rather, it was a world associated with brutal poverty and hunger and families too big to manage.

At the end of the narrative she alluded to having told similar stories to her children or grandchildren. She used the metaphor of "gold" to describe the con-ditions into which today's generation was born. A generation accustomed to comfort cannot appreciate hardship and could not survive it. Her generation, by contrast, was tough. They suffered through the absence of the most basic of necessities, such as food and shoes. The condition of being without shoes in fact contrasts starkly with the postwar *benessere,* or well being, characterized with the metaphor of gold. Her tragic death story about her father sends a strong moral message about her childhood in the 1920s, one in which life was lived on a slippery slope. Life could be particularly precarious for poor parents with seven children and probably in plenty of cases they failed to provide the kind of food, clothing, nurturing, and education that their upwardly mobile, postwar children would feel driven to make available to their own children. Elvira revalued the *cucina povera* knowing very well that what her family was eating at the potluck was dramatically different from those rotting chestnuts that her father left her with the last day of his life.

POVERTY VERSUS PROSPERITY

Cost of living alone does not explain why people modify their family-making practices. The notion of "expensive" implies that if people had more money, and hence life were more affordable, people would have more children.

Poorer couples in 20th-century Italy tended to have more children than richer ones: take, for instance, Nicoletta's parents, who had six children and were poorer than Nicoletta and her husband, who had two children. Nicoletta and her husband had more resources than her own relatively prolific parents. Did poor families have a lower cost of living? Certainly, they did not have the option of purchasing a stylish Sailor Moon backpack for their elementary school child. Elvira's family would have considered themselves lucky if they had enough wooden clogs to go around.

The Marshall Islands, where on average women have 6 or 7 babies, nowadays ranks among the country's with the world's highest fertility rates.[3] People there do not have bulging pocketbooks. I was a student research assistant in 1989 when I worked there, on Taroa Island, a small coral atoll that served as a Japanese military base in World War II. The family I lived with had a sparsely furnished, cement block home. Clothes hung from rafters. The only electricity came from a loud generator fired up for special occasions, like powering a TV for group viewing of a video. There were no stoves or refrigerators. Kitchens were outside in a covered area beneath coconut palms. Consumer goods were sparse. The best drink for the crew of archaeologists cutting through thick jungle growth to find, map, and survey Japanese war fortifications, came from coconuts cut on site by a local teenager. Our meals, one after another, mirrored the local diet: fresh reef fish, white rice, and breadfruit. Occasionally our hosts would cook up an old, free-roaming chicken into tough stew meat. There were no cars on the small island; yet in the capital city the way to flaunt status was to drive a shiny, new pickup. The global economy was cultivating new desires in people. What once seemed economically sufficient can grow to feel embarrassingly insufficient. In central Italy, even houses of sweater makers had marble floors. Inexpensive consumer goods did not clutter houses; rather, people valued fewer yet higher quality items. What counts is what people believe to be necessary to make a life and to display self-worth.

[3]The Population Reference Bureau Data Sheet, http://www.prb.org, accessed June 30, 2002.

Since Malthus (1985[1798].67–79), poverty has been associated with large families. Impoverished parents were looked down on for having numerous children. In fact, they were blamed for their poverty. Marx (1906[1867]:703–711) came to their defense when he pointed out that the profit-driven economies of early industrialization led the poor to have numerous children because in fact youths were more employable than adults. Their labor was cheaper. In the short term, when labor demands were strong, families found advantages to having numerous offspring. Over the long haul, pauperism and the reserve army of the sub-employed were endemic.

Late capitalist society's organizing and moralizing principles have come to equate morality with work, thrift, production and consumption. Couples in Italy postpone having children and limit marital fertility as they strive to achieve "moral" satisfaction, middle-class respectability, and the prestige it carries. Carlotta's observations about distancing one's self from *genterella,* or low-class folk, and Elvira's story about having once persevered in and risen above that infamous *terra terra,* or dirt-poor, social class, together indicate that life is not any more costly for the rich than for the poor. Somehow, though, the world of consumer goods expands the possible expenses beyond previously imagined limitations, and hence makes life *seem* suddenly more costly. That is class ideology's sleight of hand.

5/Labors of Love, Love's Labors

"It is only in the mysterious equations of love that any logical reasons can be found."
—John Nash, *A Beautiful Mind* (2001)

We're that race that screws so little . . .
We're among the strangest race
For caterpillars we are born and caterpillars we remain . . .
Poverty screwed us and we ended up pregnant.
—From *Berlinguer Ti Voglio Bene* (Bertolucci 1977) with Roberto Benigni

"Mi hanno rubato il mi' figlio—They've robbed me of my son."
—Sara, mother of a soon-to-be-wed groom

Love is a mystery. To speak of love is to speak of desire. And what is desire? Great minds have pondered this deep mystery. Sigmund Freud attributed modern culture and civilization to human instincts, particularly those of the fleshly order. Margaret Mead argued the turmoil of adolescence resulted from modern taboos on sexuality. A half-century later, French philosopher Michel Foucault described desire as intimately linked not only to pleasure but also to power and pain. His treatise on the *History of Sexuality* (1978) connected desire with ideas about normal and acceptable behavior. Institutions like the church, with its practices of confession, and the state, with its hunger for disciplined bodies, came to define the codes of normalcy and hence shape desire as experienced in the modern world. There is no pure, unmediated love. We only know love, desire, and sexuality through the ways in which we have been socialized to experience them.

In Italy, the experiences of love have changed dramatically with the economic boom. The cultural and economic contexts provide a structure, like a picture frame, for the range of feeling. Just as there is a before and after to the boom, there is a before and after to the hues of love.

REAL LOVE

One Sunday in late March 1996, my mind and body crashed after the big mid-day lunch. My head whirled with dizziness. Was the culprit a strange inner ear infection? Was it depression? Each moment at the table with Nicoletta's family and my own tried my patience. I excused myself. Once in my room, I fell into a disturbed sleep. The heavens were opening up. I ascended into white clouds. I was dying. I wearily emerged from my semiconscious state to hear laughter outside. Soon, all was silent. Oliviero and Luisa had left with Chris and Hollis for the Sunday afternoon *girata,* or outing. They had not even bothered to check on me. I was angry. To comfort myself, I made a pot of espresso. I climbed the stairs to find some company in Nicoletta and to offer her some fresh brew.

"*Sei ripresa*—Are you revived?" Nicoletta asked me.

I told her of my dream and, in exchange, she offered me one of her own. Hers was of lost love. Niccolò, her late husband, had come to her. He was holding the skeleton of a box that contained some sort of energy. His face was soft, almost squishy, yet lovely and round as always. He spoke to her: "I'm not like I used to be. Now all that's left of me is this energy."

"Who knows if we can believe these things?" Nicoletta asked. "They are feelings we keep inside of ourselves."

For 3 years after Niccolò's death, she felt his presence next to her in the bed as though they were still making love. He had been the one to teach her everything about sex. Her memory trail led her to recall her courtship with Niccolò. Now that was *real* love.

"Yet love, like everything in life, has to be reconstructed every day. These young people, on their third or fourth marriage, this is not love."

Life is like a sack, she used to say. At the beginning of each day, the sack is empty. Everyday, it has to be filled. Similarly, love has to be remade constantly and continuously.

Nicoletta disappeared into her bedroom to fetch something she wanted to show me. She returned with a plastic baggie that held about 15 postcards that Niccolò had sent her between 1952 and 1953. Also in the baggie were announcements dated from April 1965 of Luisa and Liliana's first communion held at the local church. She took out the postcards and showed them to me. Most pictured the same handsome Italian film couple embracing in a romantic moment.

"*Era troppo bello e Gesu l'ha preso troppo presto*—It was too lovely and Jesus took him too soon," Nicoletta said, recalling her husband's death in his fifties 8 years ago. Nicoletta and Niccolò were engaged in 1952. They married about 5 years later, when she was 24 and he was 26.

The postcards always said, "*sempre tuo,*" or always yours, Niccolò. The messages were brief, a genre of their own. It was the English equivalent of "thinking of you. . . ."

We giggled together as she flipped through the postcards. It felt like we were teenagers all over again. [*Fieldnotes,* December 9, 1995]

A widow like Nicoletta never expected romance again in her life. Unlike her mother-in-law, who lost her husband young and wore black until the end, Nicoletta dressed in colors other than black. Her color choices, however, were consciously subdued for her public outings, including regular visits to the cemetery to take flowers, freshly cut from her garden, to her late husband's gravesite. It saddened me that she did not consider seeking out another companion. I came from a cultural context where divorced or widowed women and men, pretty much regardless of age, were free to seek new love. This difference in life expectations became a point of tension and humor between us. One time, I meant to tell Nicoletta that she needed to *riposare,* or rest, but I misspoke. I told her she needed to *risposare,* or remarry! She burst into embarrassed laughter. After that, I used to intentionally make the mistake and tell her she needed to remarry. It was a way to get a rise out of her. It was also a playful tactic to acknowledge our differences.[1]

UNEASY LOVE

Luisa and Oliviero fell for each other in middle school. After graduating, the teenagers went straight to work, she in the sweater-finishing sector with her mother and sister, working in a basement workshop that had become my apartment, and he in a textile factory in Prato, where he rode his bike some 10 miles to work each day. They were engaged for 15 years before they married. Long engagements were common in central Italy. Part of the delay resulted from a couple's need to prepare and outfit a home before moving in. Furthermore, many young people were in no particular hurry to move out and assume the daunting task of managing a household and home *perbene,* or carefully and respectably.

Luisa spoke openly about her life as we became friends. She had a canny ability to tell stories, to find humor in things, and to make others laugh. During our stay, she developed a strong, motherly attachment to Hollis, my daughter. She encouraged her to come play hide-and-seek in the workshop amid the piles of large woolen-yarn spools. She was always willing to watch Hollis in a pinch.

Luisa kept two photos of the couple in her wallet from their honeymoon period: in one, they were running on the beach, in the other, they were sitting

---

[1]Nicoletta's aversion to thinking about remarrying has a history. Italian folklorist and sexologist Raffaele Corso (2001:87–89) documented cultural aversions to second marriages in his book *La Vita Sessuale Nelle Credenze, Pratiche e Tradizioni Popolari Italiane.* The book was first published in German in 1914 and only recently translated back into Italian; the original manuscript was lost. The reasons against the second marriage taboo varied from region to region. Corso noted the aversion to bigamy, and explained that the Church at times viewed second marriage as a form of adultery. Nevertheless, second marriages did happen despite proverbs warning against them. The religious motive for avoiding a second marriage was expressed in a popular tale: "After death, a man arrived at the gates of Heaven and presented himself to Saint Peter, who asked him what he had done in his life. The man responded that he had been married. 'And then?' asked the saint. 'Then I got married another time,' continued the man. 'Fine,' replied Saint Peter, 'you were twice hanged: away with you, I won't grant you entry to Paradise!'" Corso noted that "relatively recent laws" permitted remarriage after a minimal period of 10 months—recall, he first published his book in 1914. In practice, however, widows were allowed to marry "only after many years." Proverbs and sayings from diverse regions warned men against marrying widows not only for religious reasons but for secular ones. In the Veneto, in the northeast, it was said that widows were "sexually insatiable." A song from Abruzzi, in the rugged southeast, warned of the widow's persistent memory of her deceased first husband. Similarly, a song from Piedmont, in the northwest, cautioned that a widow lamented her first love when she went to sleep. My sense is that such persistent memories could be hurtful—and even emasculating—for the second husband.

arm in arm on a rock, trim and sexy. On one outing, she described herself as *pic-cioncina,* or lovey-dovey romantic, with her husband, as she kissed him and he pulled away. Their relationship was given to rockiness. As time wore on, Luisa revealed to me a deep dissatisfaction with her life. I felt our presence again magnified her absence.

> As we walked down to the main drag to get her some cigarettes, she told me: *"Sono giù. Sono in crisi."* I'm down. I'm a wreck. Ever since our arrival, she has grown very attached to Hollis, as has Oliviero. When my daughter isn't there, and when Oliviero is off to the bar, she feels very alone.
>
> "What have I made of my life? What's it all for? And if I didn't have any mother to go sit with in the evenings, I would really feel alone. But lately, I've really been sensing the absence of a child. Now I'm 42, he's 44.
>
> "Do you know why we've never had a child? We've always been a bit angry, tense, lots of ups and downs and fighting. He's always been afraid that we wouldn't stay together. And then what kind of life would the child have?
>
> "Now I feel I've made a mistake," she admitted. [*Fieldnotes,* January 23, 1996]

I would venture to say that all relationships have their ups and downs, and there are moments when everyone has regrets. So I did not take this to be the final word on Luisa and Oliviero's family-making status. Her outpouring highlighted, if anything, one of the hues of love. It was also evidence of my hunch that family planning was not just about rational decision-making; it also involved living life in deeply ambivalent ways.

> The five of us sat over pizzas at a local *pizzeria.* Hollis turned to Oliviero and Luisa and said in Italian: "You need to have a baby. You are in love so you need to have a baby. If you don't have a baby then you're not in love."
>
> We all laughed, rather awkwardly. There was another one of those heavy silences.
>
> Then Luisa offered up an analogy for herself: *"Un albero senza frutta,"* a tree without fruit. [*Fieldnotes,* March 30, 1996]

Children are like social sponges when it comes to dominant values. In this context, the dominant value was that a child transforms a couple into a complete family. Love was not enough. The rest of us were uncomfortable because the 5-year-old was in a sense asking the unaskable. She was treading on private ground but, because of her age, she could get away with it. I sensed that Luisa welcomed the probing: it provided her a fair outlet to express what she was feeling. Her analogy of a tree without fruit occurs in Italian folktales. One from Florence called "Apple Girl" begins, "There was once a king and a queen who were very sad because they had no children. The queen kept asking, 'Why can't I bear children the same as the apple tree bears apples?'" (Calvino 1980:308). The queen expresses the commonly accepted notion that reproduction is not about choice but about inevitability. The lack of bearing fruit, therefore, becomes by association the ultimate lack. In the folktale, the queen finally gives birth, but to an apple rather than a son, and the strange tale soon reveals a beautiful maiden living inside the apple. It ends happily with a lonely, single king breaking the spell of the maiden and the two of them marrying, against the wishes of an evil stepmother who flees. For Luisa, such endings may only manifest themselves in her sister's imaginative stories, or the fantasies of my then 5-year-old.

RAGS, ROMANCE, AND NEGOTIATED LOVE

The rag trade brought together Carlotta and Antonio, parents of only child Irene. Carlotta's father was a peasant who managed to accumulate enough money to buy several hectares of land in the sprawling valley of Prato. He rented building space to postwar rag-makers doing business there. One rag dealer hired a teenager named Antonio. He was 14 then. It would have been the late 1960s, and he came and went on his *motorino,* or moped, to drink from a water fountain near Carlotta's house. She was only 9 at the time, but she noticed him. Over giggles with her girlfriends, she chatted about his good looks. Then he changed jobs and she didn't see him again for some 8 years. One day she and her parents were on their way to a wedding. The route to the church took them through his neighborhood. There, among the passersby, was Antonio. By that point he would have been 22, and she 17. Even after so much time she recognized him immediately. Months passed and she ran into him at a local dance club. His friend asked her to dance. She was disappointed. She was not much attracted to the friend but danced with him anyway. She was hoping to meet Antonio.

One evening at the dance club, Antonio showed up alone. His friend was sick. Finally, Carlotta recalled, Antonio asked her to dance. They started seeing each other and after 6 or 7 months became an official couple. The engagement lasted 7 years. I sensed the persistence of that youthful love in the way Carlotta blushed and smiled as she recounted the story. I sensed she and Antonio were still very much in love. They had mutual respect for one another. They each seemed sure of themselves and of their gendered divisions of labor.

Carlotta and Antonio had been married for 13 years when I left the field in 1997. They made their home in an elegantly restored farmhouse where Antonio's family had lived as sharecroppers. It was another world. Back then, the family worked under a local noble family—indeed, the very father of my historian friend. The section of the house where stables once held farm animals had been converted into a *maglificio,* a family sweater firm. They contracted out much of the work; however, the adult family members—Carlotta and Antonio, his brother and mother—did much of the hand finishing tasks involved in making a sweater appear perfect and perfectly new.

Antonio's unmarried older brother and widowed mother lived in one floor of the house and the couple, along with their only child, then 8 years old, lived in the other. They struck me as a very loving family. They were not, however, in agreement about their family size. Irene wanted a sibling. There were moments when Antonio and Carlotta wanted another child but these moments were always out of sync. Their sort of love was modern in the sense it was not hierarchical but equal; it involved an understanding that they would only have a child if both agreed. Their approach was a realization of the 1975 reform of the family laws that replaced a patriarchal family founded on authority with a family founded on mutual cooperation.[2]

---

[2]This modern family form represents a break from the patriarchal model, which began to fall into crisis in the last decades of the 18th century. This process involved a lessening of the hierarchical social distance between husband and wife as well as between parents and children. The transformation acquired a class character, moving first through the intellectual bourgeoisie (late 1700s and early 1800s), then catching hold among the aristocrats (1850s to early 1900s), next affecting

At times, Carlotta felt ~~~~~ ~~~~ ~~~~ her decision to have only the one child. She told me that nearly half of the children in her daughter's class were *figli unici,* or only children. At other times, she felt inclined to have a second child. Among her daughter's classmates who had a sibling, there were often 3, 4, even 10 years between one child and the next. When a woman sees her friends waiting many years before having another child, and then hears those same friends speak positively of the experience, she begins to rethink her ideas of family-making. "I used to think it was a bad thing to have a child after a big gap, like me and my brother. But these two or three friends of mine, they tell me it's better like this." Her friends experienced little jealousy between their children, and the younger child admired the older brother or sister.

One afternoon in July 1997, Antonio had left with his mother and brother for a neighbor's funeral. Carlotta gave me permission to turn on the tape recorder, on the condition that I turn it off when her husband and in-laws returned. As was typical of our visits, she held a sweater in her lap and continued mending imperfections while talking to me. She spoke openly of her conflicted experiences regarding having an only child. I sensed the conflict in the halting quality of her talk, and I have indicated these self-interruptions or abrupt endings with a dash [—] (after Bakhtin 1984, Philips 1998).

"There's another friend of mine, she's beside herself. She has two little kids, a year and a half between them. They're always fighting, beating on each other. They don't get along. Jealousy. Is that any way to live, Betsy?"

I nodded.

"I don't know. So for years I've been back and forth. 'I'll do it, I won't do it.' See. Then at one point we were like, 'let's do it now.' Antonio was really into the idea but at the time it didn't appeal to me very much."

"Ah, yes," I nodded.

"It's a little that we've had opposite periods. Y'see. When I was liking the idea he wasn't much into it. But who's always been more decided has been Antonio."

"Oh really?"

"Yeah than— than me. You see," Carlotta said.

"I understand."

"When he had committed to do it I was undecided. Then when I had decided he was undecided. But his was an indecision that— that we could have overcome."

She smiled. I laughed. I think it was the feeling of intimacy in the moment.

---

bureaucrats, merchants, artisans, and industrial workers, and finally transforming social relations among the agricultural classes. The change followed this class-based course, according to Italian sociologist Marzio Barbagli, *Sotto lo stesso tetto: Mutamenti della famiglia in Italia dal XV al XX secolo.* 2nd ed. (Bologna: Il Mulino, 1996[1984]), 26. A crisis of the *ancien regime* and accompanying transformations in the political-economic system meant the old aristocratic class's models for social relations lost their legitimacy and the bourgeois class, which had long sought to imitate the behavior of the aristocracy, began to forge a new, more egalitarian model of domestic relations. Barbagli suggests that just as the rigid asymmetries between classes were diminishing, so too were the asymmetries breaking down within households. The peasant classes eventually followed suit. Italian sociologist Chiara Saraceno, *Sociologia della Famiglia* (Bologna: Il Mulino, 1996), 145, points out that by the postwar era, as agricultural reforms took hold and the peasant sharecropping system unraveled, the formal patriarchal family gave way to more egalitarian models.

"Understand? Because it was a decision that I had to make too," she said. Suddenly, her expression changed. She drew her lips, she looked straight at me with intense eyes. "I, I became overcome with fear, anxiety, fright."

"Oh I see," I said.

"Another pregnancy, you see. And I would say, will I be able to do it? To make it?

"You see the personality that I have. I'm a little nervous. I like to keep things precise, the house orderly, to go,— selfishly, to have fun, to do little trips in the summer, in the winter I like to go skiing, a little, get it?"

I remembered well the day Irene, her daughter, had bragged about being *una bambina precisa,* a careful child. Now her statement made sense to me.

"The love for children should be strong, should be excessive," Carlotta said, alluding to worries about whether she would have enough to go around. "And me, I'll tell you I feel selfish. What can I tell you, Betsy? I don't know . . . because I feel that it gives me some anxiety this thi— this thing about children because am I doing right or wrong to leave her alone?"

"Yes, I understand," I said. *"Perfectly."*

"And then and then I'll tell yo— I have to tell the truth," Carlotta continued. "Really the truth and I tell it regretfully. But by now I can tell you. I feel a little — because things happened in my house that shouldn't happen between siblings. Between my, my parents, between my dad and my— and his sister and brother. They went to an attorney."

"Hmm, I see," I said, noticing her words were filled with fits and starts. I sensed this topic was very difficult for her to talk about.

"To divide the inheritance. Follow me?" she asked.

"Understood," I reassured.

"My aunt wanted more, well my dad didn't want to give it to her, and my dad— Since he took care of my grandparents, his parents, he did so much for them, my aunt didn't do a thing and my dad expected more. And my aunt wanted more."

"I see," I offered.

"And my dad didn't give her anything," Carlotta explained. "And so they had to go through an attorney."

It turned out that even Carlotta's uncle in America had come back to get money though none was due him. Eventually, the uncle took the aunt's side, and turned against his brother, Carlotta's dad.

"And I think about this Betsy. Among siblings there's always this thing over that damned nasty money, Betsy. But here don't you think that it's only my dad. Here nearly every one— how— one for— a good percent when a parent dies. Something always happens."

"Oh really?" I asked.

"Always something. If you're an only child nothing happens."

"Of course," I said.

"But if there are just two, that's enough! Betsy. But a lot of this happens here. Of these kinds of things. And therefore I say—I really felt bad, I suffered a lot due to this affair, of late. Even to have myself another child, who'll have me do it? At least when I die it's everything for Irene or *nothing* for Irene, if I don't

have anything. Everything or nothing. See Betty? And without discussion. Even
if she'll suffer because they'll say: 'Sisters, do you have any?' They'll say,
'Brothers, do you have any?' I've seen at times brothers and sisters also give you
joy."

"Of course," I said.

"They also give you pain," Carlotta said, "but I admit they can also bring
joy."

The conversation with Carlotta led me to several insights. First, the ideal of
love may well be equal, but couples tend to believe that having a baby weighs
more heavily on women than on men for biological as well as cultural reasons.
It is women's bodies that carry, birth, and breastfeed babies; it is women's
thoughts and schedules that are seen as bearing a heavier load in terms of
parenting.

Second, when it comes to having a child, modern couples commonly nego-
tiate this decision although babies still do "just happen." When having a child is
the result of planning, ultimately the decision to have another child tends to rest
on the woman. In this respect, men acknowledge how much work is required of
women in terms of childbearing and child rearing.

Third, women often expressed sentiments of fear in talk surrounding the possibility of having a child. One saleswoman in a local boutique used the word
"terrified" to describe her fear. Meeting the expectations of the social role of
mother, as well as confronting pregnancy and labor, add up to a heavy burden.
Carlotta framed her fear about having another child in terms of her own character. A personality flaw became the source of her failure to commit to another
pregnancy. Even her desire to have fun became viewed in terms of "selfishness,"
an assessment of herself that can be read negatively given her humble peasant
background and her Catholic upbringing.

Finally, Carlotta at one point hinted at a concern of whether she would have
enough love to go around for a second child, then revealed fears linked to something besides love that parents give to their children: inheritance. A moral struggle underlay Carlotta's story about an inheritance battle between her father and
his two siblings—her uncle and aunt. She took her experience with a familial
inheritance battle as justification for having just the one child. Ultimately,
though, many things figured into her decision, and her roots in the rags to-
sweater-riches industry, though not something she pointed to directly, I believe
also figured into her view of family-making.

UNMAKING AND REMAKING LOVE

Being in the field can take its toll on a long-term relationship. Granted, Chris was
practically a saint for dropping his life and following me to the field. For most
of the history of the discipline of anthropology, it was women who followed
their husband anthropologists into the field. Of course, nobody thought of those
women as saints. They were just doing what they were expected to do. Times
have changed, somewhat. Chris had followed me but he was not at my side as
an assistant with camera and notebook. Nor did I expect him to be. He did his
share of housework, childcare, and laundry. And then he found his own way: he

made musical connections and landed regular gigs, mostly playing fiddle with Maurizio Geri (1998) and his Django-style jazz quintet. One evening in early July 1996 Carolina invited me to attend a theater production with her. A local playwright had written a comedy about peasant life. As we walked toward the amphitheater, I confided in Carolina. Chris was back after a 24-day European tour playing bass with a San Francisco Bay Area bluegrass band, Laurie Lewis and Grant Street. Things were not clicking between us. His low-key demeanor was irritating me. My anger prompted him to shut down. Carolina opined that he was so calm he often lingered at the margins of life. I defended him. Among friends he could be charismatic. In social situations with new people, though, his style of participation tended to be shadow-like. Earlier that day in the car, he had been serious and down. He lacked humor. I wanted to be entertained with escapades from his travels, and I felt he was withholding tales. Not that I was a pleasure to be around either. What had happened to us?

Carolina's take on long-term love had reasonable as well as shocking aspects. A relationship has to made and remade. That was the reasonable part. Then came the rather shocking advice. She emphasized that a relationship had not only to be made and remade, but *unmade* and remade.

She could be harsh. "You and me, we need men who are our *altezza,* our level," she said. The comment had its insulting dimension but I continued to listen. She said that people like my companion did not understand the unmaking. "People like that are good at the maintaining," she said.

"You should find yourself another man, have a relationship with him, it might last 15 days, but *non rinunciarlo.* Don't renounce it," Carolina insisted. "Don't tell, and don't feel any guilt. These are your affairs, your matters."

Boy was this a different take on maintaining a marriage.

Carolina's irreverence aside, her way of thinking was not so unusual. I encountered a great deal of fear concerning fidelity. Once Marco, the father of Hollis's best friend, asked me why so many Americans divorced. I reckoned that couples had high expectations of their spouses, and that often when one spouse stepped out, the other filed. That was a simplified version of the truth, but I thought it said enough.

"Not a marriage would be left standing if people here left the moment somebody stepped out!" he mused.

Even he had his lapses of trust. When his son was born, he told Gabriella that he looked at the blood type "just to make sure."

"What trust!" she had replied.

I encountered numerous references to *le corna,* or the horns, a hand gesture that involved raising the index and pinky fingers as a sign that a man was *cornuto,* or the victim of an extramarital affair. This is the Italian version of the English term "cuckolded," which derives from the notion that female birds have a habit of changing mates. The Italian version finds its source in the image of a broken wedding ring: "As with every semicircle, a ring broke in two pieces represents a pair of horns," wrote Italian folklorist Raffaele Corso (2001:90). I recall vividly one time the butcher waving *le corna* at a customer's back as he left the store.

I was relentlessly teased when Chris was gone on tour for 3 weeks. One night while eating a spicy spaghetti dish believed to be an aphrodisiac, Luisa and

Oliviero cautioned me against continuing since I still had a week to go! Playing along, I pushed my bowl away.

One morning about 6 months later, at a bar where I regularly met about five mothers for breakfast, the *barista* replied to one of my friend's comments that we had finished our pastries by rattling off our drink orders:

> "Two cappuccinos without foam, boiling hot, a normal cappuccino, boiling hot, a milk with a touch of espresso, boiling hot, a tea," he announced.
>
> Minutes later, the *barista* delivered our drinks on a tray along with an eye-catching sugar dispenser: bull-like horns protruded from a rectangular box. Uncomfortable shifts in the chairs echoed in uncomfortable chuckles.
>
> "*Però*—however . . .," one of my friends uttered, as though to say, don't bring us this container anymore. It might be unlucky.
>
> I asked Anna, one of the mothers, for clarification: "The one who is *cornuto*, or horned, is the one who suffers—the one who has been stepped out on," she explained. "It's sad, isn't it?" [*Fieldnotes*, February 28, 1997]

This period of fieldwork was full of sex-related public lessons. Just the day before I was at the breakfast table with my women friends as they passed around a small shopping bag inscribed with *Lenti e Occhiali*, or lenses and eyeglasses. I wondered what could be so funny as each woman snickered as she had a look. As the bag came to me, I opened it. Inside was a vibrator! Little did the *barista* know what we were snickering about. Once outside, the proud owner took it out of the little shopping bag and brought it into the light of the day, "Wow, it looks real—even the veins!" one of us exclaimed.

Just weeks before, our group had agreed to and planned a rare women's-only dinner in Florence. The atmosphere was giddy as this group of women had husbands and children and did not normally go out on the town. As the night wore on, all of us shared intimate details about our sex lives and preferences. Topics of conversation included oral sex, vaginal vs. clitoral orgasms, the "69" position for sexual intercourse, and even the taboo subject of anal sex. Several women spoke of concerns about privacy, and of changes in sexuality after the birth of a first child. At the end of the evening, I felt an intense bond with these women—one I have never again felt with a group of women anywhere. I also had gained insight into a general consensus: the conviction that as women age, they mature and sex improves.

Nevertheless, they found themselves grappling with local lore that threw into question their positive view of the relationship between aging and sex. One day they told me a story about a former count's youngest son who had left his wife for an eccentric, younger woman. Every day he went to his mother's house for lunch, where he would eat not only with his mother but with his wife. The wife kept waiting for him to come home. And eventually he did. My women friends who told me this story viewed him, and men in general, as pathetic. This man, like most men, needed his digressions. Eventually, the women reasoned, he would see the light, dump the girlfriend, and return to his wife. It just required patience. Love and relationships required a lot of that.

Patience is written into law in Italy. Divorce became legal in Italy in 1970, but even so, getting a divorce is, by American standards, a slow process: a minimum of 3 years were required for the divorce to become final.

I found myself back at Marco and Gabriella's house for dinner on the evening of January 31, 1997. One of Marco's grown sons from his previous marriage had brought his Florentine girlfriend to dinner. She was stylish in an earthy way. The topic of conversation was the Church's official annulment of the marriage between Marco and his ex-wife. "Now, my name is Pietro Innocenti!" the son joked. The last name "Innocenti" was the surname given to children born out of wedlock and abandoned at foundling homes.

Gabriella thought it ridiculous that the Church would annul a marriage that lasted for 10 or 12 years and that produced two children. The implication was that the marriage was invalid all along, that it had never happened. Annulments, she said, were usually reserved for extreme cases, such as if the husband were impotent and the marriage brief.

I asked Marco and Gabriella whether they thought 3 years was a long time for a divorce to be final. They shrugged. It did not seem excessive. Marco did not see anything particularly wrong with the time frame.

I mentioned that one of my sisters, who has had more than her share of experience in the marriage realm, in one month finalized a divorce that ended a marriage of some 13 years. It cost her only a couple hundred dollars. The couple found the American time frame outrageous.

"After 10 or 15 years of marriage, to be able to divorce like that, in that manner, so quickly, just *whoosh,* erase everything and start all over? It seems crazy," Marco said. "I think it has to do with the American myth of constant renewal."

SUNFLOWERS AND AN ETRUSCAN TOMB

Come summer, my own renewal came. I suppose I had taken the spirit of Carolina's advice.

Iginio invited me on an outing to an Etruscan tomb under restoration and closed to the public. I was excited to have an insider's peak at a future tourist destination. The plan was to go in a group—with Iginio and his conscientious objector buddies. This group composition, with me as the lone female and the five of them, was a bit disquieting, but I am a journalist-turned-anthropologist and spent enough time working in an all-male newsroom with macho reporters that I figured I could hold my own.

Chris and Hollis were groggily milling around the house when I took off around 10 A.M. My plan was to meet them by 1 o'clock for a Sunday lunch; we had an invitation at Nicoletta's brother's house just down the street. I left them with instructions to remember to take the peach pie I had baked.

I questioned whether my plan was sound when I encountered a roadblock at the *Casa Rosa,* or the pink house. Traffic police refused me from turning off the *via Statale,* the main thoroughfare that runs between Florence and Pistoia, onto the road that led to Seano. The detour forced me to head a mile further down the Statale. I blindly wound my way through country roads and finally ended up in Carolina and Leo's neighborhood with its earth-tone houses topped with red tile roofs. I parked in front of Carolina and Leo's house. I walked through the iron gate around to the side door and tapped on the kitchen door. Iginio was not yet downstairs. He was given to late nights of summer carousing as was typical of the area's youth come the hot season. Leo offered me a *caffé.* I sat down at the expansive wooden table. I complained about the detours, and they recalled a major bike race set for the day. Soon, Iginio appeared. We headed out the door.

"Does your husband know you're going off with such a *bel uomo,* or handsome man?" Carolina teased.

We laughed. Our age difference alone, with me some 13 years older, made the likelihood of anything happening between us seem ridiculous.

Iginio wanted to drive, so I tossed him the keys. "*Va bene, fai l'uomo*—OK, play the man," I teased.

He sped along the dirt road that snaked up the hill, steeply, and cut through terraces of grapevines.

"This car resembles you," he said of my 16-year-old Fiat 127, so compact it could fit under the chassis of your average SUV.

"Oh yeah? How so?" I laughed.

"*È fatta per bene*—it's well made," he said, commenting on the force it had to climb the hill in second gear.

We emerged from the side road onto a main artery of Carmignano. Spectators lined the sides of the road in anticipation of the bike race. The police stopped us and gave Iginio a hard time. The roads were closed until 2 P.M. We had entered the no-car zone through his shortcut.

"Police and conscientious objectors don't get along so well," Iginio observed.

The police made us pull into the piazza. Iginio spotted a friend. They schemed a route to the nearby village where the other objectors waited.

After several detours, we met up with the other guys. We caravaned to the tomb. Just as we closed in on it, a small car zipped by with three elderly women as driver and passengers.

"They are sisters," Iginio said. "*Zitelle,* or spinsters." The way he said it was hardly flattering. He made a remark about them being crazy. Odd, I thought, coming from Iginio—he was hardly a conformist. The women were descended from old-style nobility. They lived in the big villa down the road with their older brother. The tomb was located on their inherited property.

Two parts of the tomb were worth exploring. One was the burial itself—a doorway framed with stone led into a cavelike area. The other was the future museum space under construction. Wooden stairways led up through a tangle of scaffolding. Iginio had the guts to jump down, stretching his svelte body as he reached from bar to bar to get a better look at what lay in darkness below. He was fearless like his mother.

We headed back, but we ran into the race detour in Poggio A Caiano. I suddenly felt frantic. I worried whether we would be able to get across the main road to the house where I was supposed to be for Sunday lunch. I hardly wanted to embarrass Chris, or raise suspicions, by not showing up. I stopped at a *caffé* and called Nicoletta's brother's house to see whether they had brought the peach pie and to alert them to my problem.

Iginio assured me he could find a way back. We headed out of Poggio, south of the race route, and crossed to the other side of town. Iginio turned onto a dirt road wounded with potholes and marred by erosion. The road slivered alongside of the Ombrone River. Soon we were engulfed in sunflowers.

"Stop!" I said.

We stopped and got out from the car. I spied a huge sunflower. Its stem was so thick we could not break it off. Iginio scavenged a junk pile and returned with a piece of metal. He cut through most of the stem and broke off the rest. He gave me the bounty.

I laughed and tickled him. He called me *tremenda,* or just awful.

We headed back to the main road. We were beyond the blockade. Iginio dropped me off at Nicoletta's brother's house just as the guests were gathering around the table. Chris and Hollis had remembered the peach pie. I do not recall, and my notes do not mention, the fate of the sunflower: Had I left the evidence of my transgression in the car or did I bring it in and give it to Hollis? I took my seat among the guests. I had lost little face in light of my family, old as well as newly extended. I caught up with my car later. A few days later I wrote my old college roommate now living in Seattle.

> Chris and I talked until dawn. . . . We talked about the distance between us, how we both felt our relationship was not very good at the moment, and that neither of us quite knew what to do about it. This past week, we have managed to become closer again. I really can't say exactly how, but several of the talks we've had must have helped. Long-term relationships can at times be mysterious, how we drift apart and then come back together [*Letter from the field,* August 1, 1996]

A CHALLENGE TO THE PRIEST

Carolina did not harbor a romanticized view of love. For her, love's labor was just that: work. One day while working in the workshop in November 1996 Carolina told me a story about a priest who came in the hospital to bless her after she had given birth to her first child, in the late 1960s. She viewed this particular benediction as a rite of purification; the connotation was that the woman needed to be purged of her sins. She offered me her explanation of why this practice started. "The Church was afraid of women because through their bodies women could exercise power over men. Hence the Church invented the virgin, the prostitute, and sex as a sin." She recalled Iolanda, the now deceased "sold woman" wet nurse, who had told Carolina her experience of a priest coming to perform this rite after she gave birth. Carolina was not so deferent to the priest. "*Lo mandai a quel paese*—I told him where to go," she said. "I already gave birth, I already paid. If you want to purify somebody, go find my husband!"

Carolina clearly understood the priest's action as an effort to define her as a sinful person, and she did not want any part of it. Her rejection of the priest was a strong statement against the Church's history of defining women as subordinate to men.

"I'm a feminist, but I don't like the word. I know what's right and what's wrong."[3] She then turned to me and said, "Okay, the lesson is finished now. *Faccia l'operaia*—Get to work!"

---

[3]On Italian feminism, see Bono and Kemp 1991.

SON ROBBERY

The marriage of a son or daughter is not always cause for celebration. My sense from conversations, popular culture, and participation was that the marriage of a son was typically more traumatic for a mother than the marriage of a daughter.

The marriage of Nicoletta's nephew was one such case for the mother, Nicoletta's sister Sara. A woman known for her tailoring skills, Sara herself had remained faithful to a promise she had made to herself: "Before marrying a peasant I'll remain a spinster," she told me in an interview, "because a peasant was something terrible." She, too, had migrated from Calabria and, in 1965, at age 23, wed a local day-laborer. He went on to develop a successful high-end family painting firm. The couple had two grown children, and Sara seemed to fret equally over her son's pending marriage and her daughter's lack of visible interest in a long-term relationship that would eventually culminate in a nuptial rite and subsequent trappings, of a house and family.

The house was a big deal in central Italy, and in discussions of potential newlywed households and wedding ceremonies, the house became an even bigger deal. When I was still new to the neighborhood, I unwittingly walked in on a family blowout. Luisa had taken me over to her relatives' house to introduce me, and as we entered, Aunt Sara and Uncle Enrico's mood was so low I felt embarrassed to have appeared at the door. Of course, I refrained from prying. I felt bad enough just being there. Months later, the story came out. That night had been the occasion that the aunt and uncle's son had given the big news to his folks. He and his bride had changed their minds: They were not going to move into the apartment attached to his parents' house. Never mind that his parents had spent an inordinate amount of time, money, and work fixing up the newlywed suite. The bride's parents had a full *portafoglio,* or pocketbook, and had at the last minute put up money for a stand-alone house in a nearby town.

Forced to accept this news, the groom's parents turned toward the wedding season. Preparations included Sara's sewing of a gorgeous and subtle gold silk dress for her beautiful yet independent-minded daughter, Nicolina, as well as readying the house since it would be the site of a *rinfresco,* or informal reception. This event was mainly for second-tier guests who did not make the primary list of those 30 or so invited to the formal reception, which had to be scaled back as a result of the change of heart related to housing. I was among the second-tier guests. This status struck me as perfectly appropriate since I had only barely met the groom and did not personally know the bride. I was also invited to the August wedding ceremony itself.

I went with Nicoletta to her hairdresser's a few days before the wedding. "Young people today, *non partono più con l'idea della famiglia*—they no longer set off with the idea of the family," Nicoletta told her hairdresser friend. While I waited my turn, I jotted notes as she spoke. "*Vogliono essere liberi*—they want to be free. I don't know if it's just my idea. To me, it's completely changed."

Italian couples can choose between two types of ceremonies: religious, in a church, or civil, at the city hall.[4] This wedding was held in the picturesque local

---

[4]Prato's rate of civil marriages is much higher than the national rate. In 2001, 45.5 percent of the 685 marriages celebrated were civil ceremonies as compared with 54.5 percent religious rites. Nationwide, just under one quarter of all marriage ceremonies in 2001 were civil. There has been

Figure 5.1 Wedding guests waiting for the bride to appear

parish, which perched on a hill overlooking the valley that stretches from Florence to Pistoia. It was a simple ceremony, with two witnesses seated in chairs, lovely roses tastefully displayed in the church. There was no fuss over bridesmaids. I noticed that only about half the guests partook in communion. The politically left-leaning people I knew remained in their pews. Afterward, I asked Nicolina, the groom's sister, what she thought about the ceremony. She was a sophisticated woman who had no problem embracing strong leftist intellectual politics and simultaneously presenting a stylish cosmopolitan self.

"Would you ever get married in a church?" I asked her.

She laughed. "Never. Did you hear what that priest said? 'God created man, then man was lonely, so he created woman?' Give me a break. What crap."

I caught a glimpse of Sara. The mother-of-the-groom was crying. Her well-coifed hair was speckled with rice, her eyes filled with tears, and her lips clenched tight. She hugged her newlywed son.

Nicoletta looked on with sisterly sympathy. She leaned over to me and in a hushed voice explained, "It's the exhaustion, and then, of course, she's just lost a son." I had heard much talk about the intensity felt by mothers toward their sons, and in that moment I felt deeply for Sara.

a gradual increase of non-Church rites. In 1961 only 1.6 percent of marriages took place at the city hall; in 1971 the rate rose to 3.9 percent; in 1981, it jumped to 12.7 percent; by 1991, it rose again to 17.5 percent, and in 2001 a rate of 24.4 percent was projected. The decades have also seen a decline in marriages. A high of 404,464 were registered in 1961; the most recent data showed 280,330 marriages for 1999. Data available from the Istituto Nazionale di Statistica (ISTAT), "*Italia in Cifre* 2002," or Italy in Figures, http://www.istat.it/Prodotti-e/Italia-in-1/02_popolazione.pdf. Accessed March 31, 2003. See also "Prato in Cifre," http://www.comune.prato.it/prato/htm/matr .htm. Accessed March 28, 2001.

When I noticed she had gone in the carport to get some of the flowers, I went in, with Hollis in tow, and offered to give her a hand. She asked me to take the big arrangements of roses to their house. I carried the flowers outside and ran into Sara again in the parking lot. Leave it to Hollis to ask her, "Why are you crying?"

"Because my son has left," Sara explained. *"Mi hanno rubato il mi' figlio—*They've robbed me of my son." It struck me that she used the word *rubato*, literally to rob.

*"Quando si piglia, mai ritorna—*Once they take them, they never return." [*Fieldnotes*, August 12, 1996]

MOTHER ROBBERY

I, too, was once accused of "person" robbery. It was during our trip to Calabria in late August 1996, when we went back to the family home with Nicoletta, Liliana, Luisa, and Oliviero. They had invited us for the summer vacation to the South—a trip they used to make every year back when Liliana was well and her father was living. Our presence must have inspired them to indulge in a holiday and give us a sense of the world Nicoletta had left behind. They braved the 9-hour drive in their car. We opted for the train as we did not entrust our little Fiat to Italian highway travel. The three of us plus the four of them stayed in a small, three-bedroom structure that Nicoletta had inherited. It was sparsely furnished. A naked light bulb dangled from the ceiling above the kitchen table. A foul rotten tomato pulp odor lingered in the late afternoon air from a polluted stream outside. The selling point of the house was its proximity to the Ionian Sea: We walked a trail to an expansive, solitary sandy beach.

My first trip to the South impressed on me the vast differences between the two regions. Oliviero and an in-law had a terrible time understanding one another during a conversation on a cell phone—and the culprit was not a bad connection but rather dialect differences. Nicoletta complained about the trash that littered the streets and the skeleton cement houses that dominated the landscape. These structures were evidence of *abusi*, or construction without permits. Calabrians added on a room or floor as they had the money to do so. They had a different sense of spending, of planning, of timing. Oliviero delighted in proving to us the degree of corruption and patron-client relations that infused every aspect of life.

"You see this white salt on the table?" he asked. "It's from a neighbor who's an uncle. He drives a bus. There's this one old man he lets on for free. Then in exchange the old guy gives him this special salt. Look how white it is." I looked closely. Sea salt was a valued commodity, and my Italian friends swore they could tell the difference between good and bad salt. Horrors that most salt sold in U.S. supermarkets was not sea salt but mined salt!

I also learned about the source of the rotting tomato smell: a sauce processing factory. The plant owned a purifying system but it was cheaper to keep the thing off, I was told, so the plant seasonally dumped nasty, rotten tomato remains directly into the stream, which went straight into the beach where we planned to swim for the next week.

One day a group of us had gone to town, and Nicoletta, Hollis, and I were shopping in a store that sold handmade items unique to Calabria. We were walking along the sidewalk when Nicoletta complained of a sore arm. By this point we knew Nicoletta had heart problems. In the spring, she had a pacemaker installed. I thought of it as medical evidence of her broken heart. Just as we turned the corner, Hollis's jacket slid off her waist and we stopped to pick it up. An elderly man tried to pass us and slipped off the sidewalk. Who grabbed him but Nicoletta and with her bad arm to boot. She and I exchanged glances. I shook my head. She started to laugh and so did I. The poor man and people around us must have imagined we were laughing at him but not at all: We were laughing at the bad luck of Nicoletta and her persistent insistence to help others. When we caught up with our group, Liliana glared at me.

"You've robbed my mother from me," she accused. I was taken aback. There was a frightening tension brewing.

A few days later, I had closed the door to our bedroom to have some time alone with Hollis. Liliana barged in and demanded my face-to-face attention. She stood very close to me as she spoke. I felt threatened and uncertain what to do. I wanted to just ignore her and focus on my 5-year-old daughter but I could see Liliana was not going away. I relented. I followed her into the other bedroom, which she and her mother shared. She launched into a sad story about her life and her lost love. She sang a refrain she had sung numerous times: How tragic it was that she would never marry. How tragic it was that she would never have children of her own.

A HARD MOVE

Little did I realize how difficult it would be to move. Moving was not just a matter of finding a new place to live. It was, rather, like *undoing* a living arrangement. It was like *undoing* a life and the deep personal bonds we had made. It was hugely offensive to them. It was utterly gut-wrenching for us.

Our housing crisis taught me much about the differences between my own assumptions about housing as compared with those of Nicoletta, Oliviero, and Luisa. It opened my eyes to profound contrasts between my American notions of mobility and their Italian notions of staying put. I embraced mobility. They feared it. For me, changing houses and lives and friends had become a way of life. For them, changing houses could only mean one thing: betrayal.

A number of precipitating factors convinced me we needed to change our housing situation before another winter settled in. First, there was the issue with the heating. By law, households were only supposed to run their furnaces for 8 hours per day. Translation: a couple of hours in the morning, 6 hours in the evening, and the rest of the time freeze. Or give into serious layers: cotton-lined wool body suit, turtleneck, and up to three sweaters depending on the drafts and proximity to a blazing fire. Hollis's subterranean bedroom was given to outbreaks of mildew, and her bout with bronchitis the previous winter had me wanting to avoid another cold season there. Plus, there was the issue of the thermostat. It was on the second floor, in Nicoletta's apartment. Contrary to her best intentions, Nicoletta was not used to rising and shining as early as we were, and so we often found ourselves dressing in a cold and dank unheated basement as we scuttled about to get Hollis off to preschool on time.

Second, there was the issue of security. We wanted privacy and peace of mind. Liliana was prone to outbursts, which included incidents of shattering breakables upstairs. Her relatives assured us she was harmless; the opinion of a psychologist friend suggested otherwise. I did not take lightly the confrontation with Liliana and the accusation that I had robbed her of her mother. Furthermore, our social habits were a source of stress. Chris had enlarged his circle of musical friends. He wished for a place where he felt free to play his fiddle and free to have music friends over to pick or rehearse. We sensed disapproval, however, whenever we invited friends over. Because the ground-floor eating area was a shared area, we did not feel at liberty to entertain frequently. It could create feelings of jealousy or even suspicion.

A third precipitating factor was Nicoletta's declining health. The day she was found in a pool of blood, with Chris on the other end of the telephone and my parents and youngest sister in town, was a day that changed my view of her well-being and our place in her life. Chris was off on tour with the Maurizio Geri Swingtet; I was playing host for my parents and sister, and had taken them to the local Thursday market. We were sitting at a corner café, eating *schiacciata* and *panini,* when Nicoletta and Liliana spotted us. I did some translating, they left, and we lingered for a while before heading home.

> When we pulled up the street at about 3 o'clock, I could see something was wrong. The cars of all the nearby relatives were parked outside the house. Liliana was driving off in a car with the aunt from Prato. Luisa was on the stairway, her face all puffy. Oliviero was outside, looking worried, and he rarely ever looks worried.
>
> "Nicoletta has fallen," Luisa mumbled. "She's at the hospital."
>
> Oliviero explained she had gone downstairs to answer the phone. It was 1 o'clock. Chris was calling from Urbino. And there she was in the middle of a conversation, and she collapsed. She hit her head. There was still blood on the floor where she had fallen. Luisa helped her upstairs. Liliana was there. Chris was confused. Luisa hung up the phone. Ten minutes later Oliviero came in to ask whether his wife had called the ambulance.
>
> "*Sì.*"
>
> "*No.*"
>
> "*Sì o no?*" he asked. "Lu, these are situations in which *bisogna muoversi,* you've gotta move it!"
>
> He had driven Nicoletta to the hospital. "It's a good thing I turned up when I did," Oliviero told me.
>
> What a distressing day. I am exhausted emotionally. I am completely upset that Nicoletta is gone—that she is at the hospital, that she is not upstairs, that in the morning I won't hear her opening the blinds, that tonight she wasn't there with Luisa, watching the Maurizio Costanzo show, laughing, visiting, arguing here and there, recounting the day's goings-on. I have grown so close to Nicoletta. I love her dearly. It is complicated to have such strong sentiments for someone who is also a "key informant"—such a cold, inappropriate word.
>
> I have become so attached to this family. It's odd. It's odd because it's messy. I don't know where my research ends and my personal life begins. [*Fieldnotes,* May 30, 1996]

Perhaps I was mistaken, but I read Nicoletta's collapse while speaking on our telephone as a sign that we were a source of stress. She and I had agreed verbally, after several months of ambiguity the previous fall, that my family and I would rent the apartment for 9 months minimum and one year maximum. I understood that Nicoletta wanted back the space after that period. Once I found out my Fulbright grant had been renewed for another year, I wanted to stick by my promise. Come early fall 1996, I kept her abreast of our housing search. Not only was I driven by what I thought to be an agreed on deadline, but also by our plans to make a trip back to the States in November. I had an anthropology conference to attend. I also had a dog in need of changing caretakers from a stressed friend in Tucson to a willing nephew in St. Louis. Oliviero and Luisa, who had never been on an airplane, who had never traveled outside of their country, and who spoke no English, were planning to come with us. We joked that they would be my *campione,* or sample subjects, of Italy's record-low birthrate and zero population growth! We were a little nervous about being responsible for their experience of all these simultaneous firsts, but we were happy to have the chance to reciprocate all the hospitality they had shown us.

Finding a rental on my budget was difficult. When the real estate agent took us to look at one of the first options, he warned us that it was unfurnished. I thought, fine, we'll pick up cheap, secondhand furnishings. There were no garage sales per se in Italy, but we would find a way. The apartment was in a neighborhood between Poggio A Caiano and Florence in a town known for its dense population of Chinese immigrants who worked in the leather sector making MADE IN ITALY purses. The stairwell up the apartment building smelled of filth and urine. I had a quick lesson in what unfurnished meant: there were no kitchen cupboards, no stove or refrigerator, no light fixtures. Even the bathroom was missing some basic amenities! Friends confirmed that this was typical when you rented a place unfurnished or bought a new house. We quickly modified our search criteria for only furnished housing.

One late afternoon in early October, after a super-frenetic shift sewing 300-plus white buttons onto ugly yet-to-be-dyed off-white cardigans with irritating wool thread that broke ad nauseam, I ditched out of the workshop to look at two apartments with Chris and Hollis. Both vacancies were in a hamlet of Carmignano, and both were owned, believe it or not, by the *zitelle,* those elderly single sisters I initially glimpsed while visiting the Etruscan tomb. The first apartment, a nicely renovated space above the hayloft, looked down onto the courtyard and the crumbling stucco façade of the old family villa. It was a picture of nobility in decline: long in property, short in cash flow. The old folks' pet dog had fashioned the courtyard of its own dirt design. The proximity to the Lodovica's front door—a statement of fortification that harked back to an era of noble families living in luxury but also fear of peasant revolt—promised another variation of landlord surveillance. The second property, across town, was a partly restored *casa colonica,* or farmhouse, with two sides facing the town and two sides facing the countryside. A grove of olive trees comprised the front yard. The house itself perched up on a hill overlooking an expanse of grapevines.

"We would be idiots not to take it!" we said, laughing as Hollis picked flowers.

Elizabeth L. Krause

Figure 5.2 A restored farmhouse in Carmignano

The only problem was the rent of 1.2 million lire. It was more than half of my monthly stipend. We were paying a couple hundred dollars less than that for our current apartment, and the rent had included utilities. One solution was a friend who had expressed interest in co-renting a place if we found one in the country. We disclosed this information to the real estate agent.

This was a mistake. When I returned home after another day of exhausting sweater work, I learned the news:

> Chris tells me the *zitelle* are undecided. Not sure they want to rent to us. What angst now. We got dressed a little nice, went directly there. [*Fieldnotes*, October 11, 1996]

The intimidating iron gate to the villa was locked. The Lodovica sisters and their brother had never met us face-to-face. I rang a bell. A small, elderly man came to the gate wearing a stern and disturbed expression on his face. *"Coraggio,"* I told myself, repeating the Italian directive to be brave. The dog barked viciously as I geared up to lay on the charm. Through the locked gate, I presented the Signore with my official, stamped Fulbright letter of introduction and the contract confirming my monthly stipend. It turned out the Lodovica sisters and their brother did not want anyone else in the contract, particularly an Italian. Rental laws favored tenants and mandated leases of several years' duration when renting to a native. The preferred tenants were foreigners—Americans or Europeans—who would actually leave at the end of a year or so. We assured the Signore it would only be us living in the house.

Second thoughts always come later. I worried about leaving Nicoletta's family and the familiar neighborhood. I worried about living in such a spacious, stand-alone house. Gabriella volunteered to have a look at the place, and once there, she introduced us to some of her old friends, a middle-aged childless couple who lived around the corner with the man's mother. I was feeling better about moving—until several days later when we realized the consequences of our decision to move.

Chris took the brunt of the anger unexpectedly when he walked into Nicoletta's kitchen. Oliviero and Luisa confronted him. They were deeply *offesi*, or insulted, by the news of our move. Oliviero accused us of cheating them. Luisa claimed that "our friends" were to blame for trying to get us to move. Nicoletta had suddenly transformed into a mute. Chris felt betrayed, especially by her silence. I was perplexed to find myself in a situation where my landlords were so angry with me for moving. I had tried to be open with Nicoletta. Months back I had told her we were looking, and even she had raised concern about Hollis in the dank bedroom. She had intended to resolve the problem with the thermostat but acknowledged her health had prevented her from following through with a solution. Apparently, she had not communicated all of this to her daughter and son-in-law, with whom we had never discussed the rental agreement. Suddenly, Oliviero was performing the *capofamiglia,* or household head.

"It seems like you're leaving so fast," he said, angrily. "You're giving us so little notice."

> At this point we're screwed if we stay and screwed if we move. I can't sleep. I am so worried about what I've done. Was it wrong to be unhappy in this cavern? Actually, as I sit here in my corner of the couch I feel very comfortable, and the thought of us moving in that big house terrifies me. . . . What saddens me is the hard feelings. [*Fieldnotes,* October 14, 1996]

The episode taught me much about housing. I had learned that my Italian friends did not take moving casually. Once when I had told Leo, whose sweater firm I worked in, that I left home at 18, he had assumed I was a rebel. Quite the reverse was true: I was simply heading off to do what was expected of me: go to college. This was the norm for middle-class Americans. I even remember when I was 28 and pregnant with Hollis, a friend my same age who had decided never to have children, reminded me: "Wow, now that's a commitment: 18 years." In Italy, the relationship with the familial home was much longer and much less definite.

"I'd never move," Luisa told me as we were packing up. "My father built this house with his own hands." I reflected on the well over a dozen moves I had made since I graduated from high school.

The move and subsequent falling out threw into question the trip to America. Three days before we were scheduled to depart, Oliviero phoned. "Do you still want us to come?" he asked. Of course we did! Once in Missouri, they marveled at the orderliness with which people drove and the absence of people smoking along the streets or in houses. They took in two Thanksgiving dinners, one in St. Louis and one in Springfield, and they were shocked by how little time went into eating the feast. My father-in-law was particularly curious about "our Italians" and delighted in asking them lots of questions. Everybody wondered if they had kids. I interpreted that query for my sister-in-law, mother of three.

"Well, you would have thought two grown-ups like us would have done something," Luisa answered. "But no, we haven't done anything. *Nulla.* Nothing."

Oliviero, as was his way on this topic, stayed remarkably quiet on the personal front. As for "why" the birthrate was so low, he directed the question to me, *"la ricercatrice,"* or researcher, then offered the expense and the *egoismo,* or self-centeredness, of young people, as explanations.

As we began our road trip across the plains, they were awestruck at the huge distances and vast open spaces of the West. In a Mexican restaurant in Santa Rosa, New Mexico, they fell apart. It was classic culture shock. Confusion over a menu in a strange language with unfamiliar offerings impressed on them how far they were from home. Unanchored from their regular routines, their identities were thrown into crisis. Luisa insulted her husband in front of us. *"Sono sempre sotto controllo*—I'm always under his control," she ranted. "Be quiet. Hurry up. Do this. Do that." She stomped off to the restroom. Oliviero's eyes welled with tears. The food came. It was mediocre. We left as soon as possible.

We found refuge in the small old town of Shamrock. We spotted a café that boasted Italian-style espresso, a fact that surprised us in 1996 in a rural, western town. Oliviero ordered an espresso. The coffee was bitter and thin. The spoon was so huge it dwarfed the cup; he was accustomed to tiny spoons for stirring sugar. The woman serving us invited her Italian guests' feedback and warmly accepted Oliviero's offer to have a look at her Italian espresso machine and fixings. Not only were the beans over-roasted, he explained, but they were ground too fine. Oliviero and Luisa felt better after this flavor of familiar territory.

"Long highways, long coffee," Luisa said once in Arizona. At times, she really had a way with words.

It was in Tucson that the couple observed the odd practice of one grocery store/deli that sold beer and wine but prohibited customers from consuming alcohol on the premises. They also opened my eyes to the strangeness of American eating habits. Heading back east, Chris stopped at a highway drive-through, pulled up to the window, and took the sack of fast food. "What are you *doing?"* they asked, incredulous. They were horrified that someone would not only get food "to go" but eat it in the car.

Through their eyes, I saw my own world anew.

PUBLIC PRYING

A few weeks after the five of us had returned to Italy, on a Sunday afternoon in December 1996, we were sitting *a tavola,* or around the table, with Luisa and Oliviero in the small kitchen adjacent to their sweater workshop. The computerized looms were shut off, and we were digesting a family-style *pranzo,* or midday dinner. Luisa had served up a feast *alla mano,* or casual, family-style. Stretched over several hours we had eaten a first course of tagliatelle with mushrooms; a second of roast pork, white Tuscan beans, followed by a salad tossed with local extra virgin olive oil, vinegar, and salt. We drank bottled water and local red wine. We finished the meal with local vin santo, the famous biscotti of Prato, and *caffè.* We were still munching on nuts and sipping after-dinner drinks when the father of a mutual friend—the one responsible for our landing where we did—showed up unexpectedly. Alessandro was alone: no wife, no kids, not even Carlo, his eldest son and my friend from my study abroad days in 1984. The conversation is interesting for the way in which the topic of a childless couple came up.

> "Where's Franca? Where's Franca?" everyone demanded, asking about Alessandro's wife.
>
> *"Povera donna,"* he said, poor woman. "She works all week for Orlandi [the same psychiatrist who treated Liliana]. Come Sunday, she's spent. Then Orlandi calls her and gives her hell for leaving a film of soap on the terracotta tile.
>
> "Ultimately," he reasoned, "it's Franca's fault. Twenty-five years ago when she came home in tears after working for that woman that first day, she made the fatal error: She never should have tried to do a week's work in one day. Instead, she should have checked off the items on the list she could finish. She should have set the boundaries then. Orlandi"—he never calls her professoressa, like the women do—"has unrealistic expectations."
>
> In his mischievous, Florentine way, Alessandro joked about having a new flame—his eldest son's girlfriend, who was some 15 years older than Carlo hence old enough to be his father's lover. Soon, he had us all busting up with laughter. Liliana came in, sized up the situation, and told us how lousy she felt.
>
> "I've gotten as thin as a fish," she asserted. "It's the clothes that make me look fat."
>
> There was a brief pause. Alessandro soon shattered the silence. "You're not a *pesciolina,* a little fish, you're a *balenina,* a little whale!" Liliana turned and left, nonplussed. Alessandro then laid into Luisa and Oliviero for not having kids. Luisa became lightheartedly defensive, saying she had wanted kids.
>
> "Well either you find someone who can or go to a sperm bank," Alessandro ventured, cutting straight to the quick.
>
> "A sperm bank?" Luisa replied. "It's not that we can't have kids."
>
> "Well I don't know. Maybe you can, maybe you can't. Have you ever been to a gynecologist?" he continued.
>
> "A gynecologist? What does that have to do with it?"
>
> "To see if something was wrong?"
>
> "No, no." Luisa said. "Maybe I'm old fashioned, but he's been the one to always say no. It takes two."
>
> Oliviero remained silent. [*Fieldnotes,* December 22, 1996]

Alessandro's confrontational prying into the couple's childlessness made public a private matter. In the company of friends and an anthropologist whom he knew to be studying this very topic, he made the matter a topic of conversation. I believe there are two important insights to draw from this. First, Alessandro's action of bringing a supposedly private matter into the public sphere of culture, through talk, was evidence of a prevailing sentiment that couples like Luisa and Oliviero were not conforming to long-standing notions about the meaning of family. Alessandro's line of questioning revealed an expectation for married Italian couples: to create a culturally legitimate family required having children.

Second, when a couple does not have a child, one cannot expect a "true," straightforward explanation. I found silences to be frequent. In this case, Oliviero's silence struck me as an assertion of his right to his private life. He was much more private than his wife. He viewed talking about their relationship openly with others as inappropriate. His refusal to discuss the issue of family-making, however, was also a sign of his ultimate authority: As long as the topic of having a child was not discussed, it was beyond negotiation.

NUPTIAL BEDS AND VIRGINS

Come summer, another wedding was on the horizon. The only bride whose wedding bed I was ever invited to make was the daughter of Nicoletta's brother. I was curious to partake in this nuptial rite, one which Italian folklorist Raffaele Corso (2001) documented in his *La Vita Sessuale nelle Credenze, Pratiche e Tradizioni Popolari Italiane,* or Sexual Life in Popular Italian Beliefs, Traditions, and Practices. His study probed courtship, marriage, birthing, and postpartum practices as well as erotic proverbs and songs dating from the late 1800s and early 1900s. He mentioned wedding night pranks like the one we pulled, and were Corso alive today, he might view such a thing as a "survival," but its participants hardly viewed it that way.

I had received a call from Luisa confirming the bed-making appointment. Her voice cracked on the phone; Liliana's mental condition was at a low point. I assured Luisa I would be on time for the misdemeanor, taking care to calculate my necessary stop by a tailor's workshop. The tailor was altering a suit jacket and skirt I had acquired especially for the wedding; it was the most beautiful piece of clothing I had ever bought. My graduate student wardrobe did not contain anything appropriate for a wedding the likes of this. My Fulbright stipend of 2.4 million lire per month, which at the time was about $1,400 for a family of three, hardly permitted extravagant clothing expenditures once rent, food, utilities, a growing child's clothing, now gas and car insurance, and meager office supply costs were figured in. Many of my clothes, particularly winter clothes, had just happened upon me as sweaters are known to do in a place where everybody makes them. For the special occasion, I was lucky to discover an outlet in Prato that sold designer brand *campioni,* or samples. I fell in love with a suit fashioned of a gorgeous periwinkle 100 percent viscose fabric so stylish and shimmery that I have rarely if ever been able to wear it since, living in places like super-casual Tucson and ultra-earthy Amherst. I went to retrieve the altered suit from the chatty 74-year-old tailor, who boasted to me that her doctor reprimanded her because she still rode a *motorino* around town. I explained I was in a rush since I had to go *"fare il letto,"* or make the bridal bed. I confessed to the tailor that, contrary to custom, I was not a virgin.

> "Ah, nobody's a virgin anymore!" she said. "But you know, it's not like it's anything so new. I remember being told that my grandmother got married when she was already pregnant. Of course, back then it was a scandal. Now it's not a scandal. Both of my two sons married because their girlfriends were pregnant: the youngest was very young 23 (with girlfriend barely 18); the oldest 25." [*Fieldnotes,* June 26, 1997]

I went with Luisa to the "bridal suite"—a house built adjacent to the bride's parents' house. Everything was in perfect order; the dishes and silverware and serving platters were the maximum of simple elegance. The house was custom outfitted with the fine artisan work of the bride's father, a contemporary metal worker who made containers but was also an artist in his own right: the table

Elizabeth L. Krause

Figure 5.3 A bride prepares to throw her glove to bachelors.

base, curtain rods, among other fixtures were all beautifully cast iron. I had found the mother of the bride-to-be months before catching a nap on the porch following a dinner with 34 people *a tavola,* at the table, to celebrate the completion of the roof on her daughter's future house.

Once at the house, Luisa and I met two of the bride's cousins and her sister, all smartly dressed single women in their twenties. Somebody remarked, "The women who make the bed are supposed to be virgins!" Everybody laughed. "Right, we're the virgins!"

Making the bed required that we short-sheet the nuptial linens. In effect, this halved the usable length of the mattress. One imagines the happy newlyweds absorbed in marital bliss, ready to plunge into bed, and suddenly the "magical moment" is disturbed as they find themselves in a tangle of doubled-over bedding. The bride and groom would discover other surprises as well: almond-covered candies distributed freely beneath the bottom sheet tautly stretched over the mattress. The sister, cousins, and anthropologist chuckled as we engaged in this ritual preparation. The grandmother, Nicoletta's octogenarian mother who dressed daily in widow's black and witnessed our prank, began recalling old Calabrian traditions. The grown grandchildren rolled their eyes in collective embarrassment. It was a distancing gesture: they were fully Florentine-Prato identified—meaning modern, intellectual, urban, northern as opposed to old-fashioned, uneducated, rural, southern. They took refuge on the balcony. So they had made the bridal bed but they did not consider themselves traditional. Making the bridal bed was not a survival of custom. It was just a good gag with its own history and meaning.

My own preparations for the wedding itself tested my limits of knowledge related to style, and I wrote a letter to a friend that doubled as a fieldnote:

> I just got back from buying stockings for this wedding tomorrow. You wouldn't believe how expert these women are in dressing. I mean, I never knew there was an art to buying stockings: how they have to be according to what dress you're wearing, the fabric, the shoes, etc. It's really complicated for me. I felt like I was acting when my friend (informant?) asked me what my opinion was between two pair of pantyhose, one darker than the other but otherwise the same. I nodded, pretending, because really she has no idea how out of it I am when it comes to pantyhose distinctions. (Later I fessed up as she was giving me advice.) Anyway, you wouldn't believe how dressed up I'm getting for this affair. [*Fieldnotes,* June 27, 1997]

UNREQUITED LOVE

With her female cousin's pending wedding, Liliana plunged into a crisis. "*Sta poco bene*—she's not well at all," Luisa, her sister, told me just before the wedding, herself reduced to a bundle of worries. I knew that Liliana's story involved a relationship—truly the love of her life—that was cut short. Her parents's discovery of certain encounters of the flesh had coincided with a realization that their daughter was not well. They had pressured Liliana's boyfriend to marry her, and though he did love her and wanted to stay with her, he wanted to give it a little more time before marriage. At a certain point, the relationship had come to an end. Liliana rehearsed her life and unrequited love time and again. The love of her life had been taken from her, why should others get theirs? She landed in the psychiatric ward of Prato's hospital a few days before the wedding.

The day after the wedding, I offered to drive Nicoletta to visit Liliana. The hospital of Prato was a public facility. The entrance corridor had a large no-smoking sign at the entrance. On the way up to the psych ward, smashed cigarette butts covered the floor. Nicoletta rang, and a buzzer noise indicated the door had been opened. The ward was plain, clean, sparse, in a word, institutional. We entered, and there was Liliana, her large frame moving toward us, down the hallway.

"Liliana! You're up! You're dressed!" Nicoletta said. These small signs of well being counted a lot for Nicoletta. She monitored her daughter's condition daily. There was always some hope for Liliana to get well. In the meantime, it was a matter of maintaining equilibrium, of keeping her obsessional behaviors, her exhibitionist tendencies, and her emotional outbursts in check.

Liliana and I exchanged kisses on each cheek, and she motioned for us to come into her room.

Nicoletta handed Liliana a bottle of Gatorade. Liliana guzzled the orange fluid as though she was in a chugging contest.

"She's thirsty," offered her roommate, appearing from under the sheets. She was a young woman, late twenties probably, dark hair, dressed hippie-style. She wore lots of jewelry, an exaggerated number of bracelets, and a huge necklace made of yellow plastic beads. Pink pants with patches on them were unusual for a place where colors tend to be subdued.

Liliana finished the Gatorade. "Have you gone into my room? Has everyone gone into my room? And all the jewels from my lovers?"

"No, Liliana, no one has gone in there," Nicoletta said. "It's closed, just as you left it."

"But have you cleaned it? Dusted it? Put it back in order?"

"Don't worry. I've cleaned and dusted it, and now I'm going to paint it. It will be all nice when you come back, so don't you worry."

"But ma, I don't want to go back in that room. I've had time to reflect on my life, on things as they are, and I realize I've spent too much time closed up in that room. I don't want to go back in there, it makes me feel—. Now I want to come sleep with the *morbidonna,* or the soft woman." She laughed.

Nicoletta laughed. I laughed.

Liliana had a mesmerizing effect when she talked. She had a way of drawing you in, even if you did not want to be drawn in. Every moment was a performance for her, a *spettacolo,* or a spectacle, a chance for her to win your attention. She knew that, and she played on the drama. She was always scheming about how to make a scene. I was convinced of this. She was a master of the spontaneous scene. After all, she said, life is just *un gioco,* or a game, and what else did she do all those hours in self-confinement, in her own mental prison? She analyzed and re-analyzed the people around her, the relationships, the envies, the hates, the desires. These colors were life for her. These games were what kept her going.

She directed herself toward me: "My mother can't stand to be with me. She never pays any attention to me." I smiled at Nicoletta, apologetically. It brought to mind all the times Liliana had accused Nicoletta of never feeding her.

"But she's an old woman now. What will they do with me when she's gone?" Liliana asked. "Ma, when can I come home? I'm tired of being here. You said I'd be here for 3 days and now it's been a week and a half." Her tone changed, became angry, resentful. "*Non mi volete bene,* you don't love me—that's why. Nobody wants me there at home. They'd rather have me locked up here so I don't cause any trouble, so there's no fighting. Luisa and that husband of hers, they want me here too. *Non mi vogliono bene*—they don't love me either."

The roommate wants some change for coffee. I give her all I have, 600 lire (about 35 cents). Liliana would like to take a walk, go down to the bar, and get a coffee. We ask permission and then head out.

At the bar, Nicoletta offers to buy us all a coffee and encourages me to get a sandwich, too. Liliana wants a sweet pastry. Nicoletta gets on her case for getting a sweet, reminds her that she needs to diet. There's a little scene between them but it passes. . . . Liliana gives me a long, loving kiss, one on each cheek. The length of the kiss makes me uncomfortable, so I pull away.

On the way out, Liliana wants to go to the *chiesina, la cappella,* or the chapel. She asks one person, then another, then a third. We weave our way through the corridors, finally arriving at the chapel.

Liliana prays. Silence. She approaches a podium. There's a book opened. She starts writing on it.

"Liliana!" Nicoletta runs up to stop her.

Nicoletta tells me this has been an obsession of Liliana's lately, to write on everything. My mind flashes back to when my parents were in town and, during dinner, she called me into her room, gave me a pen, and asked me to write on the wall. When I refused, she grabbed my arm and forced me to write an "X" on the clean surface. It was then that I noticed all the graffiti.

She mutters self-degrading things in the church: "I'm just a cigarette for men . . . My family, they'd just as soon get rid of me. No one loves me, no one cares about me . . ."

Nicoletta and I step outside to leave Liliana some space. I gaze into a courtyard, the old part of the hospital. It is beautiful, Renaissance-style architecture. Perfect symmetry. The height of reason, I think, cynically.

We head back to the chapel to fetch Liliana. She's nowhere to be seen. We spy her behind some restoration scaffolding, crouching below a madonna in a cave, surrounded by burning candles. "I'm asking for forgiveness. *Chiedimi scusa*—Ask for my forgiveness," she asks us. Nicoletta replies, *"scusa."* She repeats, insistently, *"Chiedimi scusa."* So I say, *"scusa."*

Liliana smokes a cigarette as we head back to the psych ward. She seems relatively calm given her general state of anxiety. She kisses her mother longingly on each cheek. She takes Nicoletta's right hand, kisses it, then her left, and kisses it. "What a strange child," Nicoletta says to the roommate.

I approach Liliana to give her a kiss. She coolly extends her hand to me.

I remind Nicoletta of the Gatorade bottle. No glass allowed in the ward. She asks Liliana to give it to her. Liliana throws a fit. "I can't even keep a little bottle," Liliana protests.

Nicoletta explains it's for her collection for when she puts up tomato sauce.

Liliana throws a fit: "The things I've had to put up with this family. And tell me, why didn't you let me marry Mario Mazzini? I'm destined to this life, alone."

RATIONAL LOVE

The visit to the psych ward starkly reminded me of the rational behavior that modern society demands of us (see Foucault 1965, Roberts and Allison 2002). Love is no exception. Whether choosing a mate or having children, expectations to display rational behavior are high.

Love in the postwar, late demographic transition context of central Italy was an exercise in rationality. One way people could demonstrate their capability to be rational was through the choice of a partner. In the postwar period, the peasant became stigmatized. For a woman to marry a peasant man was viewed as the last thing to do. The booming economy of the 1950s and 1960s made for a context that devalued peasants. They were seen as backward and uncivilized. They were seen as unlikely providers as compared to artisans or factory workers.

Moving to the farmhouse put me in touch with former peasants, Enrica and Pietro, both from large sharecropping families, and themselves parents to one child. Enrica was born in 1920 in the very farmhouse where we were living. It would have been a much different place in her day: no indoor bathroom, no electricity, and no demarcated space for the animals. After she and Pietro were married in 1950, they lived in the farmhouse, this time with his extended family.

They had long since abandoned rural life and moved, it just so happened, two doors down the *via,* or lane, from the farmhouse. I made friends with the couple. We would sit in their small kitchen and chat about bygone days, and they were happy to let me tape-record the conversations—a fact I was grateful for since they spoke with rural dialects that were at times difficult for me to understand. Pietro recalled that, in the textile factory where he worked, nobody admitted to having been a peasant. Enrica spoke with pride about working as a straw weaver, from when she was 5 years old until later years, continuing to work as an artisan with various materials—raffia, wool, acrylic—as determined by the demands of the global market. The couple had vivid memories about family changes (see Krause 2001).

They and others came to associate small families with being modern and with being in control. The small family even pointed to a willingness "to suffer," meaning that people were relying on coitus interruptus or abstaining from sexual relations, because there did not exist "the methods of today," that is, contraceptives. Pietro enjoyed getting a rise out of me, and he sometimes played on the image of the ignorant, backward peasant to do so.

"*Gli era un problema sa!* There was a problem, y'know!" he said.

"These were big families, they used to call them 'patriarchal,'" Enrica added.

"But is it true that the patriarch used to decide how many children he wanted or did they just come?" I asked.

"No," Pietro sad, "They normally just came. They didn't even know if it went straight or crooked! *Un lo sapeano mica*—They had no clue."

"Come on!" I said.

"Really! They didn't know. *Dimorti rimaneano zitelloni*—A lot of them remained old bachelors," Pietro insisted, "because they were afraid of women."

Pietro's way of talking about peasants threw into question their masculinity. His reference to men not knowing "if it went straight or crooked" implied sexual incompetence. This led to male celibacy: the men neither had sexual relations nor did they marry. Furthermore, their fear of women was the ultimate outward expression of ignorance and backwardness. Peasant men were stigmatized. Poverty robbed men of their manliness.

The emasculating effect of poverty was a strong theme in native Roberto Benigni's most well-loved film, *Berlinguer ti voglio bene,* Berlinguer, I love you (directed by Bertolucci, 1977). Everyone I met seemed to know and admire this film, set in the outskirts of Prato where Benigni grew up. The film features the escapades of four sexually awkward jokesters. A key scene, one which leads up to a poem about caterpillars that never metamorphose into butterflies (the epigraph, p. 92), traces the aftereffects of a prank: Benigni's buddies interrupt his dance with a transgendered "woman" at a local festival with the fabricated news that his mother has died. Devastated, Benigni stays out all night. He arrives home to an outraged mother. She blurts out her lingering resentments about her failed attempts to abort him. A beleaguered Benigni is then pictured walking through a field, where he stops to gaze longingly at a poster of Enrico Berlinguer, then-leader of Italy's communist party and, in the 1970s, an icon of hope for the poor and working classes. He sets off on a bicycle; his friend, riding on the handlebars, recites the caterpillar poem, which I had heard several people recite before I ever saw the film. The poem draws on the caterpillar as a figure for poverty. The comparison of this "race" of people with a species that is born a wormlike larva and remains a wormlike larva suggests a hopeless destiny. Poverty emasculates these sons of peasants. Poverty, the poem suggests, flows in the blood. Like the peasant woman who could not abort her son, there is no aborting poverty. Being pregnant with poverty means one is destined to reproduce poverty itself. The poem does not offer a path to salvation, but one can infer that if there is a path, it is in finding a way out of poverty. The poem seemed like a cautionary tale against having children if one is poor.

STIGMA AND FAMILY-MAKING

Small families in central Italy were so in favor that a couple who had more than two children risked stigma, particularly if they were of modest means. This prejudice was driven home to me when I went to talk to Cinzia, pregnant with her third son when I met her.

Carolina had suggested I interview Cinzia, whom she described as a *donnina d'oro,* or a woman of gold, the backbone of the family. When Cinzia became pregnant with her third child, the two older sons were in elementary school. Initially she was not happy about the pregnancy. In fact, she recalled really laying into her husband for not having been more careful, for not showing more self-control; she told me they were relying on *marcia in dietro,* coitus interruptus, as their method of birth control. She recounted to me her feelings of embarrassment for not having taken greater precautions. In a young couple, desire excuses such "accidents." Indeed, the couple had ended up pregnant once before because of a lack of "self-control," as she put it, but that was back when they were young. For a mature couple, such indulgences were cause for humiliation. Her identity as a responsible adult woman left little room for these slips.

Desire had to be tamed. Untamed desire was akin to peasant sexuality: backward. In contrast to peasant sexuality, a key symbol of modern sexual relations was control.

Cinzia had considered abortion but then decided to follow through with the pregnancy and face the consequences.

"Yes, three children are a lot," she told me. "There was this one person who was like, Here in town, to have three kids, we must be half-witted, understand! As I said there were also people who told me, 'Fine!' It's like—."

"That's good," I offered.

But the way she talked, positive comments were rare.

"Three kids I mean," she said, "you don't have to make such a big deal about it, y'know. Like they make such a big deal in going, "THREE KIDS?!""

Friends and relatives expressed their sense that Cinzia was showing a lapse in judgment, calling her "idiot" and using pitying phrases such as "poor woman." The degree to which she was stigmatized revealed how dominant was the central Italian notion of keeping the family small. In violating the social norm, Cinzia prompted people to express the norm in clear and certain terms. With one child, people would say to me, *si sta troppo bene,* things are fine as they are.

Even so, there were times when having even one child led a couple's peers to question their reasoning abilities. I recall well a dinner in Florence with a group of handsome couples in their late twenties and early thirties. One friend of the hosts was pregnant. Another couple had a small child who had been left with grandparents for the evening. At a certain point the couple with the child received a call from the baby-weary grandparents. The mother half of the couple quickly headed for the door; meanwhile, the father launched into a long version of a joke that went something like this:

> There's this guy from Prato, he's very materialistic. He loves his Rolex, his Mercedes, that sort of thing. Well, one day he's up in Montecatini (a posh spa town in Tuscany), and he has an accident. He's distraught. Someone comes over to him and points out that his arm is missing. The guy looks down and exclaims, "My Rolex!" [*Fieldnotes,* June 24, 1999]

The dinner guests laughed politely and then the jokester left with his by-now aggravated wife. Our host made it clear that she did not find much humor in his joke. "The baby has gotten to his brain," she explained. "He used to be so serious, now he's always telling jokes, jokes like that and jokes about women." Love, sex, and family-making tested the limits and meanings of rationality.

LOVE AS RISKY BUSINESS

Practices of the heart can be a risky endeavor for working women, as I learned firsthand when I returned to Prato in June 1999. I went looking for Gina, the young woman who had flashed her scar at me when I was learning to operate the cutting disk at the sweater factory. I had met with Gina and her family during my first year of fieldwork in 1996. They had invited Chris, Hollis, and me for dinners and Sunday outings to Florence. We became friends. Gina confided in me. She shared with me intimate details of her life. During summer 1997, she was falling in love, and it felt like the real thing. Her mother, Simonetta, expressed to me trepidation because Gina, in her early twenties, seemed awfully young. Plus Simonetta herself had found love to be full of empty promises and painful pitfalls so she was jaded.

Simonetta's husband had been abusive, and after having three children together and enduring years of violent outbursts, she had finally divorced him. Simonetta had migrated to central Italy from Salerno, a southern city where as a young woman with eight siblings and a third-grade education, she married as a young teenager. Now, she was a single mother with three working adult children who lived together in a modest two-story house. She and her eldest daughter operated their own sweater-finishing workshop near the town piazza, where with sergers they sewed together sweater pieces like the ones Gina cut on the factory machine. (Her son co-owned a small store.) When work at the factory was slow, sometimes Gina would lend her mother and sister a hand.

Simonetta was a youthful 48 years old when I met her. "Look," she once said, while we chatted in her sweater workshop. She pulled up her pants above her knees. "Even after five pregnancies, I don't have any veins."

"*Five* pregnancies," I asked?

Two of them had ended in abortion, her first spontaneous, the other illegal, before abortion was legalized in 1979. She had become pregnant when Gina, her third child, was just a few months old.

"I was only 40 days pregnant," Simonetta said. "I realized it right away. So the creature would have been tiny." She held up a finger and pointed to the end of it.

"I just couldn't handle another child," said Simonetta, raised a Catholic. "It would have been impossible."

The decision was difficult and risky. She offered an explanation that spoke to her sense of accountability: "The pregnancy wasn't my fault. It's not like I went with some other man. It was my husband's fault." They were using coitus interruptus, so she viewed his ineffective withdrawal as irresponsible. She sought out a woman who used knitting needles.

"My god," I cringed. "What pain."

"You bet there was pain," Simonetta told me. "It was horrible."

Hemorrhage followed. But she did not go to the hospital. "Fortunately, I am strong and my body healed by itself."

Just then, several men arrived to pick up a load of black cotton sweaters. She switched her intimate talk to shop talk. She pointed to my presence, the *americana*. I asked if I could take some video. One of the guys joked, asking if he could give me a kiss instead.

Simonetta changed the tone, complaining to him about the sweater job; the material got caught in the machine, making the sewing slow. And, of course, the earnings were always the same, no matter the material. She could sew 200–600 sweaters per day depending on the weave, earning 450 lire, or about a quarter, per sweater.

Simonetta viewed herself as an artisan and put in long hours to contribute the lion's share to the household coffer. She worked hard to maintain her home and to build up a *corredo,* or trousseau, for her daughters. Over the years she told me she had spent about 50 million *lire* (some $30,000) on her daughters' trousseaus; they were filled with high quality and name brand linens, dishes, and household items.

Simonetta's workshop was one of the first stops I made during my June 1999 trip. I tapped on the door. My fear that I might be disturbing work soon vanished. Simonetta jumped up from behind her serger and grabbed me. She gave me a bear hug. Her stout sweaty body poured out affection. Within a minute, her eldest daughter pulled up on a scooter, and within another minute, Gina strolled into the shop. The spontaneous moment could not have been better planned. Their faces were all too precious.

"Did you come from work?" I asked Gina.

There was a heavy pause.

"They fired Gina," Simonetta said.

I was shocked, for I had perceived Gina as a dedicated sweater-maker. She had worked in the factory for 9 years.

"She is getting married and they fired her," her mother said.

The scene Gina described was brutal: Martino, the factory owner, had pushed her out one day in January. "There's no work for you here," he had told her.

Gina believed that the firm—indeed, also a family firm—had laid her off indefinitely after learning she was to be married that June. Gina was pursuing a lawsuit against the firm through the *Camera di Commercio,* the labor office, but the best she could hope for was one year's compensation.

Gina invited me to see her and her fiancé's new home. It was a small but charming apartment, completely refurbished, in the historic center of the nearby town. There was a cubicle of a second bedroom for the eventual one child the couple intended to have. She insisted I come to her wedding. I gladly accepted the invitation.

The wedding was a lavish affair on a rainy June day in a humble town. Neighbors huddled beneath umbrellas in the cement courtyard outside Gina's family's home, waiting to catch a glimpse of the sweater-maker girl-turned-bride. They gasped as Gina, known to wear t-shirts picturing a buff Sylvester Stallone, made her wife-to-be appearance: a well-fitted white wedding gown accentuated her voluptuous figure. Gina glowed gorgeous. She slid into a polished, antique black car that transported her around the corner to the church. A traditional church ceremony was followed by a multi-course sit-down lunch at a villa in the foothills near Pistoia. Her mother told me that the wedding dress and accessories alone cost some £7 million (about $3,200). Seeing her get married, for me, was bittersweet. I wondered how she would endure this transition to life as an unemployed newlywed. I thought how unfair this all seemed: how the sweater firm owner had welcomed the baby of her sister yet thrown out one of her most loyal workers presumably to save on potential maternity care costs. On the books, Italy's maternity leave laws were progressive and as of 2000 even extended to men. But in practice, the progressive intent of laws often backfired when employers caught in the tightening wedge of global economies felt they could not afford to pay benefits and hence sacrificed employees to circumvent the laws. In hard times, profit-monger logic defined social relationships in bottom-line, cost-benefit terms.

HUES OF LOVE

Various hues of love color different and divergent desires. Romantic love, the love that involves sexual desire, does not necessarily have as its only outcome children. Filial love, the love felt for or expressed from a son or daughter, may yield satisfaction and meaning but also may deliver disappointment and heartache. The love of friendship may bring joy but also jealousy. As the Nobel-Award winning mathematician John Nash came to realize, love cannot be reduced to an equation. But neither can people do anything they want in their love-related relations. Even something like love, which can feel so natural, results from deep historical traces and cultural constructions.

There is not a single truth but many truths about love. Romantic love has undergone tremendous changes in the past 50 years, reminding us how even desire and sexuality are subject to historical and cultural shifts. The vast majority of Italians in the early part of the 20th century lived in rural conditions and, especially women, were subject to strict sexual surveillance. Sexually active Italian women have come of age in a time when speaking about their own desires and pleasures is neither taboo, nor something only men can do; they too may share intimate information and find it to be a source of empowerment and interpersonal connection. Where once the institution of marriage meant not only sanctioned sex but also the inevitability of children, for fertile couples, today having children is only one possible motive for marriage or cohabiting.

In central Italy of the late 1990s, one of the strongest cultural notions with regard to romantic love was the idea that it had to be made and remade anew each day. Carolina took that notion one step further to suggest that love even had to be unmade in order to be remade. Although couples did not always last, as I would learn, there was awareness of love as something you had to make happen. It was a process that required the art of living.

But the art of living was hardly a perfected art, and as with any art, there were unfinished projects and castoffs. Each occasion of joy seemed at once to be an occasion for sorrow. As Liliana's cousin was about to marry, Liliana plunged into her deepest yet emotional crisis. She felt herself banished from social life. She felt like a castoff. She was not fit to love, not fit to marry, not fit to mother. She was fit to be medicated and to live her tragic life. Her sad story mirrored what Foucault (1978) predicted with regard to modern society and modern forms of power. No longer was power something that merely kept people down. Power had become productive. In other words, it produced effects. Society and its hosts of experts cranked out knowledge and categories that were anything but neutral. Rather, the knowledge produced new standards. Experts, as well as lay citizens themselves, tended to measure themselves against these norms. When people's behavior fell outside of those norms, they were marked as deviant and their morality was subject to questioning. They became unfit to make a family.

Even love, and perhaps especially love, was subject to these modern forms of power. When Cinzia, a woman of average means, was expecting her third son, she quickly realized that she had violated a social expectation about displaying rational behavior. Ending up pregnant for the third time left her peers wondering about her rational capabilities. The stigma burned. Why might people living in a fully modern society such as Italy be so concerned with displays of rationality? What might these feelings have to do with love in a way that makes sense of the current demographic dynamic?

I am convinced that the shadow of a pre-modern past haunts Italian memories. This past marked people from certain impoverished classes as backward. Recall that Nicoletta's sister proclaimed that she would have remained single rather than marry a peasant. Selecting a mate was a strategy people could use to distance themselves from a peasant past, one that in the postwar era was becoming stigmatized. The former peasants Pietro and Enrica associated small families with being modern and with being in control. Reproductive practices in central Italy, as with many places in the world, distinguish someone as modern or, conversely, as backward (see Kanaaneh 2002 for Palestinians in Israel). Furthermore, for women the pre-modern past meant relations of love within the patriarchal family. Women were left little power as they were subject to the rigid pecking order of institutionalized patriarchy.

But even those marriages that were a product of an asymmetrical gender regime—and hence to a college-age woman seemed backward—sentiments were strong of deep and lasting love. Nicoletta held on for dear life to the love she had known for her late husband. When she had entered marriage, she had truly meant it as a vow for life, and that was the expectation of her family. Her octogenarian mother continued to wear a black dress years after Nicoletta's father's death. A good southern woman like Nicoletta, even if she was a northern transplant, would not think of a second marriage. The deepest corners of her subconscious remained anchored in the love she had known for her husband, fully aware it would be her one and only.

Her own daughter's generation played with and against new rules. Even if couples did stay together, as did Luisa and Oliviero, they did not necessarily feel the same obligation to have children as did their parents. Yet this change did not come easy. As Luisa likened herself to a tree without fruit and as Carlotta expressed deep ambivalence about having only one child, they gave voice to regrets.

The stories and silences of my Italian friends and acquaintances revealed a complex range of how people experience the transformations related to patterns of demographic shift. Family-making did not occur on neutral territory or a blank slate. Rather, historical tracts have lent definition to the possibilities for the deep and intimate ways that people feel. The most intense fertility decline came on the heels of the 1975 family reform law (see Table 1.1), which reflected social demands to reject the already contested patriarchal model—recall the peasant protest that was long underway in Tuscany. The reforms recognized the family as a "collective body of persons, linked by bonds of affection and solidarity."[5] Creating a democratic micro-community was not so easy as it might appear.

The preceding stories hinted at the gender divide that figured prominently into the realms of love, sexuality, and family-making: Luisa, who likened herself to a tree without fruit while Oliviero sat in silence; Sara, who lamented the loss of her newlywed son; Pietro, who spoke of backward and unmanly men; Cinzia, who was stigmatized for having a third child, a son; Gina, who lost her job to love. Conventional and emergent ideologies related to gender were challenged, debated, and lived within the context of the new Italian family. People in love struggled to figure out what these new possibilities for being a sexual and social being meant in the context of a new family model, one that granted newfound respect to individual inclinations. Delaying marriage, not having children, or having very few children were consequences of the politics of love in the age of the new family.

[5]European Commission, Family Benefits and Family Policies in Europe, Italy, June 2002, 47.

6/Gendered Myths, Gender Strife

"When you go and give people contraceptives, especially the pill and intrauterine devices, you liberate women from the home and childbearing. That gives them time to pursue higher education, complete their schooling and training. And that is a great, great achievement."
—Dr. Joseph Chamie, Director of the population division of the United Nations

"*Non ce la faccio più*—I can't do it anymore."
—A common women's lament about responsibilities

"Children are really just the mother's. They're all her responsibility."
—Roberta [Fieldnotes, March 19, 1997]

Struggles over gender arise subtly and explode fiercely in the context of Italy's record-low fertility. They are cultural struggles that play out in daily life. Women are the scapegoat in discussions about the population trend. But the struggles involve men nearly as much as they involve women. Patriarchy is not over; it is merely threatened and uncertain of itself. A generation of women does not want to become the women their mothers were. A generation of men finds itself in a quandary with mothers who want them to stay home as long as possible and with girlfriends who cringe at the thought of becoming another mother, rather than a wife, to their lover. Gender is not just code for "women." Rather, gender refers to the complex ways that male and female beings are socially constructed and sexually oriented. Social and cultural expectations about being a man or being a woman set a range of limits and possibilities for how people live up to and rework expectations about their gendered and sexual identities. Of course, people can challenge and test those limits, and in a sense the quiet revolution consists of a whole new set of possibilities. But possibilities are not endless, and they are not always revolutionary. The old ways persist. "The tradition of all the dead generations weighs like a nightmare on the brain of the living," as Karl

Marx wrote more than a century ago (1994[1852]:15). We are all social beings conditioned in one way or another.

Three myths concerning gender circulate in relation to the quiet revolution. The first myth has to do with the "why" of low fertility. It proposes that "before" women did not work and now they do, resulting in their choosing work over family. The second myth involves the "what" of low fertility. It suggests that fertility decline leads to women's equality. The third myth has to do with the "who" of low fertility. It presumes that the quiet revolution is primarily about women.

NOBLE CLUES TO AN IGNOBLE MYTH (MYTH #1)

Little did I realize where the move to the farmhouse would lead: square on a trail to clues about the myth of the non-working woman. My arrival on this sleuthing trail, however, was circuitous. Important steps turned out to be time, trust, and an unlikely friendship with my new landlord, the former count.

Each month, Chris, Hollis, and I made an outing to the count's estate to deliver our rent payment directly to the count himself. I refer to him as "the count" even though the postwar reforms of the 1950s did away with noble titles. Nevertheless, I use the term because locals continued to refer to our landlord as *"il contino,"* or the little count, and *"signorino,"* or little sir, because of his small stature. The suffix *–ino* is an Italian diminutive; it adds a quality of smallness or affection to a person or an object. In Tuscany, the ending implies endearment. As applied to the count, however, I suspected there was a hint of disrespect, or at least irony, as I commonly heard people refer to him as *signorino* but never call him that to his face. We headed down our *via,* or lane, past our neighbors' wall-to-wall houses. Their doorsteps emptied onto the street and looked out onto a valley of vineyards. We drove a few blocks to the other side of the *paese,* or town, came upon the mound of earth that defined an Etruscan tomb, then turned onto a rocky, pothole-ridden road lined with cypress. The regal trees had weathered the centuries far better than our landlords' expansive yet decrepit villa.

The first time we paid rent, Signore Lodovica called us into his formal office. The lighting was dim, and his desk and bookcases overflowed with the trappings of a man educated in jurisprudence: papers, ledgers, contracts. I handed him the stack of lire, and he counted each of the 100,000 lire bills precisely, one through twelve. He was a well-seasoned administrator who treated each business transaction with severe attention. I imagine he had inherited such attention from his father, once the mayor of Carmignano. Satisfied, he wrote us our receipt.

This formal landlord-tenant relationship made me uncomfortable, so I was glad to see it give way to something more familiar as time passed. Chris and I began to turn our rent payment outings into occasions to purchase olive oil, wine, and *vin santo.* This sweet wine, a hallmark of Tuscany, is made from semi-dried grapes aged for up to 5 years in small barrels; the drink crosses class lines and is commonly paired as dessert with the famous almond biscotti of Prato. The estate's products were harvested from grapes and olives grown in the very fields surrounding our farmhouse. I experienced new meaning to the idea of locally grown. There was something simple and beautiful in this. I caught myself more than once romanticizing the past. Archives and memories served as antidotes to *toscanismo,* or a romanticized view of the Tuscan past so common to travel writers. My encounters with the past prevented beauty from masking aspects of history that were short on kindness.

One very wet and sloppy Saturday morning in February 1997, we went to the villa on our monthly errand. A cavernous building held large vats where grape nectar fermented into wine. Dozens of cats milled around on the rafters above us, making a strong impression on Hollis, my daughter, by then 6 years old. A large fellow with a limp chatted as he helped us. A former peasant and retired Prato textile factory worker, he was *alla mano,* or very friendly. Some customers brought glass *damigiane,* or containers, for their wine, but we arrived empty-handed. He lent us plastic containers. He put them beneath a vat, released a valve, and the fresh wine bubbled forth. He weighed it on a scale that might have belonged to another century, and then sent us, as he did with all buyers, across the driveway. The count peeked out from the *cantina,* or wine cellar, and we followed him back inside. Posters from wine fairs dating to the 1980s hung from the cantina walls. He and his sisters were more active in marketing their wines two decades ago. With no son or daughter to follow in their footsteps, such marketing had fallen off. In fact, most of their grapevines were now leased out to the larger, commercial winemaker of Carmignano. The salesroom itself was sparsely stocked. The count stood behind a formidable wooden table.

> The count seems nicer each time we see him. He is never eager to take our money. He seems somewhat embarrassed about it actually. He never lets us leave without a present: usually a bottle of *vin santo.* We bought 21 litres of wine, and he only charged us for 20—rare that one gives a discount for wine but he's feeling generous towards us these days. [*Fieldnotes,* February 16, 1997]

The count broached the topic of my research, I mentioned my archival work, and he revealed to me the existence of his family archive that dated to the 1200s! He recalled one diary of a family ancestor who recorded a jousting match in Florence between an ancestor and a Medici, the well-known royal Florentine family. The entry dated to around 1468.

"That's before the discovery of America!" he said.

I was impressed. My closest ties to Europe were through my father's father, who, when he immigrated to America from what is now Lithuania in the 1890s, found nothing worth remembering and all worth forgetting from his European past.

The count spoke of documents closer to my period of interest: agricultural products harvested in the 1900s. "There was much more diversity back then," he said. "Now we're into monoculture." This comment made me think differently about the expansive fields of sunflowers, a subsidized European Union crop.

I hinted about exploring some of the estate's historical documents. As keeper of the family's private archive, the count was intrigued by my interest but also warned his sisters about me. My American ideals of democracy and egalitarianism, he warned, colored my notion about their family's past as nobility. He rightly assumed I was critical of the history of unequal relations between counts and peasants that existed under the Tuscan system of sharecropping. With a scolding tone, however, he reminded me of America's tarnished history of slavery.

The next time we came to pay rent and buy wine, in March, I noticed a stark change in the way he handled the money transaction. I gave him the stack of 12 banknotes, and he hesitated. He continued holding them as we chatted about the cats—ever a source of fascination for Hollis. Finally, he looked down at the stack of bills.

"May I count it?" he asked, timidly.

"It's fine with me," I said. "I hope I haven't made a mistake."

He thumbed through the *lire* clumsily. His self-conscious movements seemed gentle; they contrasted with the hard counting style he used with us the first time. He slid the wad into his pocket, returned a pleasant yet embarrassed glance, and offered us a bottle of *vin santo*.

"It is special, from 1990," he explained. "It's one of the few remaining bottles from that grape harvest. Our *vin santo* is the best anywhere."

I accepted the gift, he discounted the wine, I paid and took the receipt.

The count's change in handling the money signaled an emerging *amicizia,* or friendship. This transformation in our relationship marked a turning point in my research project. He put aside his suspicion of my politics and granted me access to the archive. The clues emerged not only from the documents but also from his sisters' reactions to particular information that I came across and shared with them.

The count was generous in helping me navigate the ledgers and volumes. Admittedly, this also permitted him to have some control over my research activities. We began with the more modern materials, the *conti colonici,* or farm accounts. These books were stored in a cluttered closet in the salon. The count brought over a chair to stand on so as to reach the shelf. He handed me tarnished tea set pieces. I placed them one by one atop an antique flour grinder. He came across a shredded account book. He grumbled that a cat had gotten into it. He handed me a volume from 1901 and suggested I go sit at the big dining table where there was more light. Meanwhile, he took the shreds and placed them next to me. As I began paging through the accounts, he retrieved a huge jar of glue and with a brush smeared it onto a page. One sister came in and offered me tea. The count stepped away from his restoration project for a moment. Another sister entered the room and, unknowingly, reached across the table and grabbed the shreds of paper to throw them away.

"No! No!" yelled the count. "Leave those alone."

"What are you *doing?* What *is* this mess?" the sister asked.

He explained about the wicked cat and his project to piece things back together.

A few days later, we proceeded to the well-organized historic section of the archive. Beyond a large, locked wooden door was a dust-free room with shelves lined with hand-bound volumes dating from the 1700s but also from the 1200s: journals from ancestors recounting everyday life; records of lawsuits over land disputes; family trees dating back to the 1300s; old accounting records; a facsimile of the original sharecropping contract dating from the 1500s—when he could not locate it, he worried that a rare visitor had made off with it. He was looking for a ledger dating from the 1700s in which one of his ancestors recorded all the payments made to workers, including women. Some years ago, he told me, he had gone through the volume and marked the entries documenting women's work. Who knows what preoccupation with his own family history had led him to index these entries? Seated side-by-side at the huge wooden table, the count took great delight rediscovering each piece of evidence, reading it aloud to me, giving me time to jot it down in my notebook.

- In 1716, payment was made for 22 days of *opere di donne,* work by women, to repair the dock of the Ombrone, the nearby river.
- In 1716, payment was made to women for work to carry stones and to build the wall along the *violotto,* or small road, that runs along the ridge of *Poggiola,* the name of the very house I was renting.

  "That place was full of stones," he told me. "It was a *podere,* or sharecropping estate, that required a lot of work."

- In 1719, also at Poggiola, women were compensated for 35 days of work in which they carried stones to construct terraces and to dig holes and then place stones under the olive trees to sustain the earth beneath them. He drew me a picture of this technique. The women also were paid for building aqueducts to carry away rainwater as an anti-erosion strategy.[1]

His three sisters, elderly and unmarried like him, were outraged. "What? Tuscan women working like that? They did that kind of heavy labor? The women in *bassa Italia,* the South, worked in the fields, did heavy labor, but here? They worked in the house."

During my fieldwork, people frequently told me that "before" women did not work. I even heard educated women in their twenties and thirties, whose *own* mothers had worked for wages much of their lives, tell me women did not work "before." They depicted women as historically non-working—a fact that, particularly in the province of Prato, could not have been further from the truth.

The truth was that much of women's work was neither highly valued nor adequately remunerated. The source of this dominant myth of the non-working historical woman became increasingly evident to me over time: the participation of women as wage-earning workers in the past was continuously erased in the articles of the popular press as well as reports of demographic research. Reporting on a study released by the national statistics institute (ISTAT), the leftist daily, *L'Unità,* asked: "Is the Italian woman a housewife? This image no longer responds to reality if one thinks of her as a person who does not have resources other than those of her husband and family." Framing the issue in this way, the reporter was attempting to undo one stereotype—that Italian women are currently housewives—but ended up reinforcing another stereotype—that Italian women used to be only housewives and not wage earners (Treves 1997). Similarly, demographers spoke of a "massive entry" of Italian women into the paid workforce in the 1970s as a way to explain the fertility decline (Pérez Delgado & Livi-Bacci 1992). Such characterizations imply that "before" women did not work. Such arguments discount the importance of women's work before the 1970s. The ahistoricism in these explanations is particularly disturbing given that fertility decline was already notable in the early 20th century in the regions

[1] Archivio Privato, Villa di Calavria, Carmignano; "Saldi, Ecc. Di Calabria, Bacchereto e Querceto dal 1712 al 1727." Book No. 4, p. 44 and p. 58.

of Tuscany, Piedmonte, and Liguria (Livi-Bacci 1977:68). Antonio Golini, another well-known Italian demographer, also legitimizes this myth, pointing to women's entry into the workforce as one of the most important social changes related to declining fertility rates (cited in Palomba 1987:viii).

Such stories erase the generations of women who worked for wages from their homes, and who with their long hours and low wages fostered the development of a globalizing economy. In a chapter on "Factors Involved in the Decline," Italian demographer Livi-Bacci characterizes domicile work as insignificant: "the housewife working at home part-time spinning wool for a textile factory should not be identified with the industrial sector in the same way as the skilled worker operating the complex machinery in a chemical plant" (Livi-Bacci 1977:214). He offers no further explanation; he says only that it is an "obvious consideration." Why this blatant dismissal of the importance of women's work? What difference is so obvious as to go unexplained? Livi-Bacci's description of the woman working at home offers a clue to his theory's ideological perspective. Note that even though the woman is *working,* she is nevertheless labeled first and foremost as a "housewife," one who is working "at home" as well as "part-time." By contrast, the implicitly male laborer working in the chemical plant is not only "skilled," but he is operating "complex" machinery. Such descriptions value the work of some (male factory workers) at the expense of others (female domicile workers). They also construct a domesticated social space that effectively discounts women doing piecework as "real" work, thereby perpetuating an image of the Italian woman historically as housewife. It is a case of scholars becoming caught up in the very myths they write about.

Rare have been historians such as Simonetta Ortaggi Cammarosano, who probed the categories of census takers. She recognized the strategies by which women were erased from the historical record of labor participation. Women's participation in the labor force has not been a linear trajectory, as stereotype would have it. Rather, their participation has varied. Ortaggi Cammarosano emphasizes cycles of invisibility. Women appear in and periodically disappear from official statistics. For example, the numbers of women classified as *massaia,* or rural housewife, increased tenfold in the national census between 1871 and 1881. State bureaucrats' difficulty in classifying women's work led to a category called "unspecified employment," which in 1871 contained 4,067,449 women workers. State functionaries eliminated this category 10 years later, and grouped these women as housewives, a category that leaped from 393,839 persons in 1871 to 3,720,906 by 1881. Writes Ortaggi Cammarosano (1991:158): "Hundreds of thousands of women from the lower classes who added some form of productive work to their household duties in order to balance family budgets now figured, in statistical terms, simply as *'massaie,'*" or housewives. In Carmignano, by contrast, the category of *trecciaiola,* or straw weaver, was well represented historically. In nearly every household of the township of Poggio A Caiano in 1901 that I examined, there was at least one straw weaver listed. Census takers made the local shift to classifying working women as housewives in the 1950s and 1960s, a period that people remember as the boom of the sweater industry, when every household had a mechanical handloom running day and night. The explosion in the number of women categorized as "housewife," In records that I read, can only be explained with an understanding that the postwar era brought with it an idealization of the role of woman as house-wife. Even women who worked long hours over home-based looms would either place themselves, or be placed by census takers, as *casalinga,* or housewife.

The fact that the count knew that "before" women worked—indeed, engaged in heavy labor such as unearthing and moving stones—and his sisters did not know this was a clue about how myths derive their dominant status. The sisters, and others like them, imposed onto the past a modern ideal of women as house-wives. Many women themselves did not recognize or remember a good deal of women's historical work. Yet the count, as the educated lawyer and keeper of family accounts, knew about the long history of women workers. He kept track of this history, for it amounted to work on his capital goods. As a practiced administrator, such activities were of interest to him. He recognized the impor-tance of women's work.

He apparently had not previously discussed this fact with his sisters or they would not have been so shocked. They were outraged because they clung to the ideal of women as inhabiting the domestic sphere—as keepers of home, hearth, and family. The count kept this knowledge about women's paid labor to himself until, for some reason, he revealed it to me. It was only later, as I began to rec-ognize patterns of concealment with regard to the history of women's work, that I came to see as a breakthrough the moment involving the clash in knowledge between the count and his sisters. Peasant women who had large families were listed as having occupations. Peasant women had always worked. The housewife was a relatively new invention.

The myth of the non-working woman sprouted in the liberal 19th century, ripened during the fascist era, and was harvested in the postwar period: the myth that women didn't work "before" seems to have really taken hold among what Italians call the popular classes in the 1960s. This myth about how women "used to be" speaks loudly about what women's daily performances should look like: self-sacrificing mothers. That "women work" does not sufficiently explain Italy's record-low fertility. The shift to very small families is at best, and even then only partially, a result of women seeking long overdue recognition for their work (see Maher 1987).

THE JOURNEY TOWARD EQUALITY (MYTH #2)

One family story speaks loudly to the difficulty of breaking cycles of gender inequality. It finds its source in a southern Italian family, some of whose mem-bers have long since migrated to Tuscany or New York. Eleven children were born, all before the war, two of whom died, leaving nine living brothers and sis-ters. The mother was the most intelligent and was the real head of the family. The father tried to make up for his inadequacies by keeping strict control over his daughters. One day he noticed that his teenage daughter had closed herself in the bathroom. He became suspicious. What is she hiding in there? Is someone in there with her? Does she have a secret letter?

The father went to the door and knocked, then pounded. "What are you doing in there? Why did you lock this door? Open the damn door."

The girl became terrified that his rage would lead him to break down the door. Panties dropped to her ankles, she lifted herself off the toilet, and against the wooden feeling of her legs, she shuffled over to the door. The turn of the key echoed loudly in the bathroom, furnished as it was with only a toilet, a sink, a small tub and a bar of homemade soap.

Her father, his face by now swollen with rage, shoved open the door. "What do you have in your hand? What are you hiding from me, you dishonorable *figlia,* or daughter?"

Embarrassed but not knowing what else to do, the daughter slowly arched her hand from behind her back and revealed to him the blood-soaked rag that she had tried, in vain, to privately change.

This event left a scar on the family. How horrible, how invasive, for a father to lack such fundamental trust in his daughter. The next generation agreed that their father had gone too far.

This act nevertheless became reproduced in the subsequent generation. The eldest of three children was the most orderly; her two little brothers always wanted to play and mess with her things. So she began locking her door as she became a teenager. One evening, upon finding the door to her room locked, her father became outraged. He began pounding on the door: "What do you think you're doing, locking the door? What does my daughter have to hide?"

The mother became outraged. "If my daughter wants to lock the door to her room, she surely has the right to do so." But the father wouldn't listen. He persisted. "And so," the mother told me, "to make my point, to show that I was serious and to stand up for my daughter's right to privacy, I had to exaggerate. I threw plates, I threw them so that they would break, to show him that I would not bow down, to show my sons that their father was wrong. Each generation has to let go of some of the old ways."

CULTURE OF RESPONSIBILITY

The generation of Italians now in the prime of their childbearing ages has let go of the idea of large families. They have let go of the idea of the patriarch's right to rule. They have largely let go of the notion that only men can enter certain prestigious professions. But they have not let go of the idea of motherhood. In fact, a culture of responsibility surrounds Italian parenting, and it weighs particularly heavily on mothers. As I became familiar with the expectations that spun out from this cultural norm, I began to think hard about the second myth: that low fertility delivers equality. In effect, modern mothers give to one child—and more—what mothers historically gave perhaps to five, six, or seven children.

Demographers have long equated family planning with gender equality. Access to safe and affordable contraception and abortion have been pillars of women's rights movements of the 20th century. In Italy, abortion was legalized in 1978. Joseph Chamie's declaration that taking the pill—or any other form of contraception—liberates women from the home and childbearing (Altman 2002) smacks of wishful thinking. If he were correct about this prescription for gender parity, then Italy, with its ranking among wealthy countries as having the lowest fertility level of all, should be a place where women enjoy the highest level of liberation from the responsibilities of home and children. Such assump-

Figure 6.1 Parents in the school courtyard wait for their children.

tions do not bear out when tested against the demands of everyday life. The for-
mula-makers forgot the cultural politics of gender. They omitted gender ideologies, which bear on expectations of child rearing. In Italy, a culture of
responsibility emerged with the modern family, and it demarcated roles for
women and men in intense ways that are related to piecing together the puzzle
of the quiet revolution (see Tilly et al. 1992).

People in the field told me time and time again that raising children in the
1990s and keeping a home were not what they once were. With the modern economy has blossomed the modern mother, and along with this the *doveri di madre,*
or motherly obligations (Barbagli 1996[1984]:387–392). These obligations
nicely fall under what Italian sociologist Chiara Saraceno refers to as the culture
of responsibility, but she does not explain the nature of these obligations
(Saraceno 1996:143–148). My research sought to reveal how people experienced the Italian-style culture of responsibility. How did Italians live it? What
did a culture of responsibility really mean? Strong demands were placed on
mothers in terms of educating, feeding, clothing, and healing their children.

RESPONSIBILITY AND SCHOOL

The parents of children in Carmignano gathered outside the school before the
bell signaled the day's end. The children waited impatiently behind locked glass
doors in their matching *grembiuli,* or black school smocks, finished with white
collars and red bows. A bossy *bidella,* or custodian, typical of Italian school cus-
todians, kept the anxious children at bay as the parents engaged in a buzzing
social scene, a picture of civil society in motion.

A controversy exploded with the new school year of fall 1996. Responsibility appeared at stake. Just days after classes had begun, the parents threatened to strike—to keep their children home from school. The town had announced its plan to impose a half-hour change in the opening time of the school day, from 8:30 A.M. to 8 A.M, to accommodate transportation problems involving seven school sites in the district. Parents objected to the way that the time change had come down in a rash, sloppy, and authoritarian fashion—with no advance warning and no public consultation. Parents acknowledged the county's extensive territory. But the bus transportation problems had existed for years. Moreover, starting a half hour earlier in the morning would be a major inconvenience to working parents not to mention to children, who deserved to have time in the evening with their families and who needed the extra half hour's sleep in the morning.

About 150 angry parents crowded into the elementary school cafeteria to attend the year's first public meeting of the *consiglio di circolo,* or advisory committee, held September 24, 1996. Parents confronted the councilor of public instruction with strong emotion. I found a seat toward the front next to Gabriella, the mother of my daughter's best friend. She was always glad to explain things. I turned on my tape recorder and jotted notes about the public happenings. Later, with the help of a local research assistant who helped transcribe the tape, I would sort out people's comments. The strategies that people use in public settings reveal taken-for-granted cultural norms.

"Silenzio! Silenzio!—Quiet! Quiet!" somebody yelled over the voices.

One mother argued that the town was making things difficult for the children.

"But ma'am when one puts the numbers together—" began the councilor of public instruction, pushing a cost-benefit analysis.

"No! No! No! Numbers. Numbers," objected the mother, straining to be heard above the noise. "We're talking about children. We're not talking about numbers."

Another mother, Anna, piped up: "As for the things that are most important—I mean speaking of my case, which I think is common enough. What I really regret is to wake up a child at 6:30 so as to manage to give him a sufficient breakfast in order to confront a day of 8 straight hours of school."

What cultural norm did Anna's regret reveal? I took her self-portrayal to be as a responsible mother who made sure to wake up her children in plenty of time to feed them a decent breakfast. She contrasted her own parental responsibility with the irresponsibility of the public officials. Her strategy made a great deal of sense in the local context because of the heightened value placed on responsible parenting.

"Considering the interests of children—because the school, as with so many other things in Italy. . . ," Anna interrupted herself. "The school is made for children. But what happens? It's just like with hospitals. They're made for the sick. But none of this ends up being true. The hospital staff schedules, for example, are organized in a way to ensure that the director sees clean sheets. The rooms must seem like something that they are not—for the sake of the director. After that, if the sick person needs something, forget it. It's the same thing in the school environment. The child comes last."

Anno's intervention was founded on a moral failing, a gap in institutional responsibility. It concluded with the idea that the county purchase additional school buses to solve the transportation problem.

"*Brava! Brava!*" the audience shouted over applause.

Local parents struck me as passionate about education, and I came to understand this passion as directly connected with lingering memories of an elitist, fascist educational system. On the one hand, a strong ethic of egalitarianism underscored parents' dealings with the school. On the other, many viewed schooling as a vehicle for their children's social mobility, and at times this sentiment seemed almost desperate.[2] School offered a path to overcome old class hierarchies. It offered hope. The parents knew their children faced an uncertain future, rendered more so because of cycles of crisis in the textile sector connected with ongoing globalization. Many of the parents of children at my daughter's elementary school had earned only middle-school diplomas, and I met several who had only fifth-grade educations. They wanted more for their children, and they were willing to fight for it.

An unexpected turn of events cast me into the center of school politics. The three first-grade teachers kicked off the new school year with a regular meeting. Parents, mostly mothers, dwarfed the children's desks. Each teacher—language arts, science, geography, art, and music—discussed curricular plans for the year. Then it was time for the parents to elect their class representatives. Parents of the 16 children assigned to Section B left to vote. The parents of Section A, my daughter's assignment, stayed put for the election process.

Marco, the father of Hollis's best friend from preschool, launched into a nomination speech. He touted the advantages of having someone who was "cultured," who could offer an "outside" perspective on local matters. Suddenly, my name was being written on the blackboard beside that of another mother nominee. I felt torn as to whether to accept the nomination. I figured I had no chance of winning, so I would just let the farce play out.

The parents scrawled their votes onto pieces of paper. The ballots were immediately tallied, and the results announced. I had lost by one vote. I was relieved. The position required communication as well as preparation of notes for circulation, and not being a native speaker, I questioned how effective I might be in the role. Heading to my car after the meeting, however, I felt a twinge of disappointment. What insights might the position have offered me?

The next morning in the school courtyard, a woman named Elena, the newly elected representative of the companion first-grade class, approached me. My "opponent" had declined the position as class representative. The position fell to me! Thus began my legitimate participation in Italian school politics. I served along with parents from each classroom and a teacher from each grade level on the *consiglio di interclasse,* or the interclass advisors, who met monthly with the

[2]The lulls and delays in economic development limited opportunities for social mobility, rendering "stronger among us [Italians], more insistent, and at times even desperate, that demand for self-promotion by means of education," according to Italian sociologist Marzio Barbagli (1982:12). Education levels have increased rapidly and dramatically: for example, 69 percent of mothers born between 1946–51 have a certificate from the *scuola dell'obbligo,* middle school, as compared to only 28 percent born between 1971–75 who stopped at that level. See de Sandre 1997: 63–75.

superintendent (there was no on-site principal or administrator). I later learned that a national decree in 1974 established this democratic process of local school governance as a belated reform to the authoritarian school politics that persisted well beyond the 1944 fall of the fascist regime.[3]

My position as school representative placed me in a privileged place for observing and participating in the school conflict—a conflict that involved parents, school officials, and *comune* administrators. I found myself telephoning parents to solicit opinions, as well as typing, photocopying, and distributing letters announcing meetings. My activities provided me invaluable insight into the degree to which the school became a site for political struggle against a very bureaucratic state apparatus.

School politics intersected messily with community politics. Despite a mantra among the parents of *"tutti insieme,"* or everybody together, the movement operated on the edge of divisive local politics. Several parents stormed out at one meeting, just as a politician from the province-level government began to speak. Confused, I turned to a sweater-finishing mom of three sitting next to me.

"They were communists," she explained. The speaker was a member of the *Alleanza Nazionale,* or the National Alliance, a neo-fascist party. The protesters objected to the politician's presence and saw his offers of help as false and opportunistic. Old communist versus fascist tensions seemed to fester beneath the parents' protests.

In some ways, the school could not have been a more appropriate forum to call forth these tensions. Schooling was a prime political tool of reinforcing the status quo during the fascist era. Rigid barriers were structured into a "closed" education system designed to prevent social mobility.[4] Students were tracked according to social class and even religious background into schools that promised passage to higher levels or led to "blind alleys." The dead-end schools forbade students from using education to improve their social and economic status.

After Mussolini's demise, workers' movements fought for an egalitarian system of education. These movements were said to embrace a "Gramscian" notion of education. I took note of this local application of this term for I had read *The Prison Notebooks* of Antonio Gramsci (1971) in graduate school. His ideas about the relationships between the state, civil society, and the individual gave

---

[3]Presidential decree n. 416 established the structure for school governance at the local level and required a class representative: "The first thing to make sure of is that whomever becomes a candidate and/or becomes elected as representing the parents should really have the desire and the time to devote to the problems of the school. It is not important if they are the most knowledgeable but rather that they are the most motivated and not the same old self-important big-mouths" (Zanchi et al. 1994:56–57; my translation). At the bottom of the hierarchy of school governance are the *consiglio di interclasse,* the interclass advisors, the body to which I was elected to serve and which met monthly at the elementary school. The next level of governance is the *consiglio di circolo,* literally, the advisor's circle, similar in structure to a school board in the United States. Some of their meetings were open to the public while others were closed. More general public meetings were also held at the school throughout the year.

[4]The Gentile Reforms of 1923 marked the initial step toward creating a closed system. An anti-semitic School Charter of 1939 rendered the system even more closed. Moreover, the 1939 charter aimed to discourage "the educational and occupational aspirations of some students," that is, to prevent those from the lower socioeconomic strata from attaining higher levels of education. Hence Bottai, the regime's strongest ideologue, sought to squash "illusory ambitions" as early as possible, transforming the lower secondary into "a true dumping school." See Barbagli 1982:7, 204, 209.

rise to a concept of hegemony that became popularized in American anthropology especially in the 1980s and 1990s. As applied to Italian education, the reformers sought to use Gramsci's ideas to create an "open" system. In 1962, the reforms led to the establishment of the *scuola media unica,* or a unified middle school, and opened the university to students from any type of 5-year high school. Egalitarian values emerged as central and strong. The reformers put great hopes in schools as a place to equalize class differences. In addition, the reforms reconfigured the relationship between parents and the schools. New structures, like the decree of 1974 that required elected representatives from every classroom, lent a political flavor to the school-related involvement of parents.

The struggle over the school scheduling allowed insight into school-community politics and positioning, particularly as the conflict became heated in January 1997. The class representatives of the entire school set out to survey parents' views of the time change. By law, in order to distribute such a survey and letter inside the school, the parents needed permission from the *direttrice,* or superintendent.

Parents felt deeply that the law must be respected: *Non si può andare al di là della legge,* or It's not right to go outside the law; respect it until it's changed. So when Elena ran into the superintendent at the school, her response was to show her the letter. The superintendent read it quickly and said there should not be any problem. Still, she would call Elena at 9:30 the next morning. Elena went ahead that afternoon and distributed the photocopied survey to the teachers in grades 1–5 (between 30 and 50 students per grade, so some 185 letters). The following morning, the teachers put the letters in the backpack of each pupil to deliver to their parents.

At 9:30 sharp there arrived a major snafu: the superintendent phoned Elena.

"Absolutely under no circumstances can I approve the distribution of the letter!" the superintendent told her. The *comune* was putting together a committee comprised of parents, teachers, and administrators to study the problem of bus transportation and scheduling, and she did not want to appear as going against the wishes of the town.

"Outside of the school, you can do whatever you want," she told Elena. "But inside, no."

The teachers pulled the letters from every child's backpack.

The parent representatives called a semi-secret meeting. As another saying goes, *Fatta la legge, trovato l'inganno,* or Once a law is made, a way around it is found. The necessity to do something had intensified. The deadline of January 24 to sign up children for the next year was approaching. Once this deadline passed, the parents would be robbed of their ability to demonstrate to public officials their power: to use district open enrollment policy and sign their kids up at another school.

Ideas began spilling forth for how to circumvent the rules. One representative suggested that we put the letters in envelopes with each child's name written on it and pretend that it was a birthday invitation. Then the teachers would be protected from going against the director's decision. Another offered an alternative: arrive early and distribute the letters to individual children in the school courtyard before they entered the building.

I collected surveys from nearly all of the parents in my classroom. In total, some 70 percent of the parents at the school participated; 87 percent favored starting school at the regular time, 8:30 A.M., whereas 13 percent favored changing it to 8 A.M. We were on our way to realizing the ideal of *tutti insieme*, or everyone together.

As the conflict continued, I consulted frequently with Carolina. One morning our conversation turned into an argument. She thought the parents were out of line to be insisting on the 8:30 entry. She felt the parents should be arguing about substantive changes in the school.

> For 20 years, I've argued that the school should teach kids the keys to how the government functions, they should teach children about their rights, about how to be active citizens. Instead, some of my best friends, schoolteachers, go on about how they are doing all these creative things, like puppets. We need more than puppets. By the fifth grade, children should be able to attend and understand a debate at the *comune*, or county, level. Even earlier, in third and fourth grade, they should be teaching children about government. [*Fieldnotes*, March 14, 1997]

I argued that the parents (primarily mothers) were teaching about politics through example. Their intense involvement in political struggle—legitimized through legal elected representatives—perhaps set an example for their children in terms of taking responsibility and not letting government push them around. But I do not want to have the last word on this point, for Carolina's position was insightful. She was committed to cultivating a truly democratic society, one in which schools actually prepared children to become adults capable of creating a vital civil society. Could it be that more people in the United States, for example, would participate in electoral politics if children learned about politics in a meaningful way that empowered them from a young age?

Whether the parents were right or wrong in their struggle—still unresolved when I left—the structure that organized the relationship between the school, community, and parents had at least one clear consequence: it added a political dimension to the culture of responsibility. Ordinary parents, and mostly women, became cast in a role of key negotiators between their children and the state—as represented in educational institutions, personnel, and policies. One measure of women's emancipation has been their involvement in the public sphere, that is, in politics (see Scott 1986). Certainly, this school-linked democratic process created a space for parents, and especially mothers, to be involved in local politics; however, it would be misleading to say that such a structure liberated women from "child rearing." If anything, the postwar reforms politicized the educational aspects of child rearing and in this sense raised the stakes. This also raised expectations placed on mothers, for if direct participation was any gauge, mothers appeared to feel more acutely than fathers the responsibility for their children's educations.

THE TRAITOR

Tension was brewing in my relationship with Carolina. Initially, she had been excited that an anthropologist would "come all the way from America" to "study the women of Carmignano," as she thought of my project on the cultural politics of population. Despite her resentful feelings of U.S. cultural imperialism, what ever it was I was doing, she believed it would serve to recognize the importance of women and local happenings to global history. I suppose there is something seductive about being paid some attention. Yet there is a price to pay for placing oneself and one's region in a global context. It is the price of ethnographic translation. An Italian proverb would have us all traitors: *"traduttore traditore"*: a translator is a traitor.[5]

As I discussed earlier, Carolina helped me land an apprenticeship in a sweater factory, put me in touch with an oral history project, and then hired me in her own sweater-finishing firm. She became a true cultural consultant. I liked her because of her critical edge. She liked me because I listened to her. As I became involved in school politics, however, I began developing my own opinions, and the tenor of our interactions started to change. She took any and every chance to criticize my views, my work, my academic discipline, my parenting, and even my style of putting on a birthday party! Her eventual tirade spoke of someone who had come to the conclusion that her friend was nothing but a traitor. She had taken sides with the Italian playwright Pirandello, who equated translators with traitors. I, on the other hand, viewed myself as a sort of gluer of a broken vessel, to borrow Walter Benjamin's metaphor of the translator.[6] I was set on recovering hidden knowledge and stories as well as finding a way to carry them across national borders and make them meaningful in a different context.

Come February 1997, the outcome of my research was seeming intangible to Carolina, and one day while I was off in Florence, she laid into Chris, my husband.

> "At what point is Betsy in her research, anyway?" Carolina asked.
>
> She proceeded to let Chris know that she doesn't think I am serious, that nothing will come out of my research, that she doesn't plan to help me anymore, that she's already helped me too much, that I am *"furba,"* or clever, in the negative sense, and that I am just here on an extended vacation, as far as she can tell.
>
> "If I were on that committee, I would be really hard," she said.
>
> Chris let her know that it wasn't easy for me to get the Fulbright, but she didn't seem to care. "Well, I guess I'll just wait and see what comes out of her research," she said.
>
> Generally she views research as useless, that there's too much of it.
>
> Chris told me that it's clear to him that they are mystified because they can't figure out why I'm so interested in the low fertility. It's obvious why people don't have so many kids, they say.
>
> Chris said that they act like I think I am going to solve a mystery. She thinks I'm wasting my time—doesn't think I'll have anything to contribute in the end. [*Fieldnotes*, February 2, 1997]

[5]Italian playwright Pirandello was fond of muttering *"traduttore traditore."* He saw translators as traitors who could not help but betray the felt sense of his original texts. Marianna Mayer (1981:v) has rendered a wonderful translation and adaptation of Carlo Collodi's classic *The Adventures of Pinocchio*.

[6]Walter Benjamin (1968:78) wrote that, ultimately, "a translation, instead of resembling the meaning of the original, must lovingly and in detail incorporate the original's mode of signification, thus making both the original and the translation recognizable as fragments of a greater language, just as fragments are part of a vessel."

Although the seeds of Carolina's wrath had been planted, I was unprepared for the diatribe in May 1997. I stopped by her house to pick up my sunglasses one day and we got talking about the end-of-the-year school festival, which parents produced. She started criticizing their efforts.

> Carolina agreed with the teachers, whom she claimed saw the festival is nothing but a *stupidaggini,* or stupid nonsense. Really, she argued, the parents don't do it for the kids, they do it for themselves, just to make fools of themselves (essentially), just to get a laugh.
>
> "If it were me, I would put a barbed wire fence around the school, the type they used at concentration camps, and not let a parent within 100 feet of the school. Keep the parents and the representatives out of the classroom.
>
> "It's bad, too," she opined, "that they do their satire based on something from television. It's bad. It's negative. They shouldn't always copy television. It's culturally low. . . ." [*Fieldnotes,* May 8, 1997]

She was already in a spiteful mood, and so I was asking for trouble by sticking around. I was the perfect target. As an American, I was a breathing icon of U.S. cultural imperialism.

"Oh, you think you've found some *novità,* or something new," she accused.

"I don't really think I've found anything new," I laughed.

I noticed on the table the videotape of her interview with Iolanda, the deceased wet nurse who described herself as a "sold woman," and I changed the subject. The oral historian had copied the tape for me, I had transcribed part of it, but then Carolina had asked to borrow it back. "Could I consult it again?" I asked.

"No," she replied curtly. "It now goes to the son," meaning Iolanda's son. "And we've made a mistake anyway to let these interviews circulate. It's nothing but negative. These teachers, they don't know what they're doing. They use the tapes, say ridiculous things. We shouldn't have been so permissive with them."

At least, I thought to myself, she is honest.

And then she let it out: "We should only let *studiosi seri,* or serious scholars, use these tapes."

"Well," I said, daring to confront the put-down she had just dealt me, "will you give me this tape once the son has finished looking at it? After all, you've said you only want serious scholars to consult it."

She laughed. "Ha! To describe an anthropologist as serious is a contradiction in terms. What good has an anthropologist ever done?"

"Well how many anthropologists have you ever read?" I asked.

"Have I ever read? None. I wouldn't waste my time reading anything by an anthropologist."

The town had scheduled a meeting to discuss the local gypsy population and it involved collaborators of a recently published book on Rom culture. I told her that I understood that an anthropologist was among the participants.

"Oh, well I hope not!" Carolina shouted. "They're presumptuous, pretentious, and . . ."

"*Ho capito!* I get it!" I interrupted. "I've understood."

She continued, and I turned to Leonello. "Oh Leo, maybe she doesn't understand me. Can you tell her?"

Leo chimed in. "Carolina, did you hear her? She got it."

But Carolina could not stop. The bashing of Betsy continued. *"La festa della battitura,* or the threshing festival," I joked, in reference to an event that Carolina had helped organize.

Leo soon asked if I would be willing to drive Carolina up to the town hall. I agreed, by now well numbed by her assaults. Even anthropologists working in modern Western societies are not immune from objections from the "natives" to their position of power. In the car, Carolina told me of an Italian anthropologist whom she recently took out to dinner. He was telling her how he had gone to Mexico for 3 months, then had come back thinking he would write a book on Mexican religious practices. As he got to writing, he decided to stop, that he couldn't do it.

"And why? Because he is a serious person," she said, meaning that he realized he was unable to write a good book, so he shelved it.

"Well there are anthropologists who manage to write books, and those who don't manage to write books," I said. "There are those who write good books and those who don't."

She launched again into her diatribe. "There's no such thing as a serious anthropologist. Anthropologists are nothing but presumptuous. Anthropology as a discipline is worthless."

I found myself coming to the defense of a discipline I had spent so much time criticizing in graduate school. "You can't isolate anthropology like that. A lot of historians look to anthropology for its outlook on social life."

"Anyone who goes around recounting *chi siamo noi, chi sono io*—who are we, who am I—*non mi fido*—I don't trust. I don't trust you, an American. I would only trust someone who was born here, who lived many years here, who traveled the world, and who then came back here to reflect. I've been reflecting on who we are and who I am for 50 years, and I still can't tell you. So who are you to tell us who we are? I don't want *you* to tell us who *we* are or who *I* am."

"Fine," I said, "nor do *I* want to tell you who *you* are."

Her diatribe hurt. It cut to the heart of my purpose. It echoed the essence of the Italian proverb, *"traduttore traditore."* She did not view me as a bearer of meaning, an ethnographic vessel-gluer, but as a translating traitor. No matter that I did not set out to tell *her* who *she* was, my role as cross-cultural translator put me in that position even if my larger aim was to grasp the cultural politics of population. I expect Carolina came to resent the time she was spending on educating me, the American outsider. I expect she came to dislike that I was talking back and that I, as the translator, would eventually displace these original meanings as I carried them from their original context and made sense of them in another. In addition, ultimately, I would have the last word.

We reached the piazza of Carmignano, and I pulled my Fiat 127 up to the front door of the town hall. *"Lo so, io sono cattiva*—I know, I'm evil," she said. *"Spero di finire in inferno*—I hope to end up in hell."

She slid her formidable body out of the car. Just as I thought she was going to slam the door, she turned and leaned back toward me. She spoke with a softened, warmed tone as she said, *"Vieni a trovarci*—come and see us."

THE CRAFT OF MOTHERHOOD

I had other circles of knowledge to fall back on. I had befriended Anna, the vocal critic at that first school meeting, along with an unlikely group of five women friends. Our conversations taught me much about how individuals experienced the culture of responsibility. In their mid-thirties to early forties, these women represented a broad swath of class backgrounds, occupations, and political per- suasions. Anna worked as a wholesaler in the gift sector, had two children, and supported the neo-fascist political party. Chiara sewed sweaters from her home, had three children (including twins), and was a class-conscious moderate leftist. Beatrice, an avid reader and mother of three, had given up work as an accoun- tant to tend to home and family, and she was a politically moderate Catholic who loved confession. Marta traded in secondhand clothing to Africa, had one child, and was an ardent fascist who bragged about the photo of Benito Mussolini she displayed in her entryway. Roberta was begrudgingly unemployed, had two chil- dren, and was explicitly racist against southern Italians and *extracommunitari,* or non-European immigrants. Spontaneously, the group of us began meeting each morning, after dropping off our children at the school to share a coffee together before setting off for the day's work.

> A strange little man approached our table. He was always trying to get our atten- tion—my attention in particular. Is it the anthropologist's curse that outsiders in a community cling to us, a case of outsiders attracting outsiders?
>
> "What do you all do here?" he asked. "You're incredible. Why, you meet here every morning?"
>
> "*Si prende un caffè insieme*—we have a coffee together," replied Chiara, the mother of three who finished sweaters in her home. "Like this, we're better able to face the day."
>
> "What *mestiere,* or trade, do you do?" he continued.
>
> "*Mestiere di mamma*—the craft of motherhood," replied Anna.
>
> "*Mestiere di mamma?*" the man repeated. "I've never heard of mothering as a trade, a profession."
>
> "You've never heard of it?" she asked in disbelief. "It's as old as the world!"
> [*Fieldnotes,* February 28, 1997]

Various aspects of the *mestiere di mamma,* or the craft of motherhood, were discussed during the 8 months we met over coffee, from early fall through late spring, 1996–97. These women became important cultural consultants. They taught me about the meaning of the culture of responsibility. Spending time with them was an education in how one group of confidants felt and dealt with cul- tural expectations of responsibility.

Striving to promote children's education manifested itself in the ethic of doing things *perbene,* or well, and this weighed particularly heavily on mothers. Teachers integrated *quaderni,* or notebooks, centrally into their teaching. Parents—usually mothers—were expected to ensure that schoolwork done at home followed the teacher's specific guidelines. In these notebooks the children were taught to organize their work, to do things with precision and order. First- graders learned and practiced a beautiful cursive penmanship. (In my daughters' public school experiences in Tucson, Arizona, between 1997 and 2000, and in

Amherst, Massachusetts, between 2000 and 2003, cursive was not regularly used until the later grades of elementary school, and even as late as sixth grade a number of children complained about having to write in cursive.) The Italian children were taught, encouraged, and permitted time to draw elaborate pictures to accompany math, science, and writing assignments. This approach attested to a value placed on detail. Furthermore, the notebooks served as a record of the children's hard work as well as a testament to the parents' responsible child rearing. Parents kept these notebooks as a sort of archive of the child's life. When I mentioned to several of my Italian friends the absence of notebooks in my experience of U.S. elementary schools and the overwhelming presence of random loose worksheets, they expressed horror. Several people went so far to tell me that these notebooks were important to their children's identity formation. They gave them a sense of personal history and, unlike loose papers that beg to be thrown away, the in-tact notebooks bespoke of important objects to be cherished. Such an emphasis on quality did not, however, happen by itself. A significant amount of daily homework was expected beginning in first grade. Mothers of fourth-graders told me they regularly spent hours helping their children each evening with their homework. I sensed a higher premium on nurturing a child than on cultivating independence.

Roberta, the coffee mom with two sons, one day expressed concern over her fourth-grader's inadequate reading abilities. She was angry, irritated, and nervous. Since she did not have a job, she felt the full burden of her son's failure.

"Children are really just the mother's," Roberta lamented one morning to us. "They're just her responsibility."

Her son's teacher had sent home a note asking how much time her son read. In an exasperated yet self-righteous tone, Roberta told us she wrote, "He did not want to read," and then signed her name. She said she felt the burden acutely because she did not work—several years ago she had quit a temporary job as a garbage hauler—a job she attributed to equal employment laws. Now a full-time mom, she felt at wit's end. I attributed her sense of exasperation to the culture of responsibility. Ensuring that the children did well rested heavily on the mother and required self-sacrifice to *stare dietro ad un figliolo,* literally to stay behind a child, meaning to guide a child attentively.

The local mover and shaker Carolina, and even her 21-year-old son, Iginio, chastised me for being too free with my daughter. I apparently was violating the local adage to *stare dietro ad un figliolo.* My style of American parenting was one aimed to foster independence in my child. As time passed, I began to question my approach. I began to feel strange about leaving Hollis to dress herself, something she had been doing since in preschool in Tucson, where even mismatched clothes were celebrated as a show of the child's independence and creativity. But in central Italy, even my 5-year-old began to notice that the children did not dress themselves. One evening when I returned from my volunteer shift working in the pizzeria at the *Casa del Popolo* to fetch my daughter from a friend's house, the mother of the other child retrieved Hollis's coat and helped her put it on. My daughter usually put on her own coat—at least she used to. I was suddenly finding her expecting me to dress her, to choose her clothes, just as she saw her little Italian friends' mothers doing for them.

Mothers played a pivotal role not only in nurturing but in upholding a cultural value placed on egalitarianism. One manifestation of this ethic was in sending the child to school in the required *grembiule,* or smock. The smocks, Carolina told me one day while I was sewing buttons onto sweaters in her workshop, were once known as *copra miseria,* or covers for poverty. They were used to hide ragged clothes. The idea was to minimize differences and make all the children appear equal. The practice of wearing smocks was a strategy for putting the brakes on status competition. The mothers in my coffee group told me they found the wearing of smocks helpful and convenient because "it takes a lot to dress a child every day." The dressing of a child fell on the mother, who had to make sure clothes not only matched, but that they were perfectly cleaned, ironed, and orderly *che si fa figura*—so that one makes a good impression. The smocks took off some of that pressure at least for weekdays.

Given the pressures of a middle-class consumer society, however, holding fast to egalitarian ideals was no easy feat. Mothers felt constant pressures to finagle one's way around the ideal in favor of status displays. My first brush with this contradiction occurred when I was trying to purchase a school smock for my daughter.

> The smocks are not all equal. They range in price from 22,000 lire to 134,000 ($13 to $80), as I saw in a boutique window in Florence the other day. And to find the right size for Hollis has been a nightmare. Once we found the right size, she didn't like it. She preferred a plain black one with a pretty lace collar as opposed to the black smock with cutesy appliques. [*Fieldnotes,* September 10, 1996]

We eventually found a smock of the low-cost variety for Hollis at a local dry goods store. The ideal to equalize difference was obviously easily betrayed by the desire to differentiate; the possibilities for indulging in strategies that set oneself and one's children apart from the rest were infinite in a "hot" consumer economy (Friedman 1997).[7] That women were primarily responsible for the presentations of their children reminded people that low fertility rates did not eradicate gender roles or ideologies.

RESPONSIBILITY AND FOOD

Food was a hotly debated topic in Italy. Whether in the context of school or home, the topic became even hotter when it came to feeding children. Providing not only nourishment but also well-being and pleasure through food was a primary preoccupation of Italian parents and, in particular, mothers.

I encountered deep concerns on the part of parents in relation to food. At a parent-teacher meeting in January 1997, the teachers had gone through the details of the new grading system and explained the content of the educational program for the upcoming year. Not one question followed. Then the subject of

---

[7]Historian Paul Ginsborg (1990:408) writes, "By the late 1980s Italy claimed to have overtaken Britain, to become the fifth largest industrial nation of the Western world, after the United States, Japan, West Germany, and France. Giovanni Goria, then Treasury Minister, first made this claim in January 1987. It has been hotly disputed ever since." See also "The Economist: A Survey of the Italian Economy," *Italian Journal* 1988 (1): 31–48.

the *mensa*, cafeteria lunch, was raised and mothers complained with one concern after another.

"The pasta is overcooked," complained one mother.

"The kids don't eat it," added another.

"There are not enough places for children to sit on Wednesdays and some children remain standing," chimed a third.

All the children ate together family style; children were not allowed to bring a sack lunch to school. This reinforced the group ethic. If a parent objected to the menu, he or she could pick up the child and feed the child at home.[8] Most parents, however, chose to have their children eat at school. There, a hot meal consisted of three courses: a pasta or rice dish, followed by a protein dish and vegetable, and usually finished off with fresh fruit.

The intense attention to food was evident in talk, at meetings, and in the newspaper.[9] Indeed, food was a political matter. There was even a *Commissione Mensa,* a school lunch commission, whose members sampled the public lunch food. When as class representative I telephoned other parents to ask them about their concerns, they often mentioned school food. Some mothers expressed concern that their child returned home from school hungry; others asked whether a certain dish might be eliminated from the menu; still others suggested that the school give children a choice so that if they did not like a particular main course, at least they might have an alternative, such as prosciutto. A fellow U.S. Fulbright scholar, an historian also doing research in Tuscany, told me the parents of his child's school nearly went on strike when they learned that the school was importing a cheap variety of olive oil rather than using the prized local but more expensive oil. Finally, at the *consiglio di interclasse,* or the meeting of the advisory group, the school lunch was a regular subject of heated debate. My doctor friend Marco, despite his complaints of the mothers' constant talk about food, served as a quality-control inspector of the local food preparation site. Members of the volunteer committee dropped in on the district's kitchen and sampled foods in an ongoing effort to ensure not only cleanliness but good taste.

In the Carmignano elementary school, not only was quality an issue, but lunch was viewed as an important time for children to socialize. Children were given ample time (about an hour) to eat their family-style meal. In U.S. schools, where children can bring a packed lunch from home or choose hot or cold school lunches, my daughter experienced lunchtime as a period of stress because so little time was permitted for eating: 20 minutes to a half hour. In my daughter's Amherst school, the children were told not to talk at lunch, and when they did, a cafeteria monitor had the habit of punishing them by turning off the lights in the room. By 2003, a movement had begun to address food quality and ambience issues.

In Carmignano, the topic of food similarly arose during a meeting I attended to organize a childcare cooperative for infants and toddlers. The county had a public *scuola materna,* or a preschool-kindergarten, but children had to be at

[8]Grades 2–5 at the elementary schools in Carmignano went from 8:30 to 4:30 three days a week, and on those days lunch was served at school; two days a week school went from 8:30 to 12:50 and children went home for lunch; first-graders had only two long days and three short days. The extra afternoon for the older children allowed for foreign language instruction in French or English.

[9]"Cosa si dice della mensa?" *Nuova Proposta,* Gennaio-Marzo, 1996, p. 1.

least 3 years old to attend. Parents with young children had a difficult time finding childcare for their infants and toddlers. The few sites that did exist had waiting lists and required questionnaires that ranked parents according to need; for example, if the child had grandparents or other close relatives living nearby, they were assigned low priority for placement.

The jeans-wearing daughter and heir of a local count, whose wine and olive oil estate she managed, raised concerns over environmental pollution of local crops. As a candidate for local political office, Sofia informed the audience of her knowledge that grapes grown in the town with the lowest altitude and closest proximity to the busy streets that carried traffic to the industrial district of Prato contained a much higher level of lead than those grown on the nearby hilly slopes.[10]

Several mothers voiced their preference for a preschool cooperative offering a *dieta biologica,* or an organic diet, based on the Mediterranean cuisine. For children to bring a sack lunch would be unthinkable; they must have their pasta and main course for lunch, and they must all eat the same food as eating was seen as a crucial aspect of socialization. This particular group of women, some professionals, others artists, viewed themselves as progressive and so perhaps it was no surprise that they poked fun at themselves for having returned to the topic of food. As one mother put it as the meeting came to an end, *"Sempre si torna a mangiare"*—"It always comes back to eating."

A mother's concern with food starts when her child is an infant. My daughter's best friend's mother, Gabriella, told me she weighed her infant each time before and after he nursed to be sure he had eaten enough. This practice appeared widespread.[11] Coffee moms Anna and Beatrice recalled with great pride weighing their infant after each nursing. Roberta, on the other hand, told me she purposefully weighed her infant only every other day so as not to develop a *fissazione,* or obsession, with the infant's weight. As the infants grew old enough to eat solid foods, I learned with awe the special broth mothers prepared daily for them. Gabriella emphasized to me that it must be prepared fresh each day. Pediatricians regularly gave new mothers specific instructions and recipes for introducing their infants to solid foods. They strongly discouraged certain ingredients. The recipe contained great attention to detail (Figure 6.2).

Frequently I heard stories of mothers going to extreme lengths to fulfill their *doveri,* or responsibilities, concerning food preparation. One of coffee mom Marta's neighbors, originally from Russia, had married an Italian, and appar-

---

[10]A positive correlation between altitude and heavy metal contamination in olive trees is discussed in Giovanni Ignesti et al., "Polycyclic Aromatic Hydrocarbons in Olive Fruits as a Measure of Air Pollution in the Valley of Florence (Italy)," *Bulletin of Environ. Contam. Toxicol.* 48 (1992):809–814. Maura Lodovici et al. (1994) discusses similar contaminants found in the Valley of Florence in the bay evergreen tree in "Polynuclear aromatic hydrocarbons in the leaves of the evergreen tree Laurus nobilis." *The Science of the Total Environment* 153 (1994):61–68. My thanks to Luca Giovannini for these references.

[11]Elizabeth Whitaker (2000) argues that the practice of weighing infants dates to the fascist era and its obsession with modern, scientific mothering. When an infant's breast milk intake did not "measure up," so to speak, pediatricians advised women to "top off" the nursing session with formula. This practice, combined with rigid feeding regimens that forbade feeding-on-demand and night nursing, as well as co-sleeping, contributed to insufficient milk production and hence undermined a mother's ability to breastfeed successfully. Whitaker argues these practices persist.

Il brodo di verdure si prepara con verdura freschx di stagione adatte al bambino.	Prepare the vegetable broth with fresh vegetables in season suited to the infant.

Ingredienti:	**Ingredients:**

2 patate	*uno zucchino*	2 potatoes	a zucchini
2 carote	*fagiolini*	2 carrots	green beans
un gambo di sedano	*bietola o spinaci*	a stalk of celery	beet greens or spinach
(pomodoro)		(tomatoes)	

ed altre eventuali varietà di ortaggi momentaneamente disponibili.	and other garden varieties that may be available in season.
Sono da evitare cavoli, cavolfiore, verze, cipolle, che hanno aromi troppo forti e spesso sgraditi al bambino.	Broccoli, cauliflower, savoy, and onion have strong flavors and should be avoided as they often disagree with the infant.
Queste verdure da utilizzare devono essere ben pulite, lavate, tagliate a pezzetti e fatte bollire in acqua NON SALATA sino a ridurre il volume a metà (mezzo litro—uno o due ore circa di bollitura).	The vegetables used must be well cleaned, washed, cut into pieces, and boiled in UNSALTED water until the volume is reduced to half (a half litre—about one to two hours of boiling).
Per le prime ministrine, si utilizzano circa 250 cc di brodo. Dopo 10 giorni è utile aggiungere 1–2 cucchiai di verdure passate.	For the first soup, use about 250 cc of broth. After 10 days it is useful to add 1–2 tablespoons of puréed vegetables (use a foodmill).
Nel brodo si aggiunge alternando:	Alternatively, add to the broth:
▪ *crema di riso o semolino di grano duro o fiocchi (2 cucchhiai) di 5 cereali o 15–20 gr. di pastina.*	▪ Rice cereal or semolina (2 tablespoons) or 15–20 grams of fine pasta.
▪ *Inoltre si aggiunge olio di oliva extravergine crudo: Cucchiaini n. 2.*	▪ In addition, add 2 teaspoons of raw extra virgin olive oil.
▪ *Parmigiano reggiano grattugiato: Cucchiaini n. 2.*	▪ 2 teaspoons grated Reggiano parmesan.
▪ *Varie come carne omogeneizzata, liofilizzata o disidrata secondo parere del pediatra.*	▪ Various ingredients such as homogenized, freeze-dried, or dried meat according to the pediatrician's preference.
Dopo 10 giorni, la seconda minestra con formaggino.	After 10 days, (serve) the second broth with soft cheese.

Figure 6.2 Recipe for first vegetable broth

ently the wife was more interested in fashion than food preparation. Every day her husband's mother came from Prato to cook lunch for her son and grandchild, then went back to Prato, and for dinner returned to cook again for them. The other women were outraged that the wife did not accept her *doveri,* or responsibilities.

"Oh come on," Anna said. "We women are *grulle,* fools. Look, she has figured out something that works for her. Why do we have to criticize her for it?"[12]

Italian women historically have derived power from their domestic-related work, particularly food preparation. Carole Counihan has suggested that Italian

[12]*Fieldnote,* February 21, 1997, "gender, *doveri.*"

women have perpetuated their power as wives and as mothers through food: "The power of women is to a great extent the power of food" (Counihan 1988:52). Local values about food were key for understanding this source of power. Children were reared to have strong opinions about what ingredients mixed well with which foods. Value placed on eating and on food preparation also reflected an acute concern with raising healthy and well-nourished children who were socialized into coming together *a tavola,* or at the table. Women and men, young and old, expended a tremendous amount of energy talking about food (although I did meet several women, mostly single in their twenties, who rejected cooking altogether). Even teenage boys and single musicians could be heard expressing strong opinions about food preparation—for example, which dishes required parsley and which required basil.

Many modern Florentine/Tuscan dishes blended *la cucina povera,* or peasant recipes with bourgeois and noble ones (see Rosi 1996:5). Central Italians valued foods prepared with great attention to process, passion, and simplicity using the freshest of ingredients, such as herbs gathered from the field, mushrooms from the forest floor, and olive oil from the local olive trees. Unlike France, where gastronomical status was conferred on elaborately worked dishes, home-style cooking was highly valued in central Italy (Della Croce 1987:6–7). Hence, attaining status through food preparation was within striking distance for ordinary mothers.

In the rural-industrial counties where I conducted research, the freshness of foods was essential. The art of cooking had many secrets, as did the art of eating—which as my sweater-maker friend Oliviero once told me, half joking, was also a *mestiere,* or an occupation. It was principally mothers who assured that the craft of eating could take place, particularly on Sundays. Like all of the dimensions of the craft of mothering, feeding was also an expression of love; a nutritional diet that was also pleasurable ensured a healthy and happy child. The role of not only socializing children but "socializing taste" to teach that food was not merely an obligation but a source of pleasure rested largely on mothers, who remained the ultimate source of food pleasure (Ochs et al. 1996).[13] As a form of power, however, food remained an ambiguous source. As much as food has given women the power to nurture, it has also reinforced narrow definitions of women as nurturers. Perhaps it is no surprise that Carolina, a woman who was committed to forging a democratic family, had a husband who did most of the cooking so she could devote time to local and regional politics.

The proposition that decreased fertility liberates women from the home ignores the ways in which gender ideology ensures that women largely assume the major parenting responsibilities, such as educating, feeding, and clothing

---

[13]Ochs et al. (1996) documented linguistic practices at mealtime to detail differences between U.S. and Italian parents' approaches to children's eating. In both cases, children were socialized to view food as nutrition, food as reward, food as material good, and food as pleasure. But there were important differences. The American families involved in the study tended to emphasize the reward aspect of food. Desserts were frequently framed as "a treat, a reward, an indulgence" and were construed as "what their children *want* to eat" as opposed to vegetables and meats, "what their children *have* to eat" (p. 22). In the American families, linguistic exchanges often took the form of threats ("If you don't eat x, you won't get dessert") so that dessert became a "conditional pleasure" (p. 23). The researchers did not find this dynamic of threats and promises in the Italian families studied. Rather, the emphasis was on cultivating taste and experiencing pleasure.

their children. Italian women received a certain type of power and respect from these endeavors but that power was limited because it was valued less than official politics and professional labor.

THE MEN IN THE HOUSE (MYTH #3)

The third myth concerns the "who" of low fertility. It presumes that the quiet revolution is primarily about women. Truth is, family-making is equally about the relationship between women and men: how men relate to women, whether their mothers, daughters, lovers, or wives.

Children were by no means a prerequisite for conventional gender roles or for gender struggles within a marriage, as Oliviero and Luisa's relationship reminded me. One day, Luisa's university-student cousin made a timely visit that prompted commentary on ongoing gender strife.

> "Oh I have so much to do tomorrow," Luisa lamented. She listed off the things she had to do: finish sweaters in the workshop, do the laundry, go grocery shopping, and prepare meals.
>
> "Imagine her with four *bambini*," said Nicolina, the cousin in her twenties.
>
> "Poor thing," I said. "She has to cook every day, every meal. I only have to cook three meals a week. My husband and I have an agreement."
>
> They laughed.
>
> The conversation turned to men, Italian men. Oliviero would go to the *Casa del Popolo*, the local people's house, known locally as *il bar*, most every evening, and Luisa stayed home, cleaned up the kitchen, then joined her mother for several hours of television watching and chatting. Even young men are this way, Nicolina said, because their mothers do everything for them.
>
> "The men can't do domestic work," added Nicolina, who then made a fist and ground it into the palm of her hand to indicate how hard Italian men are. And then Luisa admitted she doesn't like Oliviero to do the laundry. She's picky about how the wash is done.
>
> "Look at her hands," Nicolina said.
>
> They were covered with a white chalky residue, film from the laundry detergent. She uses so much.
>
> I commented about the well-laundered, well-ironed pressed shirts of Italian men. They nodded. *La bella presenza*, or looking good; creating *la bella figura*, or a good impression in terms of appearance, was so important. And the labor required to do so fell largely on the women who were their wives or mothers. [*Fieldnotes*, December 27, 1995]

Attending to the domestic tasks and keeping her husband presentable kept Luisa running without being a mother. Furthermore, the unpaid domestic work that women such as Luisa performed for the benefit of their husbands revealed how patriarchy continued to be reproduced. The rigid patriarchal family form had disappeared but it left visible traces. Women's efforts at keeping their husbands and sons "presentable" was a case of their consenting to a gender ideology rooted in old patriarchal forms. And yet it was complex because they also derived power and respect from their well-nurtured and impressive menfolk.

Carolina objected to this limited form of power, and her daughter, Catrina, was her gender-equality project. Catrina was about as tough as her mother. She wore her hair short so it fit easily beneath her helmet as she rode her moped, regardless of the weather, to the University of Florence. Catrina in July 1996 found herself involved with an engineering student who was almost as smart and attractive as she was. Problem was Arturo suffered from an affliction of the *famiglia lunga,* or prolonged family: He was a *mammone,* or mamma's boy, a term for men who are overly attached to and excessively dependent on their mothers. One day, Catrina told me a story that revealed how the indulgences of mothers, and the willingness of sons to go along with them, shaped romantic relationships between men and women. Catrina and Arturo were on a camping trip when their contrasting views of gender roles came to a head.

"*Se mi ami*—if you love me—you'd wash my sweater," Arturo insisted. "My old girlfriend washed my sweater."

Catrina refused. Arturo got mad. *"Non mi curi abbastanza,"* or "You don't take good enough care of me," he complained.

Carolina was well aware of her daughter's boyfriend's attitude. She told him: "You've been ruined by your mother." The struggle continued a week later:

> Carolina, Catrina, and Hollis were sitting on the edge of the bed. Arturo was standing in the middle of the room, beneath a whimsical mobile. When I walked in, he left. I showed Carolina photos from Tucson and Oregon; she showed me photos of the construction of the town's museum park, with its striking bronze sculptures. Carolina called to Arturo. She asked what sort of farewell gift he was planning to buy for Catrina, who was soon heading north for an engineering job. Carolina predicted they would split up.
>
> "He's not a modern guy; he's *arretrato,* or backwards," Carolina accused.
>
> Arturo launched into offensive mode, bragging about how Catrina had washed and then ironed a sweater of his this morning. He liked a woman who did this kind of thing for him.
>
> For Carolina, it was all her struggles up in smoke. [*Fieldnotes,* July 21, 1996]

Carolina had fought hard for a democratic family and did not want to see her daughter succumbing to doing domestic chores for her boyfriend.

About 6 months later, in late December 1996, Luisa's cousin Nicolina invited me to go with her and a group of friends to the seacoast town of Viareggio for a dinner. Nicolina had told me stories about her mother's generation's fastidious attention to the house, to the point that it became an obsession. She talked of it almost as a sickness. So I was particularly struck when, in the middle of unwrapping sausages that the men were preparing to grill outside, the women poured themselves some champagne and toasted their generation: "*A noi ganzissime donne*—To us ultra-cool women. *Perchè non si pensa sempre alla pulizia*—because we don't always think about housecleaning!"

Challenges to unequal gender roles have emerged in the context of broader societal changes. In the 1960s, throughout Europe the generation of adults born in the immediate postwar era promoted new models of family-making, according to Italian sociologist Paolo de Sandre (1997). No longer did sex, marriage, and procreation go hand in hand. In most of Europe, birth control methods became diffuse as did cohabitation.[14] Italy, however, took a different course. Divorce was legalized in 1970 and confirmed in a popular referendum in 1974. Reforms in family law soon followed, but as of the 1990s, cohabiting unmarried couples were rare (3 percent in 1995). While birthrates ranked the lowest in the world, birth control methods remained relatively "traditional," and young adults lived with their parents longer than ever. A 1995 study found that 65 percent of males and 50 percent of females aged 18–34 were still living in their family of origin.[15]

The strong attachments between parents and their children, ironically, have created deep apprehension among grown-up children in terms of starting families of their own. The attentive style of modern Italian mothering creates strong attachments between children and their parents. It also plays into the hearts and minds of singles, who postpone their own family-making altogether. Education and professional pursuits among young adults figure into the family-making patterns, as does a rigid labor market. In part, adults of prime child-bearing age delay or forgo having children due to struggles over gender roles, desires for individual satisfaction, and—particularly on the part of young women—suspicions about boyfriends who are *mammoni*.

I felt this orientation rubbing off on me, especially during my second year in Italy. I began to see my parenting attitudes and practices as not "normal" but decidedly American. In my daughter's peer group back in Arizona, for example, 6-year-old girls widely and willingly had sleepovers. While my daughter fearlessly accepted invitations for sleepovers at her close Italian friends' houses, her Italian age mates did not do so. It seemed to sadden my friend Gabriella that Hollis was so free to leave me. "It's as though she's not enough attached to you," one mother lamented during a January 1997 hike. My daughter's independence had seemed perfectly natural in the context of the United States, and I had welcomed it. But then I began to realize how culturally specific her behavior was. Oliviero had marveled enthusiastically at Hollis's ability as a 4-year-old to tie her own shoes. Although I enjoyed the democratic parenting style that I had cultivated with my husband, my daughter's independence began to concern me. I was finding myself wanting her near me more and deriving satisfaction from the affection that came from tending to details: tucking in her shirt, washing her, fixing her fresh *brodo,* or broth, and lasagna once a week. In sum, I was feeling the need to *curare,* or nurture, her more attentively, and I found myself worrying about and attending to what and when she was eating. I found myself

---

[14]de Sandre (1997:66) notes that family diversification in other European nations was also marked by a precocious exit of young adults from their family; high level of instruction among youth; immediate access to work in a flexible marketplace; housing access facilitated by public assistance or easy credit; liberal and Protestant cultural context; populations that have already realized the demographic transition of the 19th and 20th centuries. Italians share the pursuit of higher education and the demographic transition; however, the other characteristics are largely absent.

[15]A series of national surveys confirmed that the trend of the prolonged family increased from 1983 to 1995. In a 1995 study, in the 18–34 age group, 64.9 percent males and 49.8 percent females were still living in their family of origin (de Sandre 1997:67–72). In a 1991 study of Tuscany, 82.6 percent of males and 74.8 percent of females from 20 to 25 years old still lived at home whereas for 25–29 years old, 54.5 and 37.5 percent males and females lived at home respectively. (Cited in Mencarini 1994:70–74.)

limiting her freedom. As an American, I had been cultivating in my child a sense of independence. In the Italian context, I began to see this independence at the expense of attachment and attentive nurturing.

In part, the gut-wrenching move from Nicoletta's apartment to the farmhouse made me appreciate how hard it must be for Italians, particularly sons, to leave their parents' homes. I began to see the pattern of Italian students living at home as having numerous benefits. The roughing it that we Americans endured after graduating from high school and going away to college seemed cruel, even barbaric, compared with the nurturing that the young Italian adults enjoyed.

A majority of children, especially males, continued living in their childhood home whether they were young adult workers from working-class families or students from well-off families. The increasingly late exit from the family postpones marriage and procreation. The average age of first birth among the generation of women born in the 1960s has risen to 29–30 years old. Ultimately, adult children find it convenient to have their parents—mostly mothers—prepare them meals, do the housecleaning, wash and iron their laundry, and, in varying degrees, support them financially. For their autonomy, these grown-up kids show their parents respect: contributing to household finances, letting their parents know when they will be home. A major use of *telefonini,* or cell phones, was adult children calling home to tell their parents whether they would be joining them for lunch or dinner. Parents did not tend to hassle children about not showing up as long as they had checked in.

The rapport between female university students and their families was the topic of study for one of demographer Massimo Livi-Bacci's protégés, Letizia Mencarini (1994), who shared with me the findings of her research at the University of Florence. She sampled several hundred women attending the university and concluded that the family served as an important source of support for these students' formative experience: the family guaranteed "economic tranquility."

Mencarini, who admitted to me that she was still living at home while pursuing a doctoral degree, not surprisingly had a mixed take on the prolonged family trend. On the negative side, a new but persistent *familismo,* or family-centeredness, from the Catholic tradition created an "eternal baby." The adult child found him or herself in a relationship of "dependence" and covered in a "warm and suffocating embrace." This led to a syndrome of *"giovinezza che non finisce mai,"* or youth that never ends; the longer young adults live at home, she suggested, the longer they live a protected life and refuse responsibility for their own existence. On the positive side, she argued that the trend represents a process of democratization and modernization of the Italian family where children postpone leaving because, in general, they like their parents' home. They have managed to carve out a vast space of freedom, respect, privacy, and autonomy unknown to previous generations. Parents and children lived according to a sort of "fraternal pact" with minimal conflict and maximal flexibility.

Mencarini highlighted a key motivation of students who lived at home: not fleeing the nest meant they were able to *"attrezzarsi meglio,"* or better equip themselves, educationally, professionally, and psychologically for the challenges and responsibilities of adult life. Living at home guaranteed *"benessere,"* or well-being, before they could assure themselves of their own economic independence. Finally, she described the prolonged family as a type of "*ammor-tizzazione sociale*," or social cushion (Mencarini 1994:70–72).

The words she chose all have strong associations with a vocabulary of economics. *Attrezzarsi,* or to equip oneself, is often used when one speaks about the material consumer goods either for oneself or for one's house. *Benessere,* or well-being, is highly associated with the material aspect of well-being, such as in the commonly uttered phrase, *il benessere del dopoguerra,* or the wealth of the postwar. *Ammortizzazione,* or amortize, is often associated with finances, such as to amortize (or cancel) a debt. The explanation that adult youth stay at home for economic reasons revealed the Italian perspective: attaining middle-class status was important, as was the role of mothers in helping their children arrive.

The practice of adult children living at home stands in stark contrast to the United States, where it is commonly said that a child is the parents' responsibility until he or she is 18 years old. The dominant view holds that they leave, go to college, get a job, get out on their own. Consider the formative experience of middle-class American college students: in my generation, setting off to college in the early 1980s, we were expected to leave home, rough it, live off Top Ramen, reside in quasi-squalid living conditions (even if we were from a middle-class family), and shop in thrift stores and at garage sales. The American undergrad often performs downward class mobility as she or he displays independence. In central Italy, by contrast, it was very difficult to find a used clothing store. Garage or "tag" sales were virtually nonexistent (although there were flea markets). As for food, students often returned home at lunchtime for a hot meal. The few times I met college students living on their own in an apartment, the standard for cleanliness commonly led their middle-class parents to pay for a house cleaner. Some Italian parents complained that their children stayed at home so long, but they continued to care for them. A divorced man in his forties described how his mother regularly came over to his house, picked up his laundry, and returned it ironed and folded.

> Now that Primo is divorced and without a wife his mother takes it upon herself to come to his house, do some cleaning and iron his shirts. "My psychoanalyst tells me to let her do it," he said. But clearly he's bothered by his mother's practices. As long as he's single, then he in effect is a part of the prior family. And as long as his mother is able, she will iron his shirts. She would feel bad if she couldn't. In fact, it would kill her. Primo is an only son. [*Fieldnotes,* April 12, 1996]

Female friends complained of their mothers' differential treatment toward their brothers in terms of cooking, cleaning, and laundering. The sentiments mothers felt toward their sons was most intensely displayed when a son married and left the family, as was made clear at the wedding of Nicoletta's nephew. The mother of the groom, Sara, cried because she had been "robbed" of her son.

One American mother, the wife of a visiting Fulbright historian, recounted to me an incident involving her 9-year-old son who, after soccer practice, called to her from the locker room. "Mom, you better come in here," he said. When she got to the other side, she saw the other mothers standing at the edge of the shower area, scrubbing their sons' bodies. I shared this story with the coffee moms, and they were not surprised. Beatrice told me that a local swimming pool had recently passed a rule forbidding mothers of sons that age from entering the locker room.

Fathers, of course, could and did also express deep attachments. During a dinner party at Beatrice's house, one of the coffee mom's husbands, in his late forties, recounted the habit of his father who called him every morning during his daily commute to another city. Another father, a neighbor of ours, regularly slept on the kitchen bench waiting for his 21-year-old son to return from the discos in the wee hours of the morning. Fathers could be affectionate, but I never heard the term *babbone* used to indicate a "daddy's boy." Indeed there was talk of the daddy's girl but this sort of attachment was not talked about, documented, nor popularized as has been the *mammone,* or mamma's boy.

The dominant cultural pull toward super-attentive child rearing echoed loudly in social commentary, individual practices, and popular culture. Even the media has taken note; coverage has presented the trend as though all Italian women willingly accept subordination. In 2001 *60 Minutes* aired a special report on *mammoni*. All the men the journalist interviewed had jobs, girlfriends, disposable incomes, and their own apartments—where they did not live. The journalist did not interview any Italian women, young or old, who were critical of this lifestyle. Rather, it showed scenes of mothers tidying up their grown son's bedrooms. A journalist interviewed an Italian sociologist:

> **JOURNALIST:** "Is this normal?"
> **SOCIOLOGIST:** "It is normal from an Italian point of view. You know why? Because the family in this country is still a powerful and essential institution. The family is there to stay forever. And the mother, the mother is the center, the pivot of the family."

The sociologist went on to explain that the prolonged family stems from the rapid transformation that left Italy industrialized overnight. "We have our feet in an industrial society, but our heads, our values, are still back in the past. . . . a beautiful past with a nice obliging mother. . . . still washing underwear."

Italians certainly arrived at yuppiedom later than their American or French counterparts (The Economist 1998); however, the perspective of the obliging mother portrays a distorted, stereotypical, and timeless view of Italian women. I played the *60 Minutes* report for an undergraduate class on Cultural Politics in spring 2003, and my students were disturbed that a news program they deemed to be respectable would reinforce such blatant stereotypes. A number of students observed that the report reinforced American ideas about what is normal and acceptable. The report exaggerated the differences. One student wrote, "Judgment is being passed from nations that perceive their populations to be more modernized to those deemed more 'backward' by their standards of gender 'equality.'" Another described the slant as a "'foreignizing' translation because it makes Italians seem like odd people with strange customs" (Tihanyi 2002:5).

Against this sociologist's depiction of a homogenous country in which all the women happily agree to washing their menfolk's underpants, my research suggested resistance to conventional gender relations. Sentiments from popular cultural sources are poignant. For example, a series of jokes that circulated on e-mail a few years ago, which a research assistant from Arizona forwarded to me in December 2000, played on stereotypes as it revealed the gender tensions:

Why are men like snails? *(Perché gli uomini sono come le lumache?)*
They have horns (i.e., they are cuckolds), they salivate and they scoot along with
a great deal of effort . . . in addition, they think the house is theirs. *(Hanno le corna,
salivano e si trascinano . . . in più pensano che la casa sia loro.)*

Why are men like sperm? *(Perché gli uomini sono come spermatozoi?)*
Because only one in a million is useful. *(Perché solo uno su milione è utile.)*

Why can't a man be both beautiful and intelligent? *(Perché un uomo non può essere
sia bello che intelligente?)*
Because he'd be a woman. *(Perché sarebbe una donna.)*

With a focus less on gender conflict and more on sentiments within the modern family, a number of popular Italian films address exaggerated attachments.
The powerful and humorous *Caro Diario,* Dear Diary (1994), depicts an adult
world turned upside down as it follows Nanni Moretti, who plays himself, in
search of a quiet place to write. He ends up on an island where everyone has only
one child. Expecting a calm environment where he can concentrate, he instead
finds a place where adults obsess over their only children, and where the only
children rule their parents' lives. In the opening scene, the mother of a toddler
says, "I can't believe that for Pietro these first years will mean nothing. He'll
never remember this period of intimacy and closeness when he needed me so
much." In another scene along the boardwalk, a father makes excuses for his 12-
year-old son who seems alienated from the adult conversation.

MOTHER: We want another child. It's only that we're afraid of his reaction. We often
ask him.
FATHER: Every two or three years. Daniele, Want a little brother? A little sister? He
gets pissed off. I'm afraid.
The mother hangs her head in embarrassment. The final, pivotal scene takes place
in the couple's house at 3 A.M., when they awaken Moretti, telling him it is "the hour
of the wolf—the hour when we're the loneliest." It is the time when Daniele, the 12-
year-old, crawls into bed with them. They then tell Moretti that their son has never
had a babysitter. "We've always stayed with him," the mother says. Adds the father:
"Always."

A pathological side of the mother son relationship is humorously addressed
in Roberto Benigni's early film *Berlinguer ti voglio bene,* I love you Berlinguer
(Bertolucci 1977), set in the outskirts of Prato. Benigni plays an emasculated
adult son of a peasant woman as he offers a comic portrayal of a mamma's boy.
He climbs in bed with his mother during a lightning storm and later grovels at
her feet, more infant than man, against her insults of "You're so ugly! I can't
stand you!" Intended as a satire of the Italian male "problem," the film provokes
us to think about the relationship between class and emotional bonds. As poor
peasants became working or middle class, they internalized a notion of the modern family that led to the phenomenon of *mammoni.* Mothers born before World
War II grew up with numerous siblings and often lived in rural poverty. They
wanted a different life for their children and tirelessly made many sacrifices. And
yet the mamma's boy syndrome foments in the potential wives of these men a
wait-and-see attitudes toward marriage.

Raffaella was a professional architect in her thirties and girlfriend of a self-acknowledged *mammone* who was a gainfully employed engineer and blues musician. She told me that women avoided rushing into marriage because they wanted to be sure their man was not too much of a *mammone*. The fear was that a mamma's boy would just be looking for a substitute mother to care for him. "In the past Italian women didn't work," she told me, reiterating that common myth, "so it was fine for them to take care of everything." She used the verb *accudire*—to look after something or to nurse, often used in reference to doing the housework. "Now women are more independent. They want a man, but they want to be sure that this man doesn't need another *mamma*. So, *si aspetta,* you wait."

Ultimately, this sentiment of attachment created a double bind for women as well as men. The men could not tell their mothers "no." Their mothers would be deeply hurt. The girlfriends cringed at the thought of becoming like their boyfriend's mothers. That women's identity in the past relied on taking care of others weighed as heavy as a nightmare on the current generation. The problem for many younger women was how to avoid making their own needs and interests subservient to those of others. Their own identities were not necessarily tied to motherhood. Paradoxically, adult men as well as women often relied heavily on the labor of the mother—Raffaella, too, still lived with her parents—as they avoided entering conventional marriages.

The prolonged family is interpreted as a sign of indulgent, suffocating, and overly attached parents, on the one hand, and as a mark of a modern and democratic family, on the other. Those who argue for the latter interpretation point to the autonomy and privacy permitted to adult children, as well as the lack of family conflict, which would result in larger numbers of adult children moving out (Rosci 1994:301–302). In any case, the prolonged family reflects both gender and class ideologies that have evolved from specific historical conditions. Italy is a country in which economic prosperity occurred very rapidly. The job market, however, was rigid (particularly for women wanting to re-enter it). Young adults living at home were well-fed, well-clothed, well-cared for, and on their way to being well-educated—all seductive aspects of attaining middle-class material conditions. These home-dwellers found tranquility in the fact that they could continue to consume in ways that signaled social victory (Wolf 1982). As Italians say, *che si fa figura,* or so that one makes a good impression. Living at home became "necessary." It was part of the "common sense" required in the flow of social relations.

MYTH PUNCTURING

The family remains a central institution of Italian society, yet because it has undergone a profound transformation in the past century, it is also a center of controversy for cultural politics related to gender. Talk about the family is inevitably moral talk. It conveys notions about acceptable norms for being a social subject in a moral universe. The three myths represent different aspects of gender strife and reveal the political character of demographic trends.

The first myth—that "before" women did not work—erases women's historic role as workers. One motive in erasing this history is to depict women as "naturally" mothers. It becomes a strategy of sneaky pronatalism—a pro birth backlash that places blame on women. Clearly, the story of the quiet revolution is much more complex than women simply choosing work over family. What needs to be remembered is that the shift to small families was in part rooted in a peasant protest against hierarchies and inequalities of the patriarchal family. Women in the province of Prato were intensely involved in the global economy as far back as the mid-1800s, through their production of Florentine hats, which were sold on the international market. Definitions of what constitutes "work" have changed, and often young women did not acknowledge the paid labor of their mothers or female ancestors. Much paid female labor occurred in the form of piecework and was often performed in the corner of a kitchen or a workshop with other women, yet women were paid minimally. The move away from a high fertility society is also about women's desire to be recognized for the important professional and household work that they have long performed and that they continue to perform.

The second myth—that low fertility delivers gender equality—ignores the power and persistence of gender ideologies that intersect with social class. Responsibility falls most heavily on mothers, who must ensure their children do things well. Much of the concern with responsible educating, feeding, and clothing is deeply connected to a postwar consumer society. In a new moneyed province like Prato, education is seen as the prime site for social mobility. In the context of the school, mothers were generally more involved in school politics than fathers. Reforms in education carved out a sphere of legitimate political participation for parents. Involvement in school politics gave women, especially, a local place to assert themselves as political citizens. Yet did this realm continue to be marked as a woman's domain, and hence was it devalued? Marco, though himself a member of the lunch inspection crew, nevertheless lamented that so many of the mothers only thought about food as opposed to curricular issues. Food at once empowered women and yet it identified them with the domestic sphere, a sphere that in the context of a market economy has long been devalued. Low fertility does not in itself bring about equality. It does not automatically unravel entrenched gender ideologies. When women have small families they often invest tremendous amounts in their one or two children. The Italian ideology that leads to intensive mothering is the culture of responsibility. Living among Italians and being a mother myself, I, too, began to feel the more intensive demands of mothering Italian style.

The third myth—that fertility decline concerns only women—can best be punctured through examining the conflict-ridden relationships between men and women, mothers and sons, mothers and daughters, wives and husbands. Gender equality is still at stake, and redefining gender relations is ongoing. Gender roles are not static; they are constantly made and remade through people's daily interactions with one another. The prolonged family creates *mammoni,* adult children who live at home ever longer. This family form has raised suspicions among single women vis-à-vis their potential male partners and has contributed to delays in marriage and family-making. The ongoing caring for adult children has depended on a gender ideology in which women's primary role has been defined as caretakers. Some women, like Carolina, fought on a daily basis to create a democratic family. Other women did their part to prolong the family and derived power from it, if only partial. This ongoing caring for adult children neverthe-less has depended on a gender ideology in which women's primary role has been defined as caretaker. Furthermore, the cultural politics of gender played out in a context in which new possibilities for class mobility and new necessities for demonstrating that mobility arose.

Just because Italian women have record-low fertility does not mean they have achieved record-high gender equality. Indeed, fierce cultural struggles around gender roles and expectations continue to play out. Some conform to dominant expectations. Others resist them. Although demographers use only women to calculate fertility rates, the record-low birthrates cannot simply be blamed on women. Low fertility is very much about struggles over male and female relations. It is about men figuring out how to be men beyond the rigid patriarchal family, and women puzzling over how to be women in this trans-forming gender regime that strives toward equality. Moreover, it is also very much about being Italian, being European, and being modern.

7/Demographic Alarms, Racial Reverberations

Cradles emptier, Italy grows only due to the immigrant supply.

—*La Nazione* (June 27, 1996)

The changing Italy remains in fact tenaciously equal to itself in inequities, with a South that chases after the North, by now aligned with the most advanced models of the industrialized West. From birthrates to occupation, from exports to consumption, the statistics seems to illustrate two different countries.

—*Il Sole 24 Ore* (December 24, 1995)

One day, while sewing buttons on sweaters in the workshop with Carolina and Leo, a repairman arrived to adjust the machines. We struck up a conversation that began innocently enough.

"Why aren't you blonde?" he asked, having learned I was American.

"Not all Americans are blonde," I said, assuming he watched too many Italian TV game shows with blonde American *bimbe* who spoke with intentionally atrocious accents.

"I don't watch TV," he countered.

"Well, do you know how many Italians came to America?" I asked.

"Those weren't Italians, they were *marocchini*, little Moroccans. Down from Rome, they're all *marocchini*. They have more Arab blood. *Non parlano neanche italiano,* they don't even speak Italian."

I glanced at Leo, sitting behind the marking machine that stamped chalk dots on sweaters for the buttons and their holes. "And what about him?" I asked.

"Where's he from?" the repairman challenged.

Leo named his town, a town near Naples, on the Tyrrhenian Sea coast.

"And do you understand him?" I asked.

The repairman was silent. He did not realize Leo was a southerner.

Carolina laughed, then shrugged. "I don't understand him because I don't speak Italian."

Leo smirked. The repairman looked embarrassed, gathered his tools, then left. [*Fieldnotes*, December 4, 1996]

The repairman's talk about southerners as another race of people baffled me. Myself a product of the racially polarized city of St. Louis, how could I grasp a form of racism not based on a black-white opposition? Moreover, I had heard stories of discrimination against Italians migrating from the South in the 1960s, but in the 1990s, with rising anxieties over non-European immigrants, I did not expect the stubborn persistence of anti-southern hostilities. The interaction opened my eyes to well-honed strategies of keeping a segment of the population down. These strategies simultaneously pointed to differences based on biological and cultural attributes. In both cases, the differences were viewed as intrinsic, immutable, and threatening.

Carolina's comment that she did not speak Italian struck me as her clever way of being contrary, a style that she took pride in and that suited her. She effectively challenged the repairman's racist diatribe. Carolina was of a family born, bred, and fed for generations in the central Italian comune of Carmignano. She was Tuscan through and through, and common sense had it that Tuscans spoke "pure" Italian. I recall one of my fellow Fulbright grantees, an American who taught Italian, assuring me in a pretentious way that I would *not* come across any dialect in my fieldwork. She was mistaken. I encountered rich variation in ways of speaking even within the province of Prato. Speech patterns, vocabulary, accent, and verb tenses varied from the "standard" and along lines of economic status, educational level, as well as rural or urban location. The Italian I learned in the field at times sounded as different as American English spoken by a TV newscaster and that spoken by a retired dairy farmer in the Missouri Ozarks.

My friends delighted in giving me examples of local expressions. Some of my favorites illustrate the drastic difference between dialect and standard Italian:

Tuscan Dialect	Standard Italian	English
dagli l'anda	*mandare via*	get out of here
in vetta	*in cima*	at the top
lessamelo!	*accidenti!*	dang!
icche glienno?	*che cos'è?*	what is it?
chetati!	*stai zitta!*	be quiet!

Dialects are full of rich variation and color, yet the instructional practices of schools, which reflect national policies, instill in people the idea that certain ways of speaking are better than other ways. For example, working-class kids in Prato grow up thinking the way they speak is ugly as opposed to beautiful, backward as opposed to modern, or bastardized as opposed to pure and proper. Despite there being numerous local dialects in central and northern Italy, the talk of the repairman revealed how language is used to stigmatize and racialize southerners as "not really" Italian. The stigmatization serves northerners' domination. It is one strategy that communicates the moral superiority of the North. How people talk can mark them as modern, as elite, as European, and as white— or conversely as backward, non-European, and racially marked.

Carolina's comment that she "did not speak Italian" identified her with the local dialect and playfully revealed her *campanilismo,* or sense of local pride.

Moreover, it was a protective gesture. Distancing herself from the standard way of speaking yet doing so from the position of a native-born Tuscan could be interpreted as a way to defend her husband and children; the repairman's linkage of southerners with "Arab blood" implicated her husband and, hence, her own children as racially inferior.

As the repairman engaged in his racist diatribe, he slipped between popular notions of race as a form of difference rooted in biology and as race grounded in culture. Biological differences in the context of racist thinking have long been viewed as innate. Cultural differences in this same context end up appearing equally unchangeable. This ethnographic encounter challenges the notion that racism in Europe is giving way to culture—that "new" forms of differences are now based on culture and not biology. In fact, the two intermingle in an ongoing dance, one in which the prominent background music finds a popular key in demographic alarm sounding.

DEMOGRAPHIC ALARMS

The notion of a hierarchy within Italy of Italianness can barely be detected in the alarm ringing over the trends of low birthrates and non-European immigration. Italians become a unified national group in the popularization of demographic trends. I have come across silly calculations of when the last Italian will be born. The *New Republic* predicted that "Italy will be a theme park in a couple of generations" (Easterbrook 1999:22). A former labor minister a decade ago called on Italians to produce more babies to stop the "armadas of immigrants" from coming across their shores (Martiniello and Kazim 1991:88). I began to wonder: How are population politics reshaping racial politics? Does the alarmism have a racial dimension to it? What role have demographers played in an expanding discourse on Italy's "demographic decline"?

I met demographer Massimo Livi-Bacci one November day in 1995 in a *caffé* in the center of Florence, in Piazza San Marco, just a block from a favorite spot of mine, Brunelleschi's Hospital of the Innocents. He was a distinguished silver-haired man who spoke sympathetically of the plight of Italian women who faced the double burden of professional pursuits and motherhood. He welcomed me to consult the statistics library of the University of Florence where he taught and oversaw research. The library held important demographic publications that I was greatly interested in consulting. I tried to be straight with him about my approach. I made clear my appreciation for his hard statistical and historical work but emphasized my allegiance to the approach of anthropologists Jane and Peter Schneider; their interpretations of fertility decline in Sicily challenged his own. He appeared nonplussed. My work really posed no threat to his. In his view, I was merely an anthropologist. I did not have hard numbers and big data sets to substantiate my claims. In the world of demography, the aggregate data set is king.

What I did have, however, was an eye for careful reading. How were cultural assumptions being constructed? I was interested in the ways scientists assert their interpretations as unquestionable truth. I was interested in finding patterns in demographers' publications. How did they speak about the birthrate issue? Did race come up? What implications might demographers' positions have for policy? I set about in the library to collect a number of articles and reports by Italian demographers. After weeks of reading and months of reflection and analysis, I identified several patterns. First, the demographers reported the birthrate as *bassissima,* or extremely low. Second, they agreed that this low birthrate amounted to a serious problem. Third, a good number of them viewed Italian procreative behaviors as irrational and even destructive.

A book with the rather nationalist title *Children of Italy* noted that the "birthrate has undoubtedly sunk to the lowest level in the world" (Volpi 1986:31). The verb choice of "to sink" suggests an undesirable process. The extremely low birthrate took experts by surprise as outlined in a report on *Three Scenarios for Population Development:* "None of the Italian scholars working on population would have thought to imagine some thirty years ago that in the '90s the average number of children per woman in our Nation would have arrived at the level of around 1.2—the lowest in the world and likely the lowest ever documented in the history of humanity for a large-scale population"(Golini et al. 1995:1). As for framing the trend as a problem, a report on *Demographic Tendencies* described the birth trends as "provoking in the population—quickly but *silently*—a true and real 'mutation,' which has in itself the potential to unhinge the whole social and economic structure of the country" (Golini 1994:8). Similarly, in an *Atlas on Aging* the authors wrote, "We have been dealing with rapid and profound transformations that have radically modified, and in some cases unhinged, the entire structure of the whole society" (Lori et al. 1995:1). Finally, the Italians responsible—those of childbearing age, and women in particular—had become irrational. A book on *Zero Growth* opens with the idea that Italian "procreative behaviors have pushed demographic trends on absolutely heterodox trajectories" and they are "very far from zero population growth that good sense suggests." Whereas some regions have "a level of denatality never touched by another consistent population in the world," other regions have indices that are "sensibly higher" (Golini 1991:vii, ix). The implication was that people living in those regions with very low birthrates had lost their senses.

The lack of neutrality in these reports startled me. Granted, I suspected that this field of study would have its biases, but I did not expect those who claimed to be scientists to be so moralistic and alarmist. They sounded the same alarms that resonated loudly in media reports and popular culture. The alarm sounding rarely struck direct racial chords, yet racial intonations could be heard as I listened closely.

RACISM CLOTHED AS CULTURE

In Europe generally and in Italy specifically some have argued that race is not based on objective somatic differences, but has become "coded as culture" (see Fredrickson 2002:8). The structures of racist ideology remain operative, but they often rely on stigmatized cultural attributes to depict groups as dangerous. Culture can seem just as innate and unchangeable. As the author of *Racism: A Short History,* notes, "It is when differences that might otherwise be considered ethnocultural are regarded as innate, indelible, and unchangeable that a racist attitude or ideology can be said to exist" (Fredrickson 2002:5). But racism is more than an attitude; as Faye Harrison (2002:148–149) reminds, it also involves an oppressive structure of inequality and power as well as related material consequences. Racial classifications themselves "derive largely from the roots and routes of international capital's tumultuous history" (Harrison 2002:149 after Wolf 1982:380). A number of prominent demographers' descriptions of social reality help to legitimize a process of rallying behind a white, European racial identity. Their narratives reveal the simultaneous cultural and biological foundations of racist agendas.

During an interview with a journalist several years ago, Italian demographer Antonio Golini launched into a defense of his alarm ringing over population decline. Golini was among the participants of a 1996 conference on population and environment in developed countries, sponsored by the Italian national research council. As Golini spoke with the journalist, he used alarmist language to describe the "inescapable" progressive aging of the Italian population. He predicted within three decades the "death" of 400 Italian *comune*, or counties: a *comune* must have a certain population to be recognized as a legitimate governing entity, and there are quite a few, particularly in mountainous and isolated areas, that have witnessed population decline. He suggested that the only solution to the problem of a rapidly rising median age of the population was to increase fertility from "only 1.1 actual children per couple to 2." The journalist challenged Golini by referring to a non-Italian demographer's estimate of an environmentally ideal population for Italy of 21 million rather than the present 57.8 million. Then he took Golini to task for waking up "the ghost of Italian extinction":

JOURNALIST: Isn't it a bit much in light of the problem of overpopulation of the Earth?

GOLINI: Effectively if we have a global view there is no problem. If the Italian population declines quickly, the immigrants will arrive and amen. But we cannot stop at this. I study Mayan civilization and just as I regret their disappearance, I can regret it if the Italian or European culture were to disappear.

JOURNALIST: So you therefore see the risk of the disappearance of Italian civilization?

GOLINI: No, it's exaggerated to say this. For the moment, we are speaking about these small villages. A fact that concerns a few hundred or thousand persons who have a marked destiny. As regards the Italian population, the discourse is more complex. (*L'Unità* 1996)

I believe the journalist effectively called Golini on an exaggeration and on well-honed alarm-sounding. Golini backed off from his initial nationalist stance, one that erased the differences, inequalities, and historic racisms within Italy and filled in that blank slate with a homogenous Italian peninsula—constructed here as the cradle of European civilization. Golini pointed to immigrants as bringing differences and hence posing dangers to national identity. He implied that immigrants were not capable of carrying forth the Italian civilization. His position assumed that Italians were the bearers of a unique humanism, and that certain cultural *and* genetic types were required to carry forth that legacy. After all, as a demographer he was talking about births.

Demographers are often silent on the subject of race, yet this silence masks the effects that alarmist claims have on racist feelings and actions. Most demographers like to appear objective but in fact many of their endeavors enable racism. They enable racism by normalizing Europeans as white and as such promoting a politics of whiteness—not as an objective skin color but as a subjective ideology that can function as an instrument of power. As I was revising this chapter, I made a trip to California to attend yet another of my father's business association meetings, the same one where I had encountered the Texans several years before. Coincidentally, one afternoon with my parents, oldest sister, and an Italian friend from Arizona, we happened on a very hip and timely exhibit, *Whiteness: A Wayward Construction,* at the Laguna Art Museum. It was particularly timely, for as an essay introducing the exhibit explained, California will be the first state in the United States to become a "white-minority society" (in Stallings 2003:9). "White privilege and presumption," writes David Roediger in the exhibit catalog, "often operate as unnoticed, as if they were natural" (2003:53). It reminded me how demographic alarmism assists in constructing Italians as homogenous, "white," and European, and that this construction is a way to guarantee and naturalize privilege. Furthermore, it is a form of demographic nationalism in which the national population is depicted at risk (see Alonso 1994, Palviarea 1996). The source of the risk is both internal—low fertility and rapid aging—as well as external—increasing immigration. Important to remember is that populations occupy territories. Through the presence of people and the production of ideas, images, and industry they create public spaces. These spaces may appear as stable as piazzas and as fickle as the media. In reality, piazzas can change dramatically as new populations come to frequent them, be they vendors, immigrants, or tourists. Similarly, the media is not as fickle as it might appear as it continues to promote dominant views. I argue the alarmism creates a raucous noise that gives legitimacy to white public space (see Hill 1998, Page 1999). The norm of whiteness only becomes apparent when potential "invaders" threaten to transform these into nonwhite spaces. The whiteness exhibit in California sought to disrupt the invisibility of whiteness as well as to make visible and validate nonwhite spaces.

Demographic discourses are a form of "elite" public discourse. Teun van Dijk (1993) observes that elite public discourses reproduce racism as well as racially based social hierarchies. Van Dijk's definition of elites includes journalists, politicians, corporate directors, academics, as well as scientists. I found that demographers' projections of zero population growth and of sub-replacement fertility levels were frequently reported in the Italian press in the 1990s and into the 2000s. Demographers, as experts, influence the media, and the media in turn influence public opinion and reproduce racist ideologies. Alarmist approaches to discussing demographic trends stimulate a climate of fear and anxiety toward immigrants.

In the contemporary era, upstanding elites tend to avoid making explicitly racist statements. Instead, they frequently use cultural differences to explain why immigration is a threat. Golini's "regret" about cultural death due to increasing immigrants who bring different cultures is a case of racism coded as culture.

The link between demographic politics and race politics has turned up in incentive programs for augmenting the birthrate. Such programs, most of which were locally based, have been run in response to the perceived threat to the Italian nation. Such programs were not meant to stimulate births of non-Europeans. A pronatalist measure proposed in May 1999 in Milan offered monthly payments of one million lire (about $600) for each birth, but it was only available to residents who had lived in the city for at least 15 years. Critics on the political left accused the proposal of being anti-constitutional and of having a racist odor. Without presenting any evidence of immigrant birthrates, the article noted, "In the shadow of the Madonna statue [atop the Duomo] are foreigners who continue to procreate while the Milanese, due to choice or economic difficulty, seem always less enthusiastic to confront the prospect of having a family" (*La Repubblica* 1999). Foreign newcomers were cast "in the shadow" of the city's symbol because they would be unlikely to qualify for the subsidy—the vast majority had not lived in the city for 15 years. Furthermore, as non-Italians they were likely to be Muslims rather than Catholics. The racist odor emanated from a sentiment of panic over perceived immigrant birthrates and from a policy of exclusion related to a particular population. A heightened sensibility to detect racist odors makes sense. Several years ago a prominent priest called for "the need to erect a Christian dike against the Muslim invasion of Italy." Given the context, smelling racism in Milan's pronatalist incentives was powerful. The seemingly innocent veil of cultural difference was lifted and its racist underside exposed. Racism clothed as culture has just as much power to exclude as does naked racism.[1]

PANIC OVER IMMIGRANTS

I did not have to look long or hard to detect a causal relationship between the increasing immigrants and the declining birthrate in terms of concerns over the future of the Italian nation. Consider a 1997 headline from *La Nazione:* "Cradles emptier, Italy grows only due to the immigrant supply." The immigrant "growth" is contrasted with native "decline." The article sets up a false cause-and-effect relationship. It suggests that international immigrants have a major impact on the Italian population. When one reads the data closely, the truth is that as many Italians migrated out of Italy in that period as non-Italian immigrants entered. The contribution of foreigners to population growth "is very modest" (Golini et al. 2000:9). Nevertheless, immigrants are often seen as a demographic threat; as opposed to being a vital addition, they are depicted at least as an uncertainty and often as "taking over" Europe.

Media coverage of demographic trends consistently depicts immigrants in a negative light and foments feelings of public panic. I have followed media coverage of immigrants on various occasions, and all too often articles contrast

---

[1]Immigration is altering demographic and cultural patterns across the country and "has led to some anti-immigration sentiment," reports the U.S. Department of State in its country profile of Italy. Religious differences have become an issue. Some Catholic higher-ups "have emphasized the difficulties in Catholic-Muslim mixed marriages" and advocated for immigration policy that would favor Catholics "or at least Christians." Church spokesmen Bologna Cardinal Giacomo Biffi in September 2000 issued a letter supporting such an immigration policy to "safeguard our nation's identity." Biffi's letter provoked protest as well as support. See http://www.state.gov, accessed March 28, 2003.

Figure 7.1 A poster hangs in the IRIS, an institute of research and social intervention: "Toward the city that changes. Piazza San Marco, Tuesday morning." Comune di Prato, Assessorato alla Cultura, BJBB Prato (graphics), Andrea Abati (photography). Used with permission.

reasonable, rational Italians and irrational, out-of-control non-Europeans. Headlines use threatening metaphors—such as "invaders"—to describe immigrants. Anxious sentiments and negative reports of the newcomer population are commonplace in the Italian media as reflected here in a sampling of headlines:

> "'The Senegalese wanted to kidnap my son,' but the police dismantled the house: In Turin, the psychosis of the immigrant" (*La Repubblica,* 1 March 1990)
> "'Casbah' in the heart of Milan; 163 Asians are living in the piazza" (*La Repubblica,* 6 November 1990)
> "Stones and clubs: the anger explodes among blacks without housing" (*La Repubblica,* 8 November 1990)
> "War in the new ghetto: Immigrants against immigrants among alcohol and knives" (*La Repubblica,* 6 November 1990)
> "Immigration, a record in Prato: 33 clandestines for every 1,000 inhabitants, nothing like it in Italy" (*Il Tirreno,* 12 November 2002)
> "Immigrants—disastrous hygienic-sanitary conditions; Three Chinese workshops closed" (*La Nazione,* 15 November 2002)

The stories rely on images that depict a society out of control. Psychosis, Casbah, stones, clubs, alcohol, knives, unsanitary conditions—all these provide a framing through which the dominant members of society can justify their intolerance as fully inevitable and reasonable.

Such themes are common in Europe. Immigration is not merely a domestic concern; it is a political concern of the European Union. After the passage of immigration legislation, the Martelli law of February 1990, Italy tried to rid itself of a negative image of having "leaky frontiers," and to align itself with other European countries to formulate a unified policy on immigration. Workers from points south and east solve European employers' demands for cheap labor. As of January 2001, Italy's national statistics institute, ISTAT, tallied 1,464,589 resident immigrants. They represented 2.5 percent of the nation's population of 57,884,017 residents. At last count, the province of Prato registered some 9,200 resident foreigners as compared with a population of 228,027, or about 3.9 percent (some 40,000 resident foreigners live in Florence and its environs, with total province population of 953,973, or 4.1 percent).[2]

The perceived threat of immigrants moving into the country sometimes takes on grand proportions with sinister consequences. The worst of these consequences is the demise of the Italian "race," a topic that is treated with both humor and venom. I have come across a number of humorous treatments of demographic decline. A cartoon that appeared in the Italian newsmagazine L'Espresso depicts a hyper-sexualized Mediterranean woman emerging from water, like a siren. A caption reads, "Italians don't want to have children anymore. They want to be free to do whatever the hell they want without too many witnesses" (see Figure 1.1, p. 3). Her eyes are half closed and seem deadened—perhaps she is drunk with sex. The figure certainly lacks the sort of sobriety that comes with responsibility. Furthermore, the female figure is racialized: dark hair, broad lips, flat nose, and she wears bracelets on her upper-arm suggestive of an African heritage. Here, Italians appear "native"; have irrational procreative practices become so modern as to make them once again primitive?

Venomous sentiments manifest fear. Alarms presume that there is such a thing as a unified, homogenous Italian race. This assumption could not be further from the truth given Italy's own history of internal racism—against not only southerners but also against Jews and gypsies. The word "ghetto" originated in Italy to refer to the segregated Jewish neighborhood of Venice.[3] The old prejudice against these historic ethnic peoples persists; however, the sentiment of widespread public panic appears reserved for immigrants.

A CRISIS OF BIRTH

I am feeling life so strongly. Fieldwork opens the anthropologist up to the world as people live it, all the pains and joys that make life just that: life. In the classroom we are largely sheltered from these realities. We window-dress emotions with a language

[2]Data compiled from "La popolazione straniera residente in Italia al 1 gennaio 2001." Roma: ISTAT, p.1. This document is available through the Internet at http://www.istat.it. Regional, provincial, and county statistics available at http://demo.istat.it. Accessed January 6, 2003.

[3]The Venetian Republic instituted the *Ghetto Nuovo* in 1516, and it was considered to be the world's first ghetto. The term *geto* is Venetian dialect for foundry; the Jewish neighborhood hosted two iron foundries. There, Venetian Jews were once confined within a walled zone and were obligated to wear red or yellow marks sewn onto their clothing as well as distinctive hats to set them apart from the dominant Christians. Two excellent books related to Italy's history with its Jewish population have been written by David Kertzer (1997, 2001).

of theory, a language of distancing life from how it is felt, how it is lived. Here in the field using theory as a distancing device becomes impossible if we are to understand the everydayness of life.

I am an anthropologist but first I am a feeling, living human being. How do I separate my work from my day-to-day life? I don't. And so, fieldwork becomes an exhausting project. Fieldwork runs into life like a stream emptying into an ocean, where the stream is my project and the ocean the world around me. [*Fieldnotes*, January 22, 1996]

Chinese immigrants are the largest population of resident foreigners in the province of Prato. The most recent available statistics showed that 4,814 Chinese make their home in the province, with the vast majority living in the city itself.[4] The presence of Chinese is further reflected in birth statistics. Officials at the hospital of Prato reported to me in 1999 and again in 2002 that births of Chinese women represent 11 percent of the maternity ward's total. The births of immigrants nationwide are 4.1 percent of the total annual births registered in Italy (Golini et al. 2000:10). What accounts for the difference is that Prato is not only an urban area but an industrial one with networks of small- to medium-sized firms that create an economy of subcontracting, hidden labor, and small workshops (see Becattini 2001). Many Italians continue to work in small workshops. A flexible economy where prices for work were frequently negotiated in verbal agreements has attracted a cheap labor supply. The above-average immigrant births may also be due to the age of the Chinese immigrant population; a good many women are in their twenties.

I was taking an adult language class at the Università Popolare in the city center of Prato when I met Maylin, a woman from China. One day, a friend of hers visited the school, asking if we had seen her. Maylin's 8-month-old baby had died in its sleep. No one had seen her for days.

Before this tragedy, I felt somewhat cold toward Maylin because she tended to make statements that struck me as intolerant. "Oh how disgusting and unsanitary that people in India eat with their fingers!" she once said. But then I read about her situation in the newspaper: The priest in the county where I was doing my research refused the previous summer to baptize her baby. Maylin and her Italian husband eventually found a priest, through her in-laws, who agreed to perform the baptism. Several months later, the baby unexpectedly died.

Maylin returned to class about 2 weeks later. After class, she rushed ahead, down the dark medieval stone stairway of the school. A political activist of Bengali ancestry from London tried to catch up and reach out to her. But his act of condolence was short-lived. He was soon turning back to join the rest of us. What should I do? As she disappeared through the door into the historic center of Prato, I dashed ahead of the others, pulled open the huge, heavy wooden door and stepped into the subdued light of the overcast January day.

---

[4]The statistics derive from ISTAT data, which reveal that among countries of origin, the largest number of foreign citizens in the province of Prato as well as the province of Florence (6,216) come from China. The next largest number of immigrants come from Albania (2,005 in the province of Prato and 5,909 in the province of Florence). See Cittadini Stranieri, Popolazione residente per sesso e cittadinanza al 31 Dicembre 2000, available online at the province as well as comune level at http://demo.istat.it/stra1, accessed January 6, 2003.

"I'm really sorry about what happened," I attempted. My voice began to tremble and I felt my tears pushing their way into public view.

At first she was silent and then she explained, "I believe in destiny. I just have to learn to accept it. But that's what's so hard."

I was awed by her strength yet worried that any moment she might run away, leaving me feeling like a rude intruder into her tragedy. I invited her to get a coffee. There was a heavy silence as she contemplated my suggestion. "Sure," she said at last. She seemed happy that I had offered.

At the bar, I ordered a *caffé macchiato,* an espresso with a shot of steamed milk, she ordered a regular *caffé,* or espresso.

"I have a daughter," I offered, as an explanation of my sympathy, and of my teary eyes.

I let my coffee sit on the counter. The story of her marriage to an Italian man, of the loss of her baby, and of her subsequent disappearance, took all my attention.

"I know I have to be strong," she told me. "I went away for 5 days, far from here, where I have a friend, to try to find work, but I couldn't so I came back. I bought a ticket to China, but I can't go back there."

"Why not?"

"No, I can't go back there because I can't run away. I can't leave this place. . . . But I would like to find another apartment. I can't live there anymore. Too many memories. . . . I just need to get out of there. . . . But it's hard. My husband is crazy, well, not crazy crazy, but he's just—. Latin men are so proud. And Westerners are so different from Chinese. He loses control."

Maylin was vague. "I just have to be strong. I have to learn how to calm him down. He's just so afraid I am going to leave him, that I am going to go back to China."

"Does his family accept you?"

"Oh yes, they're very, very good people. But they are *very* involved." She hinted about a strong Italian mother-in-law.

We finished our coffees and I offered to pay for hers, Italian style. She accepted graciously.

Maylin's painful experience of being discriminated against by a local priest and her subsequent tragedy of losing her baby were not causal events. The bad fortune of losing a baby can happen to anyone. Her experience was all the more painful given the Church's initial exclusion. One wonders whether her baby received the best possible medical care. Maylin had access to the health care system, as a local newspaper article attested her baby had recently been immunized, but she was also subject to its discriminatory treatment. Furthermore, I sensed in her an underlying sentiment of isolation despite being married to an Italian.

During my research trip in November 2002, I interviewed a Taiwanese physician who worked as a hospital translator in Prato, and we spoke of the experiences of the Chinese immigrants there. She said they often find themselves at the bottom rung of an outsourcing cycle. When the so-called giver of work says, "I want these pants tomorrow, what can they do?" They work long hours to turn around the job. "It's a vicious cycle." Moreover, the word on the street is that wages were continuing to drop. In addition to the long hours and low pay, the immigrants confront racism. As the translator put it, "It's everywhere. It's not pleasant."

Numerical, demographic descriptions of immigrants erase their humanity. They cultivate sensibilities of rejection and even dread vis-à-vis the "other" and undermine possible new worlds. Immigrants become a faceless population, reduced to pie charts, graphs, or criminals. Knowing individuals and seeing the world through their eyes leads to understanding the hardships they face in adjusting to a society that may be ready to employ them but not so ready to embrace them.

ITALY'S STRANGE RACE QUESTION

Nicoletta, my widowed landlady who had six siblings but only two children herself, told me painful stories about the racism she and her family encountered when they first moved north from Calabria, a region in southern Italy described in Frommer's as "hard-core Italy" (Porter and Prince 1997:24). The area is known for its agrarian enterprises and for its underground economy connected to the Mafia, known locally as *'ndrangeta*. Indeed, Frommer's *Italy* does not even include a section on Calabria, urging tourists to avoid it altogether. The stigma of the South remains attached to its natives as they migrate northward. When Nicoletta's family moved to Tuscany in the 1960s, the family was hard-pressed to find a place to live. The locals did not want to rent to southerners, so she and her family spent their initial years in an abandoned farmhouse. Slurs such as *terrone,* or earth grubber, as well as *marocchini,* or Moroccan, racialized southern Italians. In the postwar era of the 1950s and 1960s, southern Italian immigrants arriving in cities found job and housing ads in northern newspapers with statements such as "No southerner need apply" and "We do not rent to southerners" (Douglass 1983:183). Even restaurant doors displayed unwelcoming signs forbidding southerners to enter.

Three decades later, by the 1990s, anti-southern Italian sentiments simmered alongside anti-immigrant anxieties. Such intolerance manifested itself in the xenophobic political party *Lega Nord,* or Northern League, which in the 1990s pushed an anti-southern and anti-immigrant platform. The party's ultimate goal of dividing Italy into two countries relied on a rhetoric of superiority and old us-them dichotomies: between "natives" and immigrants, between *"padani,"* or northerners, and *marocchini,* or southerners (see Petrillo 1999:245). One of the league's recent outrageous proposals was to require that *extracomunitari,* or non-European immigrants, ride in segregated train cars. The daily newspaper *La Repubblica* lambasted the idea as "railroad apartheid" (January 17, 2003). Nevertheless, the Northern League as of spring 2003 was part of a five-party government coalition, led by right-wing Prime Minister Silvio Berlusconi (elected to a 5-year term in 2001), that included Forza Italia, National Alliance, Christian Center, and United Christian Democrats. Although extremists, the Northern League's political alliances have placed them in a position that gives them a legitimate voice in Italy's government.

The stigmatized South plays out in everyday interactions and continues to follow those who come from there like a meddlesome shadow. One day in March 1997, as I waited in the school courtyard for my daughter to emerge

Figure 7.2 A local street named for Gramsci

among the swell of children crowding at the front doors, several mothers began speaking about the recent arrival of Albanians. "Tuscans are carrying the Albanians on their backs," said one mother. She used the word *carico,* or load. She then switched her target to southern Italians. "Things are so bad in parts of Calabria that the women still have to go and bring in water from outside," she continued, pointing to the lack of infrastructure and implying that it was a backward place with backward people who prevented things from functioning. "These people don't really want to work. They're freeloaders, parasites."

A Sicilian friend of mine standing nearby took offense. She sensed hostility toward southerners and began to defend herself and her husband, who had moved to Tuscany 4 years earlier with their two children. She stressed how hard they both worked, he as a textile and agricultural worker, she as a house cleaner. "I'm allergic to dust and yet I still go and clean. I couldn't find any other work here, but I go every morning and clean other people's houses." As a southern Italian who had experienced racism and its subordination strategies, she was quick to recognize it.

A few days later, at the bar where I regularly had breakfast with a group of mothers, the conversation turned to new immigrants and gypsies. "At least the Albanians, the Chinese, the Africans, they work," Roberta said. "What do the gypsies do? All they do is rob. They freeload. There's one gypsy kid in my brother's kid's school, and that kid's parents they don't pay taxes. . . . All they do is bring children into the world and then they abandon them—throw them into the streets to beg and rob. None of them work. All the gypsy women should be sterilized."

Such comments troubled me deeply. Beyond my gut reactions, two things struck me about these conversations. First, I was amazed by how anti-immigrant talk easily shape-shifted into anti-southern Italian sentiment. The migrations of people from the south of Italy and from south and east of Italy's borders frequently blended into one another. Second, demographic themes, such as perceptions of "reckless" parenting, were often central to these daily moments of constructing one's neighbor as an unworthy outsider. Negative evaluations of reproductive practices relied on strategies of stereotyping and exclusion common to racist talk and behavior. To make sense of a form of racism not based on differences in skin color, I turn to Italy's "Southern Question."

THE "OCTOPUS," CRIMINAL ANTHROPOLOGY, AND RACIAL FORMATION

Italy's "Southern Question" refers to the persistent economic disparities between the North and the South. The South in the late 1800s and early 1900s was a land populated with a malnourished and illiterate population; the people suffered from malaria, from filth, and from the brutalities of feudal servitude due to the exploitations of a tyrannical and arrogant wealthy class (Teti 1993:12). These disparities were historically explained by way of arguments that racialized southerners, positing that they were innately inferior to northerners.

Northern Italians' prejudice against their southern compatriots extends back at least to the formation of Italy as a nation in 1861. The process of uniting Italy's disparate kingdoms and city-states was uneven. Unification benefited the North. It grew wealthy as the South grew poor. As Antonio Gramsci observed, "the North concretely was an 'octopus' which enriched itself at the expense of the South, and . . . its economic-industrial increment was in direct proportion to the impoverishment of the economy and the agriculture of the South" (Gramsci 1971:70–71). But most people did not see it that way. Rather than blaming poverty on economic processes connected to the politics of state formation, the dominant tactic to explain southern poverty relied on racial inferiority. So, the northerner reasoned, if southerners had not been able to improve their economic condition after liberation from the ruling French family known as the Bourbons, this meant the causes of poverty were to be found in innate deficiencies. Hence, southerners were construed as naturally barbaric and as biologically inferior. "Thus a polemic arose between North and South on the subject of race and about the superiority or inferiority of North and South," Gramsci wrote (1971:71). It was a classic case of elites relying on fictions related to biology to justify their power and dominance.

Among the many scientific efforts to explain the oppression, impoverishment, and "backwardness" of the South as compared to the North were studies of criminal anthropologists. Cesare Lombroso founded this racist school of thought in the 1870s. He and his followers relied on "race" to explain material differences such as class. Lombroso, an elite southern Italian physician, developed a theory of innate criminality. He believed that criminals were born bad, and that environmental factors or historic circumstances were irrelevant to the making of a criminal. This misguided theory unfortunately wielded tremendous influence on social thought and judicial practice well into the 1900s. For Lombroso, crime was hereditary. His views reinforced anti-southern sentiments. Stephen Jay Gould documents the dangerous outcome of such a perspective in his *Mismeasure of Man*. Gould details instances in which Lombroso served as an expert witness in criminal trials. Accused men were unjustly condemned. Lombroso, as the "expert" scientist, pointed out to the judge particular somatic features: "outstanding ears, great maxillaries and cheek bones . . . sinister look, nose twisted to the right . . ." (Gould 1981:138). Lombroso's criminal anthropology was part of a Western trend to scientific racism.

Lombroso's approach promoted a belief in biological determinism. Alfredo Niceforo, one of his adherents, in 1901 published a book that compared northern and southern Italians, aiming to demonstrate the "fact" that there were "two Italies" with "two races." In addition, he sought to substantiate the racial inferiority—physically, psychologically, socially, and morally—of southern Italians as contrasted against Italians of the North.

One of the strongest Italian critics of the racial theory of criminal anthropologists was Gaetano Salvemini. He denounced these theories and methods. "Race is formed in history," he wrote in 1899. Salvemini pointed to uneven economic conditions and development as well as forms of governance similar to colonialism to explain the endurance of southern poverty. The real cause did not rest in the blood of the southerners but in the unfair system of land ownership and class immobility. He claimed that policies and procedures favored large estate owners and kept the poor impoverished. Southerners (who stayed in the South) could not simply "help themselves." The reason appeared unyielding, inevitable, and immutable—like something rooted in nature. But persistent poverty was not reducible to race. It was a curse of history (Teti 1993:11–14, 69, 169–170).

DEMOGRAPHIC MALAISE

The curse of history persists. During a trip to Italy in November 2002, I made a pilgrimage to Feltrinelli's, one of my favorite bookstores in Florence, where I found and purchased a book by Antonio Golini and his colleagues called *Il malessere demografico in Italia* (2000), or *The Demographic Malaise in Italy*. On the train ride back from Florence my daughter, by then 11, asked me to translate the title. As I was groping for an explanation, an Italian woman sitting across from me offered a powerful insight: the term *malessere* is typically used with an illness; it is the opposite of well being. Furthermore, it is generally used in reference to the body. In the book title, the use of the term *malessere,* or malaise, points not only to individual bodies but also to the social body—or, more appropriately, the national social body. The metaphor implies that the national social body is suffering from a demographic illness. In this sense, the authors' take on the situation turns a demographic trend into a social pathology, a national disease.

Indeed, in this newest book Golini and his coauthors describe the fertility rates as very low—Italy continued to register annual fertility rates between 1.1 and 1.2 children per woman during the 1990s. They lament that this birthrate was, and continues to be, among the lowest in the world and among the lowest ever registered in the history of humanity for a large population (Golini et al. 2000:7). These prestigious demographers go so far as to describe the situation as an "excess" of low fertility. Their scientific alarmism reverberated in the media and among other influential elites in Italian society. Pope John Paul II, in a controversial and historic address to the Italian Parliament in November 2002, put demography at the top of his agenda. The Pope described the "crisis of births" as a "*grave minaccia*—or, serious threat" that weighs on the future of Italy (Drioli 2002:3).

When demographers talk about the low birthrate, they often do so in the context of the two other points of the demographic triangle: deaths and migration. As for deaths, the constant news is that Italians are living longer: men live almost 75 years on average and women live just over 81 years (according to 1997 data, these life spans are just above those of the European Union). The Italian population is aging. The trend spells demographic "upset" in terms of the proportion of young people to old people. In 1950 there were 16.4 million Italians under 20 years old compared to 5.7 million people over age 70. Demographers predict that by 2030, the numbers will invert: there will be 6.2 million youths and 18.7 million seniors (Golini et al. 2000:8).

An aging population troubles many demographers. It represents a potential "deformation" in the population age structure. Such concerns echo in the media. An article in July 1997 entitled "Italy? It Is Old and without Children" described Italy as having become "the oldest country in the world, a country of great-grandparents." Then-Minister of Health, Rosi Bindi, commented, "If the increase in the life span is a conquest, the low level of natality is a sign of lost civility or at least of tragic uneasiness" (*La Stampa* 1997). Her alarm sounds very much like that of Golini. It again reinforces a myth that Italians were in some unidentified past more civilized, and that their previous reproductive outcomes made them more civilized. But what a turn of events! After all, was it not the very prolific reproductive patterns of southerners that marked them as backwards and even stigmatized them as *marocchini,* or Arab-like?

IRRATIONAL SEX

Sicily suffers from overpopulation and the poverty that goes with it. The prodigious Italian faculty for producing progeny is never better illustrated than here. What Sicily needs are more fertile fields and fewer fertile women. *Bambini* positively swarm.
    —Samuel Chamberlain (1958:463), *Italian Bouquet: An Epicurean Tour of Italy*

For the biased North Italian the southerner is . . . given to fathering broods of children, and unconcerned with personal hygiene.
                                    —William A. Douglass (1983:182), "Migration in Italy"

Such portrayals of the Italian South and of southerners were based on stereotypes. As Margarita Pérez Delgado and Massimo Livi-Bacci (1992:163) wrote, "Contrary to popular belief, Italy and Spain have never had very high levels of fertility." Indeed, in the 1950s, when Chamberlain made his observations, the total fertility rate in the United States at just over three children per woman on average was significantly higher than in Italy at just over two per woman. A century earlier, between 1860–1870, so-called natural fertility levels among Italian and Spanish women were lower than those of German, Dutch, or Belgian women, and were about the same as those of English, Danish, and Swedes. Nonetheless, travelers and observers the likes of Chamberlain and his 19th-century predecessors "mistook the noisy presence of children in the streets . . .

and the active role they took in many rural and urban occupations as signs of unusually high fertility" (Pérez Delgado and Livi-Bacci 1992:162).

High fertility in modern times has been a way to distinguish between progressive and backward populations. This unstable and value-laden measuring stick dates back to Malthus's infamously influential essay on population in the late 1700s. High fertility, in the eyes of the British ruling class, became a sign of ignorance and moral bankruptcy. It justified policies designed to give the poor their just dessert: starvation. In Italy, the stigma associated with prolific childbearing varied regionally and socially; it also came much later.

Demographers such as Livi-Bacci (1977) explained the later timing of demographic transition among southern Italians as due to their clinging to tradition. His explanation, which relied on aggregate statistics, reinforced notions of a backward South. A significantly different picture emerged from Jane and Peter Schneiders' case study approach (1992, 1996). The anthropologists conducted village research in Sicily, where up until the late 1800s, having a large family bespoke of wealth. When agricultural markets collapsed at the onset of the 1900s, the gentry class was hard hit, and a new family ideal emerged. In order for elites to maintain a luxury lifestyle, they had to change their ways. They embraced small families. By contrast, artisans and peasants experienced economic cycles differently. The artisans made the transition to small families in the 1930s during the Great Depression. The peasants, on the other hand, began having small families during the 1950s and 1960s after land reform improved the opportunities for laborers. In each case, it was not that the southerners suddenly broke with tradition and rejected the customary values that marked them as backward, as Livi-Bacci would have it. Rather, to realize the old value of respectability, they had to make new adjustments, such as having fewer children. It was none too soon. In the 1950s, people in better-off classes characterized the sexual endeavors of poor peasants as "the festival of the poor." A concern with too large of families was expressed as *"più famiglia, più fame,"* or more family, more hunger (Schneider and Schneider 1992:156, 158).

Demographers, as experts, have contributed to attitudes toward family-making and family size. They not only crunch numbers, they make moral judgments that bespeak of core values: the family as the basis for a healthy society, the couple as a procreative unit, the woman as mother, protected sex and planned offspring as the rational norm. Having rational sex meant that people started to control their "animalistic" impulses. They began to have fewer children, or to limit their fertility: through coitus interruptus, rhythm methods, barrier devices, herbal remedies, abortions; even intensive and long-term breastfeeding could shape birth spacing. Couples also limited family size through traumatic means such as abandonment or infanticide.

Europeans, as the first population on record to undergo the demographic transition, or the conscious limitation of births, "appear in a great deal of early and classical population theory as paragons of rationality," write Jane and Peter Schneider, "their minds disciplining their bodies on behalf of long-range goals" (1996:5). As people elsewhere made this transition to controlled fertility—as opposed to "natural" fertility—they too joined the so-called march of progress to rational personhood. In demographic parlance, the women or couples having small families were "leaders" and those still having large families were "laggards." Reading this language symbolically, we infer that leaders were modern and laggards were backward. Nothing has more strongly divided populations into modern or backward than their procreative practices.

By the 1990s, however, the demographic yardstick for distinguishing modern from primitive reproductive behavior no longer worked. Reproduction had become so controlled as to be no longer rational. It had reached pathological extremes. In fact, demographer Livi-Bacci compared modern Italians' refusal to procreate to anorexics' refusal to eat. His analogy appeared in the introduction to *Tendenze demografiche e politiche per la popolazione,* or Demographic Trends and Population Policies (1994). This was the third report on the Italian demographic situation, funded by the national population research institute (IRP). Livi-Bacci described demographers who work on the topic of low fertility as being "in the worrisome position of the doctor faced with the case of an adolescent who refuses food." The loss of appetite, he reasoned, might just be due to social factors that could be changed. But, in a worst-case scenario, the loss of appetite was due to an alteration of core values and hence reflected "a true and real anorexia" (Livi-Bacci 1994:14). This characterization frames reproductive activities of Italians as far from rational, for anorexia is considered neither reasonable nor sensible but rather a debilitating, self-destructive disorder, not unlike hysteria and insanity. It is also very much a gendered disorder. Who is engaging in a "hard refusal" to procreate if not women? (Recall, demographers use female cohorts to calculate fertility rates.) The implication is that women, angst-ridden and body-obsessed, are rejecting the responsibility to replenish the nation. They have a disease. They have not become irrational like their high-fertility "inferiors" but rather have become struck by a pathology that prevents them from exercising their rationality. Such demographers hope that Italian women's family-making practices can be fixed but fear that they are beyond cure. Race is the unmentioned interlocutor. Pronatalist policies have yet to turn to immigrants to increase the fertility rates. The 2004 budget package offered a bonus of 1,000 euros ($1,200) to Italians upon the birth of a second child, an incentive that was set to run until the end of 2004 (Reuters 2003, *The Economist* 2003).

SNEAKY PRONATALISM AS POLICY

Alarmist statements in the media are not merely innocent coincidences but represent the use of public discourses to change women's birth patterns. In this sense, the scientific pronouncements that frame the low birthrate as a serious problem constitute a type of sneaky pronatalism. Pronatalism refers to an attempt to entice people to have babies. During the fascist years in Italy, from 1922 to 1944, a bold demographic campaign encouraged women to have numerous offspring to create a more populous and powerful nation as well as to populate Italy's colonies in Africa. Crude birthrates had declined from 39 to 26.9 per thousand between 1886 and 1926. In his 1927 Ascension Day address, which sounded demographic alarms and established a pronatalist program, Mussolini told the Chamber of Deputies: "a declining birthrate was a symptom of disease and decline" (Horn 1994:46–47). Mussolini's policies were overtly pronatalist: taxing bachelors, awarding prolific mothers, outlawing abortion, banning contraceptives, and restricting women's access to employment. The regime felt profound anxiety over Italy's future as a viable nation with a vibrant civil society. Population became an instrument for monitoring and managing the social body (see Foucault 1978:139–141).

The modern history of census taking and birthrate tracking in Italy dates back to the early 1800s when parts of Italy were under the French empire and subject to the Napoleonic Code. Italy's first nationwide census in 1861 coincided with the new Italian nation (see Livi-Bacci 1977:8–11). The most intense statistical data collection occurred during the fascist period. Mussolini set up numerous commissions and agencies to monitor the population beginning in 1926. The primary purpose of the newly established Central Institute of Statistics was to ensure that population statistics rapidly developed as a field of study (de Grazia 1992:48; Horn 1994:14). It is no surprise that the fascists increased the intensity of statistical documentation, for it was their aim to exert state control to a degree never before attained.

In the postwar era of renewed democracy, a hands-off approach to influencing reproduction has characterized national policy. Italian demographers have avoided pushing stringent pronatalist measures for a number of reasons. First, the shadow of an oppressive fascist regime hovers over demographic science. Most contemporary demographers want to distance themselves from the fascist era and its blatant pronatalist policies. Incentives for reproduction have emerged mostly at local and regional levels. The most lavish example was a "baby bonus" of 10,000 euros ($11,900) that a mayor of a hill town southeast of Naples offered to couples for every newborn baby (Reuters 2003). Second, many demographers understand the important connection between women's reproductive choice and their chances for equal opportunity. Hence, they realize that a hard-line demographic policy would dismantle gains over the past several decades toward gender parity.

A concern over gender issues arose in the context of a Region of Tuscany report on the quality of life. The report identifies Tuscany as having "one of the globe's lowest birthrates and strongest trends toward aging and demographic decline." It calls for innovation in policy to address issues of "sustainability with regard to the family as well as maternity" yet cautions against "damaging or undermining civil liberties" owed to singles and, in particular, to women. The report states "the need to recuperate the birthrate differential, to bring it up to the level of the most developed areas in northern Europe" (my translation). Nonetheless, the document avoids making specific policy proposals. "The hesitation results from respect for family privacy," explained my anthropologist friend Massimo Bressan. "The state should not heavily intervene in such choices" (e-mail communication, January 14, 2003). Such policies are very hard to make without raising the hackles of those who care about civil liberties, gender equality and individual freedoms.

A strong statement with regard to population policy appears in Golini's recent volume, *Demographic Malaise,* though even here specific policy measures are absent. Golini and his colleagues tread cautiously in confronting what they perceive as the growing "deformation" in the age structure of Italy's population. They believe that demographic deformations create a vulnerable society, weakening its ability to meet the needs of its citizens: services, buildings, jobs.

They push the idea that certain numerical relationships between generations must exist to "to assure a harmonious individual and collective development." They assume such relationships engender "adequate social cohesion . . . and one can affirm that these rapports should not be excessively altered. Just as there should exist a 'correct' dose of numerical equilibrium between the generations so should this logic apply to the distribution of various types of families . . ." (Golini 2000:99).

For example, the isolated hill town of Zerba (province of Piacenza), with a population of 153 people, has a deformed age structure that translates into social disequilibrium: 30 inhabitants over age 80 for every child under age 5. A less extreme scenario can be found in Bologna, a medium-sized city of 401,000 inhabitants known for its low birthrate. As of 1991 Bologna had 23,000 elderly over 80 years old compared to 11,000 children under age 5. This 2:1 ratio, however, is a far cry from the 30:1 ratio of a peripheral town such as Zerba. Golini and his coauthors cite the case of Zerba to warn that profound demographic deformation is a possibility if something is not done about the crisis of births. He and his colleagues call for adding a mix of immigrants and newborns. This dual strategy will not prevent the inevitable changes in the age structure. But they say that it will lessen its negative impacts.

How does foreign immigration become a partial solution? The current rate of immigration of about 80,000 to 100,000 new foreign residents per year could contribute "substantially to the demographic balance of the Italian population in the next few years," write Golini and his colleagues (2000:101). In part, their projections assume that immigrants would not immediately acquire the reproductive behaviors of Italian couples—in other words, they would on average have more than one child. They predict that the immigrant population would eventually climb from 2.6 percent to 10.3 percent of Italy's total population. The researchers, however, caution that relying too heavily on immigrants to "fill the demographic void" is risky. In the few years since Italy has been registering immigrants, their presence "has already created some social tensions to the point of manifesting rejection." In other words, intolerance on the part of the host society appears to be on the rise. Although these demographers maintain they do not approve of those feelings, their argument gives them weight. In describing the processes of integration, they write: economic integration is normally fast; logistic integration (such as home and school) is medium-long; and sociocultural and political integration is long to very long. Does their characterization of the integration process reinforce conservative, xenophobic notions in which racism is coded as culture? Their proposal takes for granted stereotypes of an old-world society resistant to change and fearful of differences. Ultimately, Golini and his associates fail in their attempt to occupy a neutral, "objective" ground. While they suggest that it is up to "the hosting society to embrace the immigrants and treat them like citizens," they also sound alarms about the existence of structured "limits to immigration" (Golini et al. 2000:101–102).

Augmenting the birthrate is the primary strategy to create a more viable and hence "normal" population structure. These demographers suggest that a successful scenario would require a fertility increase from a rate of 1.1–1.2 to at least 1.7–1.8 births per woman. To translate those averages into reality they find, would require many more women to have two and three children, and many fewer women to have zero or one child. However, the most significant change would have to come in the number of women without any children: a decrease from the current estimates of 23 percent to 14 percent. Another large proportion of women—those with three children—would have to move from the current 13 percent to 21 percent. Less dramatic, but still noteworthy, at least 1 percent of the mothers would need to have four or more children. Finally, this scenario would call for the number of women who have only one child to move from the current level of 29 percent to 26 percent.

Ultimately, Golini and his fellow demographers admit their scenario is "impossible." It seems highly unlikely, for example, of the 36 percent of women who have two children that nearly 2 out of 3 of them would procreate a third. Moreover, they offer no concrete policy advice on how to realize their scenario. Rather, they explain why they think the scenario will not happen. First, women have their first child increasingly late in life and hence they do not feel there is enough time—not only physiologically, but also psychologically as well as professionally—to have a second, let alone a third, child. Second, in Italian society, "the interests of women are intrinsically at odds with the interests of babies and with the population," write Golini and his coauthors. They portray the demographic crisis as the manifestation of a "profound and generalized crisis of values that all but supports procreative choice: as far as people have become individuals—women in particular but not only women—and couples . . . remain imprisoned within the play of social pressures and the drive toward individualism" (Golini et al. 2000:102–104). To say that women's interests are at odds with those of babies is to stake out a moral ground in which women's primary role should be as biological reproducer for the nation, much as it was during the fascist years. Furthermore, women in this argument are clearly not immigrants but Italian nationals who are "white" Europeans.

The bottom line of demographic malaise is tied to fear about a future in which the old social and class structures of society no longer exist. Similarly disappearing but not mentioned are the culturally constructed justifications that protected social institutions such as the patriarchal family, the landed nobility, and white northern Italians. It is not just about a "deformation" in the age structure.

Golini and his collaborators stop short of offering enticements to get women to fill their wombs. The main strategy is fear: fear of vulnerability, fear of change, fear of a deformed society, fear of immigrant others.

CHALLENGING WHITENESS

Immigrants are acutely aware of the racism underlying the panic that surrounds demographic profiles and predictions. To them, race panic is anything but invisible. Demographic alarms legitimize Europeans and the privileges that go along with being European—that is, white European. The alarms, for example, construct Italians as a homogenous yet vanishing white European "race." They create a sense of panic against non-Europeans who enter European spaces. The protectionist way of thinking has it that the public spaces, whether media, streets, or piazzas, belong to Europeans and these spaces are "at risk" due to declining fertility and rising immigration.

Zero population growth became the topic of discussion among three Africans who had immigrated to Italy to make a living as street vendors in a dark comedy produced by the multicultural theater group *Ravenna africana* (Martinelli Gabrieli:1998:92–94). The immigrant characters challenge the whiteness alarms and turn the subordination strategies upside down in a satire of the "crisis of births."

> IBA: I'll write a novel.
> ABIB: What will you call it?
> IBA: My Europe!
> KHADIM: Europe is beautiful.
> IBA: Europe is free.
> ABIB: There are hospitals.
> KHADIM: There are discotheques.
> IBA: The discotheque is nice.
> ABIB: Tomorrow Europe will be ours.
> KHADIM: When tomorrow?
> ABIB: Tomorrow.
> IBA: Europe will be ours.
> KHADIM: You [Europeans] don't have kids anymore.
> ABIB: The schools will close.
> IBA: The hospices will fill up.
> KHADIM: You are old.
> ABIB: Zero growth.
> IBA: Zero growth.
> KHADIM: We are many.
> IBA: Hunger in Africa is ugly.
> KHADIM: Europe is beautiful.
> ABIB: Europe is free.
> IBA: We don't want to be street vendors.
> KHADIM: Europe is beautiful.
> ABIB: We are not animals.
> IBA: Street vending is ugly work shit work.
> KHADIM: Europe is beautiful.
> ABIB: We are not animals.
> IBA: Hunger in Africa is still uglier.
> KHADIM: Our Europe.
> ABIB: . . . We will give . . . to our . . . children . . .
> IBA: You [Europeans] won't have children, one day.
> KHADIM: Zero growth.
> ABIB: Poor whites . . . you don't have any more sperm.

The reference to Africans being well positioned to inherit the institutions and culture of Europe—because Europeans "won't have children, one day"—plays on fears of the low birthrate and the future of below-replacement societies.

CONSEQUENCES OF ALARM

The expert voices of demographers create a cacophonous alarm that rings not only in the ears of Italians but also in the ears of immigrants. The alarm ringing is very much about Italy as a nation and about Italy as part of Europe: as primarily Christian and white. Demographic politics are at once racial politics even when they are careful not to engage in obvious vulgar racism. In the current context of Europe racism has become coded as culture. When politicians attribute differences to race, for example, they invite trouble. Speaking in terms of cultural difference is a strategy that masks the practices of protecting white European privilege.

Alarmist discourses masquerade as objective science. In reality, I suggest they constitute a strategy of subordination. Demographers express fears of demographic desertification from a position of authority. Hence, their opinions give weight to those fears. Alarmist claims about demographic deformations enable racism because they stimulate a climate of panic and anxiety toward immigrants. They fuel a media environment in which the norm is to depict immigrant newcomers as a threat.

Furthermore, as demographers speak with regret about a future "disappearance" of Italians and of Italian and European culture, they rewrite history. They encourage forgetting. They would have us believe that Italy was once homogenous. The kind of prejudice that southern Italians such as Nicoletta experienced when they moved north in the 1960s reminds us that Italy has its own history of internal racism. The shadow of the "Southern Question," fueled by turn-of-the-last-century racist science, lingers. Science gave credence to dominant northerners' view of southerners as deviant from birth. Yet history constructs notions of race and realities of inequality. Furthermore, history lives on in prejudices against southern Italians whom northerners continue to disparagingly refer to as *marocchini,* or Arab-like. Language becomes another way to identify populations as inferior. It becomes another code for racist thinking that subordinates certain people by constructing them as dark.

Moreover, sounding scientific alarms about an aging population implies that the country is dying. Italians—particularly women—are depicted as pathological in terms of their sexual practices. Once, Italians who embraced small families were held up as the paragons of rationality. Now they can be characterized as anorexics; instead of refusing food they are refusing procreation.

Immigrants understand who is implicated in this alarm ringing. The immigrants have their own crises, as Maylin's story illustrated. Crib death can happen to any child; however, her exclusion from the community suggested she was isolated and without support. Her story reminds people that immigrants are not merely "the problem." Immigrants have life and death problems themselves. Add to this challenges of integration and experiences of racism that emanate from the host societies that depend on their labor in a globalized economy.

Demographers' constant reiteration of the demographic "problem," of the "crisis of births," or of demographic "unhinging," does not cultivate sympathy or invite equality for immigrant populations. Cultivating a world of open frontiers, open hearts, and equal footing remains the work of alternative initiatives whose shape is still emerging.

8/Globalizing Policy, Policing Populations

crisis (krī´sĭs) n. [L. to separate] 1. the turning point in the course of a disease, when it becomes clear whether the patient will recover or die 2. a turning point in the course of anything; decisive or crucial time, stage, or event 3. a time of great danger or trouble, whose outcome decides whether possible bad consequences will follow [an economic *crisis*]-SYN. see EMERGENCY *(Webster's New World Dictionary)*

To speak of a crisis of births is to speak of an illness writ large on the Italian population. Is low fertility really the malaise of modern Europe, as demographers would have it? Are Italy and other countries like it at a crucial turning point? Is this really a time of great danger? Or is it a time of great political maneuvering, of constructing revolutionary demographic change as a crisis? Taken globally, one might wonder whose crisis is low fertility. Why, when much of the Western world is still clinging to the albeit vanishing menace of overpopulation, are Italy and its European counterparts so bent on describing the demographic situation as a crisis? Why are demographers, the media, and Europeans not celebrating? In part, an aging population leads pension calculators to forecast shortages. Furthermore, the changes lead to disappointment and uncertainty on the part of would-be grandparents. Finally, immigrants are becoming a regular part of the social landscape, and this has created anxiety that takes the form of racism veiled as cultural difference.

To frame low fertility as a crisis erases a host of histories that explain why family-making among Italians has come to take on its current form. This book reminds people that low fertility is the outcome of a deep, horizontal, quiet revolution that began nearly a century ago against the rigid pecking order of the patriarchal family. It is a consequence of society's embrace of an egalitarian model of the family, and of a generation's grappling with the implications for the cultural politics of gender in a context where the so-called culture of responsibility weighs most heavily on women. Low fertility reflects the reconciling of family work with wage work in a context where social obligations of trust and reciprocity were and are foundational to the economy. Furthermore, it marks the rejection of the stigma of a rural past, which included attributing innate racial inferiority to certain segments of the population. Distancing oneself from the rural past meant striving toward a new location of social class and all the consumer practices that went with that. Low fertility is also the contradictory victory of rationality with regard to sex—contradictory because it leads to new forms of stigma for those who violate the norms. Finally, low fertility is the embrace of the small family as a display of middle-class decency.

In recent decades, there has been no stronger symbol of being modern than the small family. China took that symbol to its logical albeit extreme conclusion beginning in the 1970s with the one-child policy (Anagnost 1995, Greenhalgh 2001). The one-child policy sought to improve the quality of the Chinese population and to convince its inhabitants that this was a wise step. Women have at times resisted the policy and have been subject to coercive and punitive measures, from forced abortions to job dismissal. At other times, couples have used amniocentesis to determine the sex of the fetus and to abort females due to male preference. The policy has also created a whole category of outcast "unplanned" persons who are "legal nonpersons" existing on society's margins (Greenhalgh 2003). But in many cases, Chinese citizens have come to believe having only one child made sense as a strategy to attain top-notch modern status. Having few children meant improving the collective. It is no small coincidence that the architect of that policy was an American-trained demographer, Yinchu Ma, set on modernizing his country. I say it is no coincidence because demography went global long ago.

This global history matters to understanding the genesis of framing low fertility as a "crisis." Moral notions about appropriate family size in modern times have circulated globally, largely following modern routes of capitalist development and colonial expansion, emanating from West to East and from North to South. A number of 18th-century French, English, and Scottish social philosophers put forth competing notions on whether large populations created a wealthy nation or an impoverished one. Thomas Malthus's pessimistic treatise on population is the most famous and enduring. Although it was challenged in the mid-1800s with Marx's critical tome on *Capital,* its influence proved to be lasting. The ghost of Malthus hovered, with its unsympathetic stance toward the immoral lifestyles and sexual exploits of the working poor, over the experiments of criminal anthropologist Cesare Lombroso, whose scientific racism stigmatized a whole segment of the southern Italian population as innately inferior. That ghost continued to drift over the First International Conference on Eugenics, held in London in 1912, and then went on to loom large over the first World Population Conference, convened in Geneva in 1927. At the latter conference, chaired by American birth-control advocate Margaret Sanger, the "population problem" emerged as an international, scientific issue. A discourse on eugenics framed the meeting. Perhaps more than any other scholarly gathering, the World Population Conference revealed how pervasive were shared assumptions about the role of government in managing populations through shaping and even policing families, notes anthropologist David Horn in his book *Social Bodies.* Despite disagreements in terms of political, cultural, and disciplinary outlooks, the participants shared significant assumptions: birth, death, migration, and marriage were "regular" phenomena that lent themselves to quantitative study; the need to collect data and conduct censuses was great; the sciences were well-equipped to undertake impartially these important tasks; and the findings should be used to formulate government policies. Moreover, the political leaders and social scientists agreed that "the greatest dangers faced by modern nations were not other states, but the internal pathologies identified by demographers, eugenicists, and sociologists—pathologies that demanded prompt intervention" (Horn 1994:51).

This language of political arithmetic echoes the first definition of crisis, "the turning point in the course of a disease." Such language continues to be crucial to constructing low fertility as a crisis. It is a trope that enjoys great longevity. I found such language in a document entitled "The Situation of Families in Italy in 2001."[1] Report author Giovanni Sgritta writes of "the appearance of the 'long family,' i.e. *genus italicum,* in which the adult children tend to stay with their parents until a pathologically late age." He goes on to describe how the undoing of the "traditional rules that once governed generational relations" have produced "tensions that give rise to downright perverse effects" (p. 4). To explain the "perverse mechanism" that the prolonged family sets into motion, Sgritta reviewed a 1999 survey on Italian attitudes to the advantages or disadvantages of children leaving home: 55 percent saw no advantage. Only 12 percent of the respondents indicated that parents would benefit from greater freedom and 5 percent from greater privacy. The so-called perverse mechanism involves each person who is part of this transition to adulthood and who contributes, "though unintentionally, to producing an unwanted result." Topping this list of undesirable results is family-making: "Young people postpone the formation of a family and procreation *sine die* [for an indefinite period] bringing about demographic outcomes that, in the long run, cannot be sustained by society as a whole" (p. 6).

What is partly to blame, in Sgritta's view, is the loss of traditional rules. He describes family relations as "halfway between tradition and modernisation." This characterization assumes that history has a single trajectory, from traditional to modern. Such a view results from an ethnocentrism that elite modern Europeans wage against their own compatriots. Such an approach becomes an instrument of eurocentric modernization that is used to erase differences within Europe—or at least make the continent appear homogenous. In such approaches, middle-class white Northern Europeans become the standard of what is modern and hence normal against which everyone else is measured. Consistent with these strategies, Sgritta writes, "in other aspects, Italian families show behaviours and attitudes that hint at a gradual process of convergence and similarity to the typical family patterns of other European and Western countries" (p. 2). Here arises the specter of backwardness that haunts Italians. They just are not modern

---

[1]The report is downloadable from the website of the European Observatory on the Social Situation, Demography, and Family, a multidisciplinary network of experts that the European Commission requested be established in 1989 albeit under a different name. The observatory has a national expert in each EU member state, and these experts monitor and report on developments, particularly related to the observatory's annual research focus. For example, the theme for 2003 was "The Family in the Health System," and for 2002 it was "Family Benefits and Family Policies." The monitoring reports are then published on the group's website. A series of related studies were posted under the heading "Families in Finland, Italy, Portugal, Spain, and Sweden." See http://europa.eu .int/comm/employment_social/eoss/index_en.html, accessed May 12, 2003.

enough. Even their "experts" attest to their odd perversions, their ways of living making that produce distortions.

In my view, these dominant constructions of the "crisis" have casualties. Experts such as Sgritta conveniently forget the peasant protest against the rigid pecking order of the patriarchal family that underlies this change in family-making. Sgritta offers a cleaned up, romantic view of traditional authority. Such stories also erase the potential immigrant contributions to a country particularly in terms of labor but also in terms of intellectual, artistic, culinary, and linguistic diversity. Yet how paradoxical, for just a few pages earlier he was depicting the traditional aspects of Italians as a source of shame! Contradictions and amnesia arise in the context of the cultural politics of population.

The terms "pathological" and "perverse" to describe Italy's demographic situation reflect discursive strategies for constructing the situation as a crisis. The language echoes what doctors use to describe a dangerous disease. Dangerous diseases call for immediate intervention. A major consequence of the alarmism over fertility decline is a movement to create incentives for Europeans to have more children. I predict such debates will persist. I also suggest that they mask dangerous cultural politics of threatened whiteness, of threatened economic privilege, and of threatened patriarchy.

GLOBAL FERTILITY AND POLICY TRENDS

Ultimately, fertility rates are the cold and calculated outward measures of peoples' most intimate practices and expressions of desire: sex. In the late modern period of today, sex is assumed to be highly rational. Demographers assume that in so-called controlled fertility populations, people use contraception and hence engage in "rational" sex. The common wisdom is that modern families are planned families, and that modern families reflect couples' cost-benefit analyses. This internalization of rationality came to mind when an acquaintance, also a college professor, told me his wife was pregnant with their fourth child: "We're verging on obscenity," he said, half joking. His comment echoed the dominant global judgment that having too many unplanned children is a sign of irrationality.

This approach to understanding people's fertility practices leaves out the emotional and cultural context. It reminds me of the conviction of John Nash, the Nobel-prize winning mathematician hailed for his advances in game theory, that all decisions could be reduced to "calculations of advantage and disadvantage, algorithms or mathematical rules divorced from emotion, convention, and tradition" (Nasar 1998:13). His biographer described him as "compulsively rational"—until, ironically, his rational mind was infected with a serious mental illness that left him a prisoner of his own delusions. He came to realize that love could not be reduced to calculation.

I am convinced that much demographic work suffers from a similar compulsion with rationality and hence overlooks the less measurable aspects that figure into people's fertility-related behaviors. I believe people are rational, and they do weigh the costs and benefits to having a child. But this accounts for only part of the story. The other part has to do precisely with emotion and convention—what you sense you are supposed to do. In other words, people's feelings, their

identities, their histories, and the norms of their cultural contexts figure prominently into family-making beliefs and realizations.

That said, low fertility, a phenomenon that occurs primarily in wealthy countries, has been a source of worry at various moments in the 20th century.
Demographers define a stable population as replacing itself, which is a fertility
rate of 2.1 average births per woman, the current rate in the United States. By
contrast, Japanese society has a fertility rate of 1.3 and an average of 9 births per
1,000 women, and it has witnessed intense alarmism over its aging "problem."
The issue finds its way into government white papers, the media, and public
debate. Nancy Rosenberger identifies young women as the target group, as such
debates attempt to "domesticate" them as reproducers for a nation-state that
assumes "no leakage of population in or out" (2001:7). In Scotland in November
2003 the first minister announced initiatives to lure back Scottish expatriates and
increase its population in light of a "baby bust" (Alvarez 2003). An article that
appeared on the front page of *The New York Times,* "Persistent Drop in Fertility
Reshapes Europe's Future," noted that "Europe stands out as the continent with
the lowest fertility rates" (Bruni 2002). Countries with the lowest rates, between
1.1 and 1.2, from 2001 World Health Organization data, were listed: Russian
Federation, Italy, Estonia, Czech Republic, Belarus, Armenia, Ukraine, Spain,
Latvia, and Bulgaria. Spain was the lowest in Western Europe. Some provinces
in Italy's wealthy, well-educated north have rates well below the national lows:
Ferrara, for example, has been below 0.9 every year since 1986. Remarked
reporter Frank Bruni, "Nationwide, Italy's fertility rate has been so low for so
long—under 1.5 since 1984—that the country offers an especially good glimpse
into the dimensions and dynamics of this trend."

Fertility rates worldwide are now calculated at 3.1 births per woman over the
course of a lifetime. In the 1980s, countries such as Tunisia, Indonesia, Turkey,
Mexico, and India all had fertility rates of more than 4.0 children per woman. By
the early 2000s, all of those countries had dropped to just over 2.0 children per
woman, except India, which had reached the global "norm" of 3.0 children.
"What we're seeing right now is a revolution in fertility," Joseph Chamie, director of the United Nations population division, told *The Wall Street Journal* in
January 2003 (Naik et al. 2003). *The Wall Street Journal* cited a number of reasons for the global trend toward fertility decline, including increased education,
improved employment opportunities, greater potential financial independence,
growing urbanization, and increased contraceptive availability. Moreover, global
fertility decline has led to new projections of the world's population: from 6 billion today to a leveling off of about 9 billion by mid-century, according to the
UN division. This represents a significant reduction from the 12 billion figure
projected a decade ago. Indeed, demographer Jon Bongaarts (1998) has identified fertility decline as the emerging issue of the current century. The importance
of reproductive politics have not been lost on ultra-conservative Patrick
Buchanan, who exploits the European and Japanese trends to campaign against
immigrants, whom he describes as risking "the balkanization of America." He
couples as evil forces immigration with low fertility, and points to low fertility
countries as stagnant and suicidal: "The cradle of Western civilization will have
become its grave" (2002:9, 13).

TABLE 8.1 GLOBAL COMPARISON
OF TOTAL FERTILITY RATES

Ukraine	1.1	Israel	2.9
Latvia	1.2	Mexico	2.9
Romania	1.2	India	3.2
Spain	1.2	Syria	4.1
Germany	1.3	Iraq	5.4
Italy	1.3	Marshall Islands	5.7
Japan	1.3	Ethiopia	5.9
Russia	1.3	Afghanistan	6.0
Cuba	1.5	Liberia	6.6
Sweden	1.6	Burkina Faso	6.8
China	1.8	Mali	6.8
France	1.9	Congo	6.9
Puerto Rico	1.9	Uganda	6.9
Tunisia	2.1	Somalia	7.2
United States	2.1	Yemen	7.2
Venezuela	2.8	Niger	8.0

Source: World Population Data Sheet, 2002 Population Reference
Bureau.

Particularly in Europe, the low fertility trend has come to be taken for granted as a crisis and has led to policies designed to help families balance work and family but at times have been downright discriminatory in terms of who was eligible. Debates of eligibility continue to rage. Many countries in Europe and elsewhere have witnessed a move away from nationalistic family policies that gave preference to a particular ethnic group. So concludes sociologist Leslie King, who compared four nations with explicit pronatalist policies: France, Romania, Israel, and Singapore each have programs that claim to encourage births. The current array of pronatalist initiatives includes lengthy parental leaves, subsidized childcare, subsidized housing for families, tax incentives, generous family allowances, as well as incentives for businesses to create job flexibility.

France's first comprehensive policy of this sort dates to 1939. Whereas these early programs extended to all legal residents, regardless of citizenship, eligibility more recently became a political hot potato, and one linked to xenophobic sentiments: "a backlash against immigrants sparked debate during the 1980s and 1990s over whether pronatalist incentives should be offered to 'non-French,'" notes King (2002:374). At the local level, towns instituted pronatalist policies that excluded noncitizens. At the national level, however, French lawmakers have pushed for inclusive policies that extend to noncitizen, legal immigrants. Despite opposition from the political right, King concludes that pronatalist programs of the French state have become more inclusive overall.

A similar inclusive trend has emerged in Romania, whose nationalistic and oppressive demographic regime ended in 1989 with the overthrow and execution of dictator Nicolae Ceausescu. The ethno-nationalist character of those policies has given way to hands-off policies that do not, at least officially, discriminate according to ethnic differences. In a parallel direction, a discriminatory pronatalist policy in Singapore has given way to an inclusive substitute. Dating to the mid-1980s, the previous policy honed in on a segment of the population: it encouraged highly educated citizens, mostly Chinese, to have children, and discouraged less educated citizens, mostly Malay and Indian, from having children. The program offered cash incentives to citizens of low educational level who agreed to be sterilized. Controversy led to the program's demise and opened the way to an all-encompassing pronatalist stance. The government slogan since 1987 has been: "Have three children, or more if you can afford it." Furthermore, realizing working women's importance to the economy, in the 1990s, Singapore's approach to stimulating births moved away from a focus on mothers and toward one of striking a balance between work and families (King 2002:380)

Israel has witnessed a similar move away from ethno-nationalist official policies, according to King's assessment. Formed in response to the devastating population losses of the Holocaust yet realized as part of an ongoing project of Western colonialism, Israel is a Jewish state in which ethnic nationalism is at the core of national identity and citizenship politics. Arab women have higher fertility rates than do Jewish women—4.7 as compared with 2.5. Although this difference may be a source of stigma for Arab women in terms of how they see themselves and how others see them, it has also resulted in a fierce demographic politics. To encourage Jewish population growth, Israel grants immediate rights and privileges of citizenship to Jews who immigrate there. Furthermore, although abortion is technically legal, a number of practices discourage women's access to abortion, including bureaucratic hurdles and required viewing of an abortion video. In addition, Israel's pro-family allowances, which up the ante with each child, initially excluded Palestinians because the benefit targeted families of veterans; recall, one mark of Palestinians' second-class citizenship has been their exclusion from serving in the Israeli military and reaping related benefits. In 1994, however, the allowance was unlinked to veteran status and extended to Arab citizens of Israel. The exception is Palestinians living in Israeli "occupied territories" where citizenship is not granted to them. Concludes King, "Thus, currently, the family allowance system does not discriminate on the basis of ethnicity or religion" (King 2002:378).

The language of policies can be a world apart from the experiences of policies. Rhoda Kanaaneh in *Birthing the Nation* portrays Palestinian women as recipients of unevenly applied demographic campaigns. The Israeli state's fear of the "Arab demographic time bomb" sets the tone for a context of mistrust that plays out in interactions between patients and doctors in health clinics. Palestinian women sense the fear on the part of health-care personnel of their preference for relatively large families—even though many Palestinian women have embraced modern ideals of the family as well as the trappings of consumer culture that go along with it. Moreover, Susan Kahn's *Reproducing Jews,* an ethnography of assisted conception in Israel, probes behind the scenes of the country with the most infertility clinics and with accompanying generous support for the services: free of charge for up to two children to any woman at least 30 years old, regardless of marital status or sexual orientation. Yet the study leaves the impression, more through absence than through direct discussion, that it is the rare Palestinian woman who would seek out these state-sanctioned services.

I witnessed a similar misfit between policy and experience in Italy. I discussed (in Chapter 5) how practices of the heart can be risky for working women. Gina was allegedly fired from the sweater firm where I apprenticed because the owners caught wind of her plans to marry. They wanted to avoid the loss of profits they would encumber from a maternity leave.

Current family policies in Italy cover two main areas: monetary transfers to families and parental leave. The government increased tax deductions and allowances for families, and as of 1999, a monthly payment of 103 Euros plus one extra month's bonus per year was granted to families with three or more minor children with minimal earnings. A similar maternity allowance is available to women without other social security benefits. This is in addition to covered medical care. Furthermore, a law effective March 2000 (n. 53/2000) modified a preexisting parental leave policy. It extended benefits to fathers. Each parent can take up to 6 months of leave or 10 months combined during the first 3 years of the child's life. If, however, the father takes 3 months in a stretch, the couple's maximum leave is extended by one month as a sort of bonus. The amount of pay is 100 percent during the first 30 days of leave. Thereafter, it is 30 percent except in low-income cases, in which it may be calculated at a higher rate. If between 3 and 8 years old the child gets sick, parents get up to 10 days of leave, and special leave is granted to parents of children with handicaps for up to three years. Leave applies to single parents as well as to parents who adopt babies (Gottardi 2000).

Laws such as this mark an effort to address gender discrimination in the workforce and to distance themselves from fascist pronatalism. The latter narrowly defined women as reproducers for the nation. The new law, in extending paid leave to fathers, in theory diffuses women as targets for discrimination so that employers have less motivation to scapegoat women as the culprits for threatened loss of production. Indeed, the new law allows fathers potentially more leave than mothers: a maximum of 7 as compared with 6 months! But who knows whether such laws will be effective in preventing the kind of harsh dismissals that Gina experienced.

Policies and the welfare system are inadequate to resolving problems related to the demographic situation in Sgritta's view. The Sicilian saying, *più famiglia, più fame*—more kids, more hunger—bears out in current statistics (Schneider and Schneider 1991:889). From the 1980s through the 1990s, families with the highest levels of poverty were the ones made up of five or more members, and a 2000 study noted a high degree of risk for poverty in families with three or more minor children (Sgritta 2001:7).

Nevertheless, politicians are hearing the pan-European demographic alarms to encourage couples to get together and procreate. The period between 1996 and 2001 witnessed revived political and social interest in family matters. Livia Turco, Italy's former Minister for Social Affairs, called for placing the family at the center of public policies. She noted that "between 1996–1999, family policies were planned as a great battle of culture and values arising from our awareness of the need [to invert the] trend [of] sterile familialism that has distinguished the last 50 years, during which the Italian family has been left alone to bear the burden of all the social and economic changes." As this book was heading into production, a town in Naples offered couples a 10,000 euro "baby bonus" and the Berlusconi government passed a blatantly pronatalist, if Band-aid, incentive of 1,000 Euros per newborn (Reuters 2003).

Policies in much of Western Europe have been slow to promote aggressive pronatalist courses of action, in part because of the lingering specter of fascist pronatalism. The nature of intervention following the 1927 World Population Conference varied significantly, as the horrors of eugenics attest, as manifested in Nazi Socialist Germany but also in the United States against various poor populations. The Anglo-American eugenicists worried about upper-class fertility decline, whereas the Italian participants favored a broad pronatalist stance. Statistician Corrado Gini, first head of Italy's Central Institute of Statistics (now ISTAT), created in 1926, viewed this trend not as a cause for concern but rather as an inevitability similar to aging. His worry reflected what an Italian writer in 1912 had described as the "nightmare of depopulation." Gini and Alfredo Niceforo (a follower of Lombroso) warned of the danger of decreasing births. Italy's fertility rates were high relative to other European countries but were declining at a rate that concerned government leaders and scientists. The trend prompted the Italian fascists to promote population growth. Mussolini was obsessed with modernizing Italy, and his primary tactic was to do it through numbers. The fascist demographic campaign outlawed contraception, made abortion a crime against the state, narrowly defined women as reproducers, and emphasized men's virility as fathers, workers, and soldiers. The strategies sought to police people in their own bedrooms as a means to increasing family size; however, the policies ultimately failed. Birthrates continued to decline significantly during the regime's two decades of power (see Table 2.1, p. 23).

Internationally, the postwar era witnessed the emphasis of demographic policy on reproductive practices, ranging from developing countries to domestic populations. One thinks of the infamous forced sterilizations of Native American women, of poor black women, or of "feeble-minded" white women. Internationally, agents of Western-style family planning-programs disseminated neo-Malthusian methods to curtail fertility rates. Threats of overpopulation were framed in the proselytizing language of modernization. So-called classic transition theory dominated social science research in Asia, Africa, and Latin America through the 1960s. Its key tenet was that fertility change was a universal, progressive, and irreversible process. Its key target was the wombs of third world women, whom the elite theory-makers blamed for poverty.

Assumptions of universal progress and of women perpetrators were initially destabilized—unintentionally—through the massive European Fertility Project, launched at Princeton University in 1963 and continued for two decades. The results disappointed its investigators, for the data disproved their hypothesis: that the onset of fertility decline would correlate with social and economic development. It turned out that women began to have fewer children under a mosaic of social, economic, health, and infant mortality conditions (Knodel and van de Walle 1986). The project nevertheless produced one seductive lead: that fertility was significantly related to "culture" (Greenhalgh 1995:5–6). A number of anthropologists began to investigate the cultural aspects of fertility decline. Jane and Peter Schneider, for example, grounded their investigation in historical, political, and economic changes in Sicily, where people from different social classes made the transition to small families in different decades, primarily through thoughtful coitus interruptus. What struck the Schneiders was the power of culture: each strata of society eventually embraced the emerging ideology of a small family while simultaneously holding onto a preexisting and persistent goal of achieving respectability.

A further challenge to the modernization theorists' scapegoating came at the 1994 watershed Conference on Population and Development in Cairo. The international meeting gave voice to women around the world who were critical of Western-style population programs that blamed poor women's reproductive practices for poverty in developing nations. The participants insisted on changing this language and perspective. They called for women's empowerment, and they called for an end of human rights violations related to coercive family planning. Ultimately, though, "the new agenda didn't challenge the idea of population growth as a cause for poverty and environmental degradation," noted Betsy Hartmann, author of *Reproductive Rights and Wrongs,* at a panel discussion I attended in May 2003. Similarly, Dennis Hodgson and Susan Cotts Watkins (1997) identify a neo-Malthusian subtext in the conference's Program of Action. It is hard to shake the effects of a movement that for nearly a half century made fertility reduction a central objective of international policy. The movement after all was founded on entrenched neo-Malthusian presumptions: low rates of population growth are beneficial; rapid fertility declines are ideal; and population stabilization is the goal.

In this book, I challenge the neo-Malthusian assumption that low fertility is "the answer" to poverty and pollution. These assumptions imply that once these goals are attained, the story is over. Clearly this is not the case; otherwise, low fertility would not be framed as a crisis but as a victory. Low fertility does not mark the end of history but the beginning of new cultural politics, a new strategy to struggle over whose history—and lives—matter most in the world.

Despite the revolution in declining fertility, the ethnocentric and elitist presumptions of neo-Malthusianism continue to wield plenty of sway. This perspective infiltrates environmental groups such as the Sierra Club, as I noted when I attended a local Massachusetts chapter's Population Action Workshop in February 2003. National groups work hard to avoid accusations of global racism through careful and sophisticated reframing of their politics in terms of women's empowerment all the while retaining overpopulation as a focus of concern.

I was further reminded of the extent of issues that flow from the topic of population when I attended a May 2003 panel discussion on the "Crisis in Reproductive Policies: The Effects on Women across the Globe." The discussion, presented by the Five College Sociology Colloquium Series at Smith College in Northampton, Massachusetts, featured four panelists: Marlene Fried, Betsy Hartmann, Sangeeta Kamat, and Leslie King reminded the audience of the contemporary relevance and range of reproductive policy issues. Perhaps the most symbolic was the Global Gag Rule, an executive memorandum that George W. Bush signed Jan. 22, 2001, his first day in office, to deny funds to overseas family-planning clinics; some organizations have called his action a violation of international rights related to reproductive health. "George Bush is bad for reproductive health," said Fried. In addition, panelists cited a host of troubling issues: sex education and the trend toward abstinence-only programs; sexually transmitted diseases, including HIV/AIDS, and uneven access to medication;

family planning and jeopardized funding at home and abroad; personhood and the Bush administration's attempts to accord this status to the unborn fetus; abortion and an escalating crisis of access in the United States and abroad; contraceptive experiments and the role of Southern hemisphere women and low-income women; health care and issues of pregnancy, birth, and breastfeeding; new reproductive technologies and debates over surrogate motherhood; parental leave and childcare issues; reproductive technologies and examples of misuse such as amniocentesis for purposes of sex selection; neo-eugenicist campaigns such as "CRACK" and the offering of $200 cash to drug users for long-term or permanent sterilization; and finally national security and racial profiling related to the "youth bulge" overseas. These issues extend beyond the scope of this book; however, I expect population and reproduction to remain controversial topics, for knowing and policing populations via the family is integral to the art of government in a world of nations and of inequality.

THE THREE PIGS: A LOCAL THEORY

Many reasons circulate to explain why Italians' birthrate is so low. One of my favorite local explanations came from Carolina. One day in 1996 while I was in her workshop, sewing buttons on sweaters, she offered me her theory of why women used to have lots of babies and why they no longer do. Women, she said, were in the middle of three *maiali,* or three pigs: the priest, the count, and the husband. The priest wanted couples to have sex only for reproduction, to increase bodies for his parish and souls for heaven; the count wanted lots of children because more arms meant a bigger harvest and a bigger share for him and his estate; the husband wanted more people to order around. Now, nobody listens to the priest, the count no longer has peasants or title, and the husband views children as drains on his time and pocketbook.

Carolina's theory speaks to an erosion of patriarchy. She viewed the trend toward small families as a positive one. Some commentators lamented the new generation as self-centered. Carolina praised it. For her, delaying family-making reflected independent-minded citizens who would not be so likely to fall for political movements like fascism. And her daughter would be able to work as an engineer. *Figli programmati sono figli fortunati,* she liked to say. Planned children are lucky children.

Carolina's parable suggests that demographic alarms deny an important aspect of the quiet revolution: that it is a revolution, though often silently so, against patriarchy and the patriarchal structures of power that hierarchically ordered social relations for centuries. The shift in reproductive practices was rooted in a festering peasant protest among women and junior males against a rigid, family form. Powers of decision making and available income were inconsistent with the distribution of workload, capacity, and responsibility (Becattini 1998:83). Women have long worked for pay, as the presence of straw weavers in household records from the early 1900s attest. They comprised the leading force behind an industrializing countryside since they offered a cheap source of labor. Their contributions were devalued, and much of their work was barely recognized, much like today's immigrants. Italy's birthrates reflect adults' attempts to reconcile ongoing expectations for family work with emerging possibilities for wage work. This has unfolded in a postwar context of tremendous structural and symbolic change.

When I returned to the province of Prato in November 2002, I visited Gina's mother, Simonetta. Her daughter's marriage did not work out. Simonetta blamed the failed marriage on an intervening mother-in-law and an overly compliant son. Gina had since taken a job working as a custodian in a Medici villa in the area. Simonetta had also gotten out of the sweater business and had found similarly low-pay custodial work at I Gigli, the area's first and very popular shopping mall that opened in May 1997 in Campi Bisenzio, a municipality in the outskirts of Prato. It struck me as a tragic effect of the sweater-industry crisis that both of these women, who had taken pride in their work as artisans, were now engaged in unskilled and demeaning low-level work.

Perhaps it is no mere coincidence that of the three Italian couples whose weddings I attended in the 1990s, all were separated by November 2002. Although this rate exceeds the national one—some 39 percent of Italian marriages, as of 2000, were on record as ending in divorce or separation (ISTAT)— it mirrors the profound challenges that confront young people who set out on the uncertain path of family-making.

Certainly, the economic context adds to the challenge. During the fall 2002 visit, my friend Oliviero put me and local anthropologist Massimo Bressan in touch with two brothers who had recently gotten out of the sweater business. Oliviero had been weaving sweaters for their firm for more than 15 years, and they had developed a relationship of profound trust with him and some 200 *terzisti,* or subcontractors. The brothers gradually shut down their operation because pressures from global competition had thrown the industry into its worst-yet crisis, making profit margins unbearably low. They had inherited the firm from their parents, and so were deeply attached to it; however, they could not bear to stay in business and pay pennies for the work of long-term subcontractors such as Oliviero. They had the option to relocate elsewhere, say Romania, as some clients had insisted. But they had wives and children, and they were attached to home and their lifestyle. Plus, just as their parents had left them something, they wanted to leave something to their children. The future in sweater-making was bleak. The choice was: "*O cambio vita o cambio lavoro*— Either I change life or I change work." They changed work so as to hold onto the things they loved about their life in Prato, which centrally included their families.

The 20th century has brought with it economic dislocations that bear on the family. As Eric Wolf wrote long ago (1969:295), "The spread of the market has torn men up from their roots, and shaken them loose from the social relationships into which they were born." Central Italy has been experiencing intense spread of the market since the mid-1800s. New imbalances lead people to seek new adjustments, without altogether severing those social relationships. One new adjustment has been the peasant protest against the patriarchal form. Yet figuring out how to cast off patriarchy and forge love in the context of a democratic family has posed profound challenges. At a deeply cultural level, the small family is an outward expression of new adjustments—adjustments involving the cultural politics of history, class, gender, love, and race/ethnic identification. The ongoing struggle continues over what is worth keeping, what is worth rejecting, what is worth revaluing, what is worth innovating, and whose story gets told.

Epilogue

A phone call from Luisa brought sad and painful news. It was spring 2000. Nicoletta had been found in her garden, collapsed of heart failure. Nicoletta's nightmare came back to me that pregnant day: the image of her holding a baby as it turned to stone in her arms. Her dream of a grandchild died with her.

Remembering her at this writing some 8 years after that first fireside talk, I pored over the notes I had made in October 1995. I came across a small memo stapled onto the first page of my primary field notebook. Its perforated edge was evidence that it had been torn from a jotting notebook and then placed strategically on a page of my main notebook to signal its importance. "Last night Nicoletta came down and sat by the fire," it read. The word LA FAMIGLIA appeared in all caps with a square around it: "Children are what make a family," Nicoletta had told me. She could not understand why Luisa and Oliviero did not have children. The note went on to capture her idea that it was important not to have just one child but two. "Otherwise they are alone when they grow up, when they marry." Then she had insisted, "You and Chris should have another child while you're here. The child would then be Italian!"

The pressure to have a second child struck me as generational. While in Italy, so many women my age had advised differently: do not have a second—*si sta troppo bene con uno,* or you're plenty fine with one. The message was why botch up a good thing? One was, after all, already very demanding. The commonly heard exasperation of women, particularly mothers, *"non cè la faccio più,"* or "I can't do it anymore," echoed through my mind like a mantra that warned against having a second child.

Back in Tucson, I noticed many well-educated, middle-class, white couples with two and three kids. The more relaxed manner of child rearing also struck me. No one I knew ironed, hardly anyone fretted about food, and fashion was so casual as to be nonexistent. I found myself in the middle of gestating a dissertation—about low fertility—yet deeply conflicted about whether to have a second child. My daughter was 9, my husband and I were 37, and we had a geriatric dog and a new kitten. Given that I would soon be subjecting myself to the academic job market, our future felt hugely uncertain. Life seemed plenty complex. We were not getting younger.

In June 1999, with a draft of the dissertation in hand, we made a return visit to my field site. We rented a restored farmhouse in Carmignano. It was there that I confronted my own ideas about fertility rates and reproductive choices. These "choices" are largely the result of our confrontation with dominant notions regarding what is a manageable and acceptable way to lead our lives. Are we the "right" age to have a baby? What are the risks? Can we afford a child? Notions of affordability are shaped by ideologies connected to socioeconomic class. What kind of clothing, house, food, health care, and education are necessary before having a child? What kind of relationship do we have with our partner? Do we have a partner? Notions of acceptable gender relations also enter into the picture. Is co-parenting possible? Is a democratic household realizable? Does this matter to the mother and father, or to the parents (if they are same sex), or parent, if he or she is single? Our notions about family-making certainly bear on the health of our relationships and our sense of love. They are connected to deep-seated beliefs about life, spirituality, and personhood. Family-making is also shaped by a broader politics: demographic politics; national politics, such as tax breaks and health care; global population politics; even environmental politics. Finally, personal histories shape reproductive practices.

Three things happened to me during my return visit to Italy that affected my own attitude toward having another child. The first was an after-dinner conversation with an oral historian friend and his wife. Lingering in the hallway of the 16th-century villa, the couple lamented the wild ways of their 23-year-old son, who had a habit of riding his *motorino* with brakes worn to nothing and his girlfriend straddled on the back. They encouraged us not to repeat their mistake. They urged us to have a second child. They were convinced a sibling would have prevented their only child from behaving with such reckless abandon.

The second was a phone call from my mother in St. Louis about the sudden death of a dear old friend, my high school sweetheart. He suffered tremendous physical and mental pain the last few years of his life from untold bones broken after falling, drunk, from his third-story apartment building, indeed, such pain that he would later end it all with a shotgun. The suddenness of death made me starkly aware of the brevity of life. My daughter had been begging persistently for a little brother or sister, and I had been experiencing strong ambivalence about whether to have a second child. At once, I felt driven to embrace life.

And then there was the third factor: an Italian historian-turned-mayor told me one afternoon in his office that as a woman academic, I could certainly only have one child! I suddenly felt determined to disprove such an assertion, which surely rested on the assumption that it was the mother who bore most of the work involved in rearing a child. The future seemed clear.

I was blatantly pregnant and well into my 34th week of gestation in February 2000 when I delivered a paper for a job talk at the University of Massachusetts. I acknowledged to the audience that I was obviously not engaging in a "hard refusal" to procreate. The comment broke a thick tension in the room, given my apparent contradictory stance to criticize Italian demographers for their alarmism while my belly was bulging into this intellectual space.

In the blue morning light of the Sonoran desert in April 2000, our son was born to Miles Davis' "Sketches of Spain." He was not Italian, but he ended up with an Italian name: Luca. Our Italian friends undoubtedly influenced our decision to have a second child as did the very different set of expectations we faced as parents in the United States. I called Italy that day to share our good news. Nicoletta answered the phone around 11 P.M., wondering who could be calling so late. Of course, she was happy for us. Two weeks later I would get the heartrending call from Luisa. When she and Oliviero met our son in November 2002, they told us, *"Siete bravi davvero a fare figli!"* You guys are really great at having kids! The compliment struck me as linked to the context of low fertility in Italy. In the United States, I experienced having kids as taken for granted. In Italy, in the context of alarmism over the low birthrate, it had become something worthy of praise.

Bibliography

Alonso, Ana Maria. 1994. The Politics of Space, Time and Substance: State Formation, Nationalism and Ethnicity. *Annual Review of Anthropology* 23: 379–405.

Altman, Daniel. 2002. "Bracing for Economic Changes: When the Population Grows No More," *The New York Times,* August 20, p. D8.

Alvarez, Lizette. 2003. Scotland Takes Action to Halt Drop in Population. *The New York Times,* November 30, p. 2.

Anagnost, Ann. 1995. A Surfeit of Bodies: Population and the Rationality of the State in Post-Mao China. In *Conceiving the New World Order: The Global Politics of Reproduction.* Faye D. Ginsburg and Rayna Rapp, eds. Pp. 22–41. Berkeley: University of California Press.

Angel-Ajani, Asale. 2000. Italy's Racial Cauldron: Immigration, Criminalization, and the Cultural Politics of Race. *Cultural Dynamics* 12(3):331–352.

Bakhtin, Mikhail. 1984. Discourse in Dostoevsky. In *Problems of Dostoevsky's Poetics.* Caryl Emerson, ed. Pp. 181–269. Minneapolis: University of Minnesota Press.

Balestri, Andrea, ed. 1998. *7th Rapporto Annuale sul Sistema Economico Pratese.* http://www.ui.prato.it/uffstudi/ rapportoeconomico, accessed July 1999.

Barbagli, Marzio. 1982. *Educating for Unemployment: Politics, Labor Markets, and the School System—Italy, 1859–1973.* New York: Columbia University Press.

——. 1996 [1984]. *Sotto lo stesso tetto: Mutamenti della famiglia in Italia dal XV al XX secolo.* Bologna: Il Mulino.

Becattini, Giacomo. 1998. The Development of Light Industry in Tuscany: An Interpretation. In *Regional Development in a Modern European Economy: The Case of Tuscany.* Robert Leonardi and Raffaella Y. Nanetti, eds. Pp. 77–94. London: Pinter.

——. 2001. *The Caterpillar and the Butterfly: An Exemplary Case of Development in the Italy of the Industrial Districts.* Roger Absalom, trans. Firenze: Felice Le Monnier.

Benjamin, Walter. 1968. The Task of the Translator. In *Illuminations.* Hannah Arendt, ed., Harry Zohn, trans. New York: Schocken.

Berry, Wendell. 2002. The Prejudice against Country People. *The Progressive* 66, (4) April.

Bonarini, Franco. 1999. L'uso della contraccezione in Italia: dalla retrospezione del 1979 a quella del 1995–96. In *Nuzialità e fecondità in trasformazione: percorsi e fattori del cambiamento.* Paolo de Sandre et al., eds. Pp. 395–411. Bologna: Società editrice il Mulino.

Bongaarts, John. 1998. Demographic Consequences of Declining Fertility. *Science* 282:419–420.

Bono, Paola, and Sandra Kemp, eds. 1991. *Italian Feminist Thought: A Reader.* Oxford: Blackwell.

Bourdieu, Pierre. 1984. *Distinction: A Social Critique of the Judgement of Taste.* Cambridge: Harvard University Press.

Bressan, Massimo. 1997. Cultura e istituzioni comunitarie nello sviluppo di un distretto industriale. Ph.D. Thesis, Università degli Studi di Firenze.

Brunella, Giovara. 2002. Gli italiani poco prolifici: Tutta colpa della mamma. *La Stampa,* February 20, p. 18.

Bruni, Frank. 2002. Persistent Drop in Fertility Reshapes Europe's Future. *The New York Times,* December 26, p. A1.

Buchanan, Patrick J. 2002. *Death of the West: How Dying Populations and Immigrant Invasions Imperil our Country and Civilization.* New York: St. Martin's.

Caldwell, Lesley. 1978. Church, State, and Family: The Women's Movement in Italy. In *Feminism and Materialism.* Annette Kuhn and AnnMarie Wolpe, eds. Pp. 68–95. London: Routledge and Kegan Paul.

——. 1991. *Italian Family Matters: Women, Politics, and Legal Reform.* Houndmills: Macmillan.

Calvino, Italo. 1980. "Apple Girl," *Italian Folktales.* New York: Pantheon.

Carter, Donald Martin. 1997. *States of Grace: Senegalese in Italy and the New European Immigration.* Minneapolis: University of Minnesota Press.

Castiglioni, Maria, Gianpiero dalla Zuanna, and Marzia Loghi. 2001. Planned and Unplanned Births and Conceptions in Italy, 1970–1995. *European Journal of Population 17:*207–233.

Chamberlain, Samuel. 1958. *Italian Bouquet: An Epicurean Tour of Italy.* New York: Gourmet Distributing Corp.

Coale, Ansley J., and Roy Treadway. 1986. A Summary of the Changing Distribution of Overall Fertility, Marital Fertility, and the Proportion Married in the Provinces of Europe. In *The Decline of Fertility in Europe.* Ansley J. Coale and Susan Cotts Watkins, eds. Pp. 1–181. Princeton, NJ: Princeton University Press.

Cole, Jeffrey. 1997. *The New Racism in Europe: A Sicilian Ethnography.* Cambridge: Cambridge University Press.

Contini, Giovanni. 1993. Le Fotografie di Scheuermeier a Carmignano. In *AFT, Rivista di Storia e Fotografia IX* (18) December 1993, 11–20. Comune di Prato: Archivio Fotografico Toscano.

Corso, Raffaele. 2001. *La Vita Sessuale Nelle Credenze, Pratiche e Tradizioni Popolari Italiane.* Firenze: Leo S. Olschki Editore.

Counihan, Carole M. 1988. Female Identity, Food, and Power in Contemporary Florence. *Anthropological Quarterly 61:*51–62.

Crehan, Kate. 2002. *Gramsci, Culture, and Anthropology.* Berkeley: University of California Press.

de Grazia, Victoria. 1992. *How Fascism Ruled Women, Italy, 1922–1945.* Berkeley: University of California Press.

de Sandre, Paolo. 1997. La formazione di nuove famiglie. In *Lo stato delle famiglie in Italia.* Marzio Barbagli and Chiara Saraceno, eds. Bologna: Il Mulino.

——. 2000. Patterns of Fertility in Italy and Factors of Its Decline. *Genus LVI*(1–2): 19–54.

de Sandre, Paolo, and Fausta Ongaro. 2003. Fecondità, contraccezione, figli attesi: cambiamenti e incertezze. In *Fecondità e contesto: tra certezze ed aspettative; dalla "Seconda Indagine nazionale sulla Fecondità" alla realtà locale.* Pp. 27–56. Milano: Franco Angeli.

de Sandre, Paolo, Antonella Pinnelli, and Antonio Santini. *Nuzialità e fecondità in trasformazione: percorsi e fattori del cambiamento.* Bologna: Società editrice il Mulino.

Dadà, Adriana. 1999. *Il lavoro di balia. Memoria e storia dell'emigrazione femminile da Ponte Buggianese nel '900.* Comune di Ponte Buggianese: Pacini Editore SpA.

Della Croce, Julia. 1987. *Pasta Classica: The Art of Italian Pasta Cooking.* San Francisco: Chronicle.

Douglass, Carrie, ed. Forthcoming. *Barren States: The Population Implosion in Europe.* London: Berg.

Douglass, William A. 1983. Migration in Italy. In *Urban Life in Mediterranean Europe: Anthropological Perspectives.* Michael Kenny and David I. Kertzer, eds. Pp. 162–202. Urbana: University of Illinois Press.

Drioli, Itti. 2002. Le 'tavole' del Papa conquistano il Parlamento. *La Nazione, Quotidiano Nazionale,* Prato, November 15, pp. 3, 5.

Easterbrook, Gregg. 1999. Overpopulation Is No Problem—in the Long Run. *New Republic,* October 11, p. 22.

Eberstadt, Nicholas. 2001. The Population Implosion. *Foreign Policy 123.*

Ehrenreich, Barbara. 2001. *Nickel and Dimed: On (Not) Getting By in America.* New York: Henry Holt.

Foucault, Michel. *Madness and Civilization: A History of Insanity in the Age of Reason.* New York: Vintage.

——. 1978. *The History of Sexuality. Volume 1.* New York: Vintage.

Fredrickson, George M. 2002. Racism: A Short History. Princeton, NJ: Princeton University Press.

Friedman, Thomas. 1997. The Hot Zones. The New York Times, Feb. 12, p. A12.

Gal, Susan, and Gail Kligman. 2000. The Politics of Gender under Socialism. Princeton, NJ: Princeton University Press.

Gelli, Silvano. 1996. Q.M.P. Le Epigrafi nel cimitero di Poggio A Caiano: Testimonianze di Storia poggese (1884–1954). Signa: Tipografia Nova.

Geri, Maurizio. 1998. Maurizio Geri Swingtet. Manouche e Dintorni. Dunya Records.

Ginsborg, Paul. 1990. A History of Contemporary Italy: Society and Politics 1943–1988. London: Penguin.

Golini, Antonio. 1991. Introduction. In Crescita Zero, Rossella Palomba, ed. Scandicci [Firenze]: La Nuova Italia.

———. 1994. Prefazione. In Tendenze demografiche e politiche per la popolazione. Terzo rapporto IRP sulla situazione demografica italiana. Milano: Il Mulino.

Golini, A, A. De Simoni, F. Citoni, eds. 1995. Tre scenari per il possibile sviluppo della popolazione delle regioni italiane al 2044. Roma: Consiglio Nazionale delle Ricerche, Istituto di Ricerche sulla Popolazione.

Golini, Antonio, Antonio Mussino, and Miria Savioli. 2000. Il malessere demografico in Italia. Bologna: Il Mulino.

Gottardi, Donata. 2000. Congedi parentali: nuovi chiarimenti dal Ministero. Guida al Lavoro, Il Sole-24 Ore. No. 30 (2000):12–15. Italian Minister of Social Affairs, www.affarisociali.it/congedi. Accessed July 2, 2001.

Gould, Stephen Jay. 1981. The Mismeasure of Man. New York: W. W. Norton.

Gramsci, Antonio. 1971. Selections from the Prison Notebooks. New York: International.

Greenhalgh, Susan. 1995. Anthropology Theorizes Reproduction: Integrating Practice, Political Economic, and Feminist Perspectives. In Situating Fertility, Susan Greenhalgh, ed. Pp. 3–28. Cambridge: Cambridge University Press.

———. 2001. Fresh Winds in Beijing: Chinese Feminists Speak Out on the One-Child Policy and Women's Lives. Signs: Journal of Women in Culture and Society 26(3):847–886.

———. 2003. Planned Births, Unplanned Persons: "Population" in the Making of Chinese Modernity. American Ethnologist 30(2):196–215.

Guglielmi, Laura. 1997. Crescita Zero addio? La Repubblica, 25 February, D47–52.

Harrison, Faye V. 2002. Unraveling "Race" for the Twenty-First Century. In Exotic No More, Jeremy MacClancy, ed. Pp. 145–166. Chicago: University of Chicago Press.

Hartmann, Betsy. 1995. Reproductive Rights & Wrongs: The Global Politics of Population Control. Boston: South End.

Hartt, Frederick. 1979. History of Italian Renaissance Art: Painting, Sculpture, Architecture. New York: H. N. Abrams.

Hatcher, Robert A. et al. 1994. Contraceptive Technology. 16th revised edition. New York: Irvington Publishers.

Hill, Jane H. 1998. Language, Race, and White Public Space. American Anthropologist 100(3):680–689.

Hodgson, Dennis, and Susan Cotts Watkins. 1997. Feminists and Neo-Malthusians: Past and Present Alliances. Population and Development Review 23(3):469–523.

Horn, David. 1994. Social Bodies: Science, Reproduction, and Italian Modernity. Princeton, NJ: Princeton University Press.

Hostetler, John, and Gertrude Enders Huntington. 1967. The Hutterites in North America. New York: Holt, Rinehart & Winston.

Insabato, Elisabetta, and Sandra Pieri, eds. 1989. Archivi Comunali Toscani: Esperienze e Prospettive. Provincia di Firenze, Sovrintendenza Archivistica per la Toscana, Comune di Carmignano, comune di Lastra A Signa. Firenze: All'Insegna del Giglio.

Jordan, Glenn, and Chris Weedon. 1995. Cultural Politics: Class, Gender, Race, and the Postmodern World. Oxford: Blackwell.

Kahn, Susan Martha. 2000. Reproducing Jews: A Cultural Account of Assisted Conception in Israel. Durham, NC: Duke University Press.

Kanaaneh, Rhoda Ann. 2002. *Birthing the Nation: Strategies of Palestinian Women in Israel.* Berkeley: University of California Press.

Kemp, Sandra, and Paola Bono, eds. 1993. *The Lonely Mirror: Italian Perspectives on Feminist Theory.* London: Routledge.

Kertzer, David I. 1980. *Comrades and Christians: Religion and Political Struggle in Communist Italy.* Cambridge: Cambridge University Press.

———. 1993. *Sacrificed for Honor: Italian Infant Abandonment and the Politics of Reproductive Control.* Boston: Beacon.

———. 1997. *The Kidnapping of Edgardo Mortara.* New York: Alfred A. Knopf.

———. 1998. *Politics and Symbols: The Italian Communist Party and the Fall of Communism.* New Haven, CT.: Yale University Press.

———. 2001. *The Popes against the Jews: The Vatican's Role in the Rise of Modern Anti-Semitism.* New York: Alfred A. Knopf.

King, Leslie. 2002. Demographic Trends, Pronatalism, and Nationalist Ideologies in the Late Twentieth Century. *Ethnic and Racial Studies* 25(3):367–389.

Knodel, John, and Etienne van de Walle. 1986. Lessons from the Past: Policy Implications of Historical Fertility Studies. In *The Decline of Fertility in Europe.* Ansley J. Coale and Susan Cotts Watkins, eds. Pp. 390–419. Princeton, NJ: Princeton University Press.

Krause, Elizabeth L. 1994. Forward vs. Reverse Gear: The Politics of Proliferation and Resistance in the Italian Fascist State. *Journal of Historical Sociology* 7(3):261–288.

———. 2001. "Empty Cradles" and the Quiet Revolution: Demographic Discourse and Cultural Struggles of Gender, Race, and Class in Italy. *Cultural Anthropology* 16(4):576–611.

———. 2003. Italy. In *The Greenwood Encyclopedia of Women's Issues Worldwide: Europe.* Pp. 341–372. Lynn Walter, ed. Westport, CT: Greenwood.

———. Forthcoming. Toys and Perfumes: Imploding Italy's Population Paradox and Motherly Myths. In *Barren States: The Population Implosion in Europe.* Carrie Douglass, ed. London: Berg.

La Repubblica. 1999. Coppie milanesi, fate figli vi diamo un milione al mese. May 5, p. 30.

La Stampa. 1997. Italia? Vecchia e senza bambini. July 25, p. 17.

Livi-Bacci, Massimo. 1977. A History of Italian Fertility. Princeton, NJ: Princeton University Press.

———. 1994. Introduzione. In *Tendenze demografiche e politiche per la popolazione. Terzo rapporto IRP sulla situazione demografica italiana.* Antonio Golini, ed. Milan: Il Mulino.

———. 2000. *The Population of Europe.* Oxford, MA: Blackwell.

Lori, Agostio, Antonio Golini, Bruno Cantalini, eds. 1995. *Atlante dell'invecchiamento della popolazione.* Roma: Consiglio Nazionale delle Ricerche.

*L'Unità.*1996. Allarme dei demografi: a causa della natalità sotto zero spariranno centinaia di cittadine italiane. *L'Unità,* October 29.

McKenna, James J. 1996. Sudden Infant Death Syndrome in Cross-Cultural Perspective: Is Infant-Parent Cosleeping Proactive? *Annual Review of Anthropology* 25:201–216.

Mack Smith, Denis. 1959. *Italy: A Modern History.* Ann Arbor: University of Michigan Press.

Maher, Vanessa. 1987. Sewing the Seams of Society: Dressmakers and Seamstresses in Turin between the Wars. In *Gender and Kinship: Essays toward a Unified Analysis.* Jane Collier and Sylvia Yanagisako, eds. Pp. 132–159. Stanford, CA: Stanford University Press.

Malaparte, Curzio. 1964[1956]. *I Maledetti Toscani.* Firenze: Valecchi Editore.

———. 1964. *Those Cursed Tuscans.* Rex Benedict, trans. Athens, OH: Ohio University Press.

———. 1998. The Little Hand. *Grand Street* 64 16(4):224–226.

Malthus, Thomas. 1985[1798]. *An Essay on the Principle of Population.* Antony Flew, ed. London and New York: Penguin.

Martiniello, Marco, and Paul Kazim. 1991. Italy: Two Perspectives. *Race & Class* 32(3):79–89.

Martinelli Gabrieli, Marco. 1998. Ruh. Romagna più Africa uguale: commedia nera. In *Ravenna africana*, pp. 68–96. Ravenna: Edizioni Essegi.

Marx, Karl. 1906[1867]. *Capital: A Critique of Political Economy*. New York: The Modern Library.

———. 1994[1852]. *The Eighteenth Brumaire of Louis Bonaparte*. New York: International.

Mauss, Marcel. 1990[1950]. *The Gift*. New York: W. W. Norton.

Mayer, Marianna. 1981. *Carlo Collodi's the Adventures of Pinocchio*. New York: Four Winds.

Mayes, Frances. 1996. *Under the Tuscan Sun*. New York: Broadway.

Mencarini, Letizia. 1994. Aspettative e intenzioni su famiglia e figli: un'indagine campionaria sulle studentesse fiorentine. Università degli Studi di Firenze, Facoltà di Scienze Politiche, Tesi di Laurea.

Metcalf, Peter. 2002. *They Lie, We Lie: Getting on with Anthropology*. London: Routledge.

Millard, Ann V. 1990. The Place of the Clock in Pediatric Advice: Rationales, Cultural Themes, and Impediments to Breastfeeding. *Social Science Medicine* 31(2):211–221.

Mother Jones. 1995. Prosperous Italy Has the Lowest Birthrate in the World. *Mother Jones* 20(5):50. September.

Naik, Gautam et al. 2003. Fertility "Revolution" Lowers Birth Rates. *The Wall Street Journal*, January 24 (online edition).

Nasar, Sylvia. 1998. *A Beautiful Mind*. New York: Touchstone.

O'Mara, Peggy. 1999. Get Out of My Bedroom! *Salon.com*, Mothers Who Think. www.salon.com/mwt/feature/1999/09/30/family_bed_rant/index.html. Accessed March 12, 2003.

Ochs, Elinor et al. 1996. Socializing Taste, *Ethnos* 61:7–46.

Origo, Iris. 1957. *Merchant of Prato: Francesco di Marco Datini*. London: J. Cape.

Ortaggi Cammarosano, Simonetta. 1991. Labouring Women in Northern and Central Italy in the Nineteenth Century. In *Society and Politics in the Age of the Risorgimento: Essays in Honour of Denis Mack Smith*. John A. Davis and Paul Ginsborg, eds. Pp. 152–183. Cambridge: Cambridge University Press.

Page, Enoch. 1999. No Black Public Sphere in White Public Space: Racialized Information and Hi-Tech Diffusion in the Global African Diaspora. *Transforming Anthropology* 8(1&2):111–128.

Palomba, Rossella, ed. 1987. *Vita di coppia e figli. Le opinioni degli italiani degli anni Ottanta*. Scandicci: La Nuova Italia.

Palomba, R., A. Menniti, A. Mussino and H. Moors. 1987. *Attitudes towards Demographic Trends and Population Policy: A Comparative Muli-Variate Analysis of Survey Results from Italy and the Netherlands*. Consiglio Nazionale delle Ricerche, Working Paper. Prepared for the European Population Conference, Finland.

Palumbo, Silvia. 1988. *Un'indagine sull'agricoltura nel Comune di Carmignano*. Firenze: F. & F. Parretti Grafiche.

Passerini, Luisa. 1987. *Fascism in Popular Memory: The Cultural Experience of the Turin Working Class*. Cambridge: Cambridge University Press.

———. 1996. Gender Relations. In *Italian Cultural Studies*. Pp. 144–159. David Forgacs and Robert Lumley, eds. Oxford: Oxford University Press.

Patriarca, Silvana. 1996. *Numbers and Nationhood: Writing Statistics in Nineteenth-Century Italy*. Cambridge: Cambridge University Press.

Pérez Delgado, Margarita, and Massimo Livi-Bacci. 1992. Fertility in Italy and Spain: The Lowest in the World. *Family Planning Perspectives 24* (4 July/August):162–173.

Pescarolo, Alessandra. 1988. Modelli di industrializzazione, ruoli sociali, immagini del lavoro (1895–1943). In *Prato storia di una città, 3: Il tempo dell'industria (1815–1943)*. Giorgio Mori, ed. Pp. 51–114. Comune di Prato: Le Monnier.

———. 1991. Lavoro, Protesta, Identità: Le Trecciaiole fra Otto e Novecento. In *Il Proletariato Invisibile: La Manifattura della Paglia nella Toscana Mezzadrile (1820–1950)*. Alessandra Pescarolo and Gian Bruno Ravenni. Pp. 23–121. Milano: Franco Angeli.

———. 1995. I Modelli del Lavoro Femminile: Continuità e Mutamento nei Percorsi e nei Valori. Istituto

Regionale per la Programmazione Economica della Toscana (IRPET). Pontassieve: Centro Stampa.

Petrillo, Agostino. 1999. Italy: Farewell to the "Bel Paese"? In *The European Union and Migrant Labour.* Gareth Dale and Mike Cole, eds. Pp. 231–262.

Philips, Susan U. 1998. *Ideology in the Language of Judges: How Judges Practice Law, Politics, and Courtroom Control.* New York: Oxford University Press.

Porter, Darwin, and Danforth Prince. 1997. *Frommer's '97 Italy: The Best of the Cities, Villages, and Countryside.* New York: Macmillan.

Rapp, Rayna. 1999. *Testing Women, Testing the Fetus: The Social Impact of Amniocentesis in America.* New York: Routledge.

Reuters. 2003. Italian Town Offers $11,900 per Baby. MSNBC International News (online edition). Dec. 4.

Riva, E. et al. 1999. Factors Associated with Initiation and Duration of Breastfeeding in Italy. *ACTA Paediatrica 88*(4):411–415.

Roberts, Mark S., and David B. Allison. 2002. Why You're Crazy: The DSM Story. *Cabinet 8:*54–58.

Roediger, David R. 2003. "I Came for the Art": Exposing Whiteness and Imagining Nonwhite Spaces. In *Whiteness, a Wayward Construction.* Tyler Stallings, ed. Laguna Art Museum, Laguna Beach, CA, and Fellows of Contemporary Art, Los Angeles.

Rosenberger, Nancy Ross. 2001. *Gambling with Virtue: Japanese Women and the Search for Self in a Changing Nation.* Honolulu: University of Hawai'i Press.

Rosci, Elena. 1994. Le lunghe adolescenze dell'Italia d'oggi. In *Stato dell'Italia.* Paul Ginsborg, ed. Milano: il Saggiatore.

Rosi, Sandra. 1996. *Firenze: L'arte della Cucina.* Firenze: Edizioni La Mandragora.

Saraceno, Chiara. 1992. Constructing Families, Shaping Women's Lives: The Making of Italian Families between Market Economy and State Interventions. In *The European Experience of Declining Fertility, 1850–1970: The Quiet Revolution.* Louise A. Tilly, John R. Gillis, and

David Levine, eds. Pp. 251–270. Cambridge, MA: Blackwell.

——. 1996. *Sociologia della Famiglia.* Bologna: Il Mulino.

Sarogni, Emilia. 1995. *La Donna Italiana: Il lungo cammino verso i diritti, 1861–1994.* Parma: Nuova Pratiche Editore.

Schneider, Jane C., and Peter T. Schneider. 1991. Sex and Respectability in an Age of Fertility Decline: A Sicilian Case Study. *Social Science Medicine 33*(8):885–895.

——. 1992. Going Forward in Reverse Gear: Culture, Economy, and Political Economy in the Demographic Transitions of a Rural Sicilian Town. In *The European Experience of Declining Fertility, 1850–1970: The Quiet Revolution.* Louise A. Tilly, John R. Gillis, and David Levine, eds. Pp. 146–192. Cambridge: Blackwell.

——. 1996. *Festival of the Poor: Fertility Decline and the Ideology of Class in Sicily: 1860–1980.* Tucson: University of Arizona Press.

Schneider, Jane C. 2002. World Markets: Anthropological Perspectives. In *Exotic No More.* Jeremy MacClancy, ed. Pp. 64–85. Chicago: University of Chicago Press.

Schrambling, Regina. 2002. The Truth Behind the 'Market Menu.' *The New York Times.* July 24, F1.

Scott, Joan. 1986. Gender: A Useful Category of Historical Analysis. *The American Historical Review 91*(5):1053–1075.

Seremetakis, C. Nadia, ed. 1994. *The Senses Still: Perception and Memory as Material Culture in Modernity.* Chicago: University of Chicago Press.

Sgritta, Giovanni B. 2001. The Situation of Families in Italy in 2001. *European Observatory on the Social Situation, Demography, and Family.* Electronic document, http://europa.eu.int/comm/employment_social/eoss/index _en.html. Accessed May 15, 2003.

Sheldon, Anna R., and M. Moyca Newell. 1904. Chapter Two, Prato: A Medieval Journey. In *The Medici Balls. Seven Little Journeys in Tuscany.* New York: Charterhouse.

Shore, Cris. 1990. *Italian Communism: The Escape from Leninism—An Anthropological Perspective.* London: Pluto.

2000. *Building Europe: The Cultural Politics of European Integration.* London: Routledge.

Small, Meredith F. 1998. *Our Babies, Ourselves: How Biology and Culture Shape the Way We Parent.* New York: Anchor.

Specter, Michael. 1998. Population Implosion Worries a Graying Europe. *The New York Times,* July 10, p. A1.

Stallings, Tyler. 2003. *Whiteness, a Wayward Construction.* Laguna Art Museum, Laguna Beach, CA, and Fellows of Contemporary Art, Los Angeles.

The Economist. 1998. Why Italians Don't Make Babies. *The Economist,* May 9, p. 53.

The Economist. 2003. Italy's Declining Population: Bambino Boom. *The Economist,* Dec. 6, p. 47.

Teti, Vito. 1993. *La razza maledetta: origini del pregiudizio antimeridionale.* Roma: manifestolibri.

Tihanyi, Catherine. 2002. Ethnographic and Translation Practices. *Anthropology News,* September, pp. 5–6.

Tilly, Louise A., John R. Gillis, and David Levine, eds. 1992. *The European Experience of Declining Fertility, 1850–1970: The Quiet Revolution.* Cambridge: Blackwell.

Treves, Simone. 1997. Studio e lavoro: donne protagoniste. *L'Unità,* February 13, p. 12

van Dijk, Teun A. 1993. *Elite Discourse and Racism.* London: Sage.

Volpi, Roberto. 1986. *Figli d'Italia: Quanti, quali e come alle soglie del Duemila.* Bagno A Ripoli [Firenze]: La Nuova Italia.

Waldman, Amy. 2003. States in India Take New Steps to Limit Births. *The New York Times.* November 7, p. A1.

——. 1999. *Envisioning Power: Ideologies of Dominance and Crisis.* Berkeley: University of California Press.

Weimer, Jon P. 1998. *Breastfeeding Promotion Research: The ES/WIC Nutrition Education Initiative and Economic Considerations.* Washington, DC: Economic Research Service, U.S. Department of Agriculture. Bulletin No. 744.

Whitaker, Elizabeth. 2000. *Measuring Mamma's Milk: Fascism and the Medicalization of Maternity in Italy.* Ann Arbor: University of Michigan Press.

Willis, Paul and Mats Trondman. 2000. Manifesto for *Ethnography. Ethnography* 1(1): 5–16.

Wolf, Eric. 1969. *Peasant Wars of the Twentieth Century.* New York: Harper Colophon.

——. 1982. *Europe and the People without History.* Berkeley: University of California Press.

Yanagisako, Sylvia. 2002. *Culture and Capital: Producing Italian Family Capitalism.* Princeton, NJ: Princeton University Press.

Zanchi, Fabio, et al. 1994. *La scuola in tasca: manuale di sopravvivenza per genitori e alunni delle elementari e medie.* Venezia: il Cardo editore.

WEB SITES

European Observatory on the Social Situation, Demography, and Family. http://europa.eu.int/comm/employment_social/eoss/index_en.html, accessed May 15, 2003.

Population Reference Bureau. www.prb.org. See in particular the annual World Data Sheet, accessed May 15, 2003.

ISTAT, Istituto Nazionale di Statistica (National Statistics Institute). See Italy in Figures 2002. www.istat.it/English/index.htm, accessed July 9, 2003.

The Women's Documentation Center Library in Bologna (Biblioteca delle Donne), Italy's primary gender research library, collects materials written by women and on women. www.women.it/bibliotecadelledonne, accessed March 26, 2002.

Index